SONS, DAUGHTERS, AND SIDEWALK PSYCHOTICS

SONS, DAUGHTERS, · AND · SIDEWALK PSYCHOTICS

Mental Illness and Homelessness
in Los Angeles

NEIL GONG

THE UNIVERSITY OF CHICAGO PRESS

Chicago and London

The University of Chicago Press, Chicago 60637
The University of Chicago Press, Ltd., London
© 2024 by The University of Chicago
Published 2024
Printed in the United States of America

33 32 31 30 29 28 27 26 25 24   1 2 3 4 5

ISBN-13: 978-0-226-58190-3 (cloth)
ISBN-13: 978-0-226-83223-4 (e-book)
DOI: https://doi.org/10.7208/chicago/9780226832234.001.0001

Library of Congress Cataloging-in-Publication Data

Names: Gong, Neil, author.
Title: Sons, daughters, and sidewalk psychotics : mental illness and
homelessness in Los Angeles / Neil Gong.
Other titles: Mental illness and homelessness in Los Angeles
Description: Chicago ; London : The University of Chicago, 2024. |
Includes bibliographical references and index.
Identifiers: LCCN 2023032848 | ISBN 9780226581903 (cloth) |
ISBN 9780226832234 (ebook)
Subjects: LCSH: Mental health services—Social aspects—California—
Los Angeles. | Mentally ill homeless persons—California—Los Angeles—Social
conditions. | Homeless persons—Mental health services—Social aspects—
California—Los Angeles. | Equality—California—Los Angeles.
Classification: LCC RC451.4.H64 G66 2024 | DDC 362.2086/
9420979494—dc23/eng/20230817
LC record available at https://lccn.loc.gov/2023032848

♾ This paper meets the requirements of ANSI/NISO Z39.48-1992
(Permanence of Paper).

For Joyce and Kelvin

CONTENTS

ABBREVIATIONS

DMH	(Los Angeles County) Department of Mental Health
FSP	Full Service Partnership (Community Case Management team)
IOP	Intensive Outpatient (Treatment) Program
LAHSA	Los Angeles Homeless Services Authority
LAPD	Los Angeles Police Department
NAMI	National Alliance on Mental Illness
SSI	Supplemental Security Income (a program administered by the US Social Security Administration)

"THIRTY YEARS LATE"

The veteran psychiatric nurse listened to my questions, nodded curtly, and told me I was wasting my time. A grizzled white man in his fifties who spoke with a northeastern accent, Vic Edson (not his real name) had earned his no-nonsense manner. He'd been in the field for three decades and seen the worst of it: crowded psych wards and jail mental health wings; chaotic emergency hospitalizations and sidewalk triage. Now he did home visits for a Los Angeles County Department of Mental Health (DMH) case management team, part of the new recovery-oriented system that would help people living with serious mental illness thrive outside institutional settings.

I'd come to Downtown LA, ground zero of California's mental health and homelessness crises, as a PhD student eager to research innovations in outpatient psychiatric services. But as we headed to a dilapidated apartment complex to check on the welfare of a formerly homeless client, Vic declared the house calls and community care a joke. To him, the only solution was to bring back the state mental hospitals.

This caught me off guard. I'd worked in mental health services after college and had been taught that the state hospitals were part of a shameful past. The United States once warehoused people with psychiatric disabilities in cavernous asylums. Then from the 1960s to the '80s, patients gained new rights, and most of these facilities were shut down. There have been lots of good intentions since then, but the nation never properly invested in the housing and services meant to replace the old model. Deinstitutionalization, as it was called, effectively abandoned many people to the streets.

But Vic's advocacy wasn't a gritted-teeth, lesser-of-two-evils sort—it was an actual preference for the old state hospital model. As we tracked down client after client, from neighborhoods like Skid Row to Eagle Rock, the gruff nurse softened. He waxed romantic about the old asylums. In his telling, people could have their medical needs met, make friends, and enjoy amenities like gardens and bowling alleys, all while being securely locked inside mental institutions. By way of contrast, he told me about a DMH client, an African American man diagnosed with schizophrenia, who endured years of homelessness and incarceration before becoming stably housed. "Do you really think he is better off being placed in an apartment, where someone has to shop for him, get him an ID, help him with this and that?" Vic's mouth curled into a snarl. "But yeah, he's 'independent.'"

I pondered Vic's remarks. On the one hand, the client in question *was* independent and living successfully in the community—at least in the sense of no longer being stuck in the revolving door between life on the streets and repeated arrests. And I knew patients' rights activists who would be outraged at Vic's suggestion that the man would be better off in an asylum. On the other hand, he reportedly abused drugs, refused treatment, and was indebted to a loan shark—so perhaps this independence was destructive. And given how hard it was for Vic and his colleagues to assist just one person, I could see why the state hospital seemed like an answer.

Later that day, however, Vic amended his claim that the DMH program was a joke. No, he said, it was just "thirty years late." The case management teams should have been in place when the state hospitals shut down, but California only developed them in the late 2000s. Against that thirty-year absence, large enough for thousands to fall through the cracks, understaffed county programs could only do so much. In this context, Vic believed that his real job was keeping poor patients out of sight. Mimicking a wealthy Los Angeles parent, he whined, "They're dirty, they're scary, I don't want my kids to see them."

Was it true? Vic's comments stuck with me as I followed the DMH treatment team, homeless outreach programs, and other state and nonprofit social service agencies between 2013 and 2015, then private agencies from 2015 to 2017. Were the workers just keeping people out of public view? What if treatment programs hadn't shown up "thirty years late"? What if the team had proper staffing and funding, and the patients had not been abandoned? Would the "independence" and client choice that Vic denigrated mean something else?

This book documents my attempt to answer these questions. I couldn't turn back time and create a new American mental health system, of course, but I could at least compare the DMH with a different model. Initially, I'd planned to travel to Sweden or another European country to find a contrasting approach and history, but it turned out I didn't need to go that far. A clinician referred me to the place I call the Actualization Clinic, a private case management program for privileged patients in West Los Angeles that dates back to the 1970s and the deinstitutionalization period. This program generously allowed me to observe treatment meetings and therapy groups, and then it introduced me to aligned mental health-care providers serving this elite demographic.

The comparison helped me answer some of my questions, but it also forced me to ask new ones. Unlike a laboratory experiment, in which scientists can control conditions and manipulate a single factor to test theories, the real-world comparison revealed differences I hadn't even known to look for. As I dug into the cases, my approach morphed until I felt as though I were holding these separate worlds up to each other as mirrors. Their striking contrasts challenged many of my presumptions. While the well-off weren't receiving care "thirty years late," this treatment world had its own problems. Sometimes these were directly related to the privilege and heavy family involvement that the DMH clients lacked. I also met middle-class people who could neither qualify for intensive public services nor access places like Actualization; their plight illustrated an entirely different side of our broken mental health system. The social safety net seemed to sag in the middle.

If I've done my job, you will come away from this book with insights about how things work in American mental health care as well as new ideas for improving it. Some reforms seem straightforward, such as increasing funding for public providers, pushing private insurers to cover services that are ironically more accessible with Medicaid, and scrutinizing boutique programs that go unregulated. But this study also raises ethical and existential questions beyond matters of policy. What kinds of futures should people in psychic distress reasonably expect? How do we define *independence* and *choice* when a person makes seemingly irrational decisions? And what should we do if our answers differ when it comes to strangers on the sidewalk, our loved ones, or ourselves?

INTRODUCTION

After time spent on the psychiatric ward, in jail, and living on the streets of Downtown Los Angeles, Rick Valentine's luck finally seemed to change. Recent policy developments to address chronic homelessness[1] had recast his devastating experiences in a new light. Now his emergency hospitalizations and arrests put him at the front of the line for an apartment. In this new Housing First model, Rick could move into a subsidized unit without requirements to follow his doctor's orders or stay sober. A Los Angeles County Department of Mental Health (DMH) case management team would conduct home visits and help him get his life back on track.

The situation wasn't glamorous by middle-class standards, but permanent housing seemed like a dream after the streets of Skid Row. And as a well-spoken white man in his early forties with a neat beard and freshly trimmed hair, Rick was better positioned than most in his situation. I'd once seen him pacing nervously, rail thin in his checkered shirt and black jeans, on guard as if he thought it might all disappear. But he also began to settle into his new life. He told me he hoped to work in construction in Northern California, as he had in his younger days.

That's why it all felt strange when Rick, his social worker, Beth, and I piled into the county Toyota Prius and moved him into a run-down East LA motel. Beth explained that it might be tricky to check him in, because the treatment team had already brought too many "disorganized" mentally ill people to this location. We'd heard that the motel receptionist was getting tired of "difficult" DMH clients, so Beth called ahead to tell her that Rick was simply getting his apartment fumigated. Of course, that was a lie.

It was true that Rick wasn't mentally disorganized in the clinical sense, for he spoke in a coherent and logical manner. But he needed a place for a few nights because he was on the run from a stalker—one that the DMH said was a figment of his paranoid imagination, or what clinicians call a fixed delusion.

Later, Rick and I stood outside the DMH clinic, where Skid Row's encampments and needle exchange sites meet gentrified Downtown's hipster cafés, and he told me about his predicament. He believed that a mysterious man was about to be released from prison and come murder him. His dread radiated from his body, and I assured him that I empathized. There was nothing necessarily paranoid about fearing violence, given Rick's experiences in jail and on the streets. Beth once joked that she would start a betting pool with other DMH workers about whether his fears were real, since we all found him convincing.

Still, parts of Rick's story simply didn't add up. He said his neighbors had spied on him with an infrared camera, snapped photos while he masturbated, and distributed these images throughout the neighborhood. As a result, he claimed, a local father now believed he was a pervert who had intentionally shown the photos to children. This was why people were after him and he couldn't go home. Now Rick even planned to give up his hard-won apartment. He told me he knew how the infrared camera story sounded, but he insisted he wasn't crazy—it was just that the anxiety of his situation would drive anyone insane. Sometimes he drank alcohol just to cope.

"Knowing that someone's watching you while you're doing that [masturbating] is really uncomfortable," he said, clenching his hands. "It just stresses you out." He felt humiliated and angry to be thought a pedophile. "This guy across the street [the angry father] is just making it worse, knowing that he's told everybody near me that I exposed myself to his kids. That is the worst, because that, to me, is . . . people that know me know that's not true."

Rick felt desperate, but in some ways he was surprisingly empowered, and this shaped what the DMH could and couldn't do for him—or to him. He vehemently disagreed with the schizophrenia diagnosis he'd received in lockup, so he refused to take antipsychotic medication—and this was his legal right. He recalled an earlier incident related to the same stalker, when he'd threatened to kill his neighbor and was placed on a 5150—California's code for a seventy-two-hour emergency psychiatric hold. After a series of detentions, he said he'd learned his lesson: "I'm very careful of what I say now, how I phrase my words." Rick had figured out how to avoid meeting the legal thresholds of "danger to self or others" or "gravely disabled," as either one could lead to coercive hospitalization.[2] The DMH respected his refusal of medication, tolerated his drinking, and began formulating a plan.

As I got to know Beth, Rick's caseworker, I learned how psychiatric social workers navigated this environment. Although some saw Skid Row as a bad assignment, Beth viewed it as a mission. In her early thirties and fresh out of graduate school, she wore her socialist political commitments on her arms, adorned with tattoos that railed against the rich. She recruited me to join her for volunteer homeless outreach on the weekends, her work as much a calling as a career. But between the full-time job and the weekend hours, Beth was getting burned out.

I once heard Laura, an African American social worker and supervisor, offer Beth some sage advice: "You have to take a period where *you're okay with things not being okay.* You ask yourself if it is necessary to do something . . . this is the vicarious trauma that comes with working in Skid Row." Laura, too, felt a moral commitment to serve the vulnerable, but she believed that professional detachment was a precondition. If Beth could not accept situations for what they were, she would never make it.

Reflecting on that day outside the motel, I wondered about Rick and the DMH team's options. How could Beth and Laura ensure that Rick didn't return to the streets nor make another threat that could land him back in jail or the psych ward? And what things in Rick's life should they simply come to tolerate—to be "okay with things not being okay"?

Across town, Joshua Roth was convinced he was dying of AIDS. The middle-aged son of a wealthy Los Angeles family, he had become fixated on his impending death. Though his frequent HIV tests kept coming up negative, he stopped performing as a pianist and quit working at the family business. The diagnosis was not AIDS but delusional disorder—a psychiatric term for a person with fixed, seemingly untrue beliefs who lacks the hallucinations that might lead to a schizophrenia diagnosis. Joshua's relatives were concerned, because he continued to try to access an antiretroviral medication cocktail that could have serious side effects. Joshua, meanwhile, questioned why he was expected to see a psychiatrist and a case manager, and he angrily accused his relatives of paying off doctors to keep his supposed AIDS secret and protect the family name.

I began following Joshua's case at the Actualization Clinic, an elite, private case management program. It originated in the 1970s as hospital discharge assistance for wealthy patients undergoing deinstitutionalization. Today it helps families navigate the world of private mental health care. After witnessing the struggles faced by the DMH public treatment team, I wanted to see what was going on across the proverbial tracks.

Joshua, like Rick, could be considered noncompliant, in that he resisted conventional medication treatment, and lacking in insight, in that he didn't agree he was mentally ill. Reportedly, he'd scared his family when he walked out onto a roof and said he might fly to Switzerland for assisted suicide. Though the Actualization team spoke of hospitalization, Joshua retained his rights to refuse medication and other treatment. This legal dynamic resembled what I'd seen at the DMH, yet there were differences in how this team made sense of his mental illness.

Consider the case manager: Ian, a slight, blond man with a gentle demeanor and the tranquil presence of a meditation instructor. Ian believed there could be great spiritual meaning in psychosis, and with his Sanskrit tattoos and master's degree in Buddhist psychology, he traced his intellectual lineage to the California healers of the 1960s. He believed, for instance, that his personal use of psychedelic drugs helped him relate better to people in altered states. He hoped to build trust with Joshua and engage in humanistic therapy.

Joshua's private psychiatrist, a psychoanalyst, had an intriguing interpretation of unconscious motives. He thought Joshua had been repressing a gay identity and was still uncomfortable with his homosexual desire. Joshua's father had recently died, and the doctor speculated that his grief combined with his sexual shame to create an AIDS delusion. Ian relayed the doctor's theory to the wider care team. "After his father died, Joshua started going to massage parlors in West Hollywood [a prominent gay neighborhood]," he explained. "He reported rape, being penetrated briefly by a massage therapist. He put a stop to it, but thinks he got AIDS. It's homophobia and homosexuality. His doctor thinks it's a shame thing—thinking about death avoids all the other things around being unsuccessful."

This interpretation of loss, identity struggles, and the horror of real or imagined sexual violation might serve as fodder for psychotherapy and other care strategies. Sitting in a meeting of Joshua's treatment team, I wondered what difference these therapeutic resources and family involvement would make. Could the Actualization Clinic avert the danger of Joshua's suicide, restore his family's harmony, and rebuild his life—perhaps even resolve his internal conflicts?

.   .   .

Seen from a psychological or psychiatric perspective, Rick's and Joshua's stories are individually heartrending—and fascinating. Readers might imagine these men profiled in popular mental health books like Sigmund Freud's *Three Case Histories*, the neurologist Oliver Sacks's *The Man Who Mistook His Wife for a Hat*, or Black and Andreasen's *Introductory Textbook of Psychiatry*.[3] Those works might delve into the men's childhoods, explain unusual brain conditions, or explore research on chemical imbalances.

As a sociologist, I am mindful of such theories, but I am ultimately focused more on social context and its consequences than explaining individual psychopathology. My aim is to understand how people are shaped and processed by systems and structures larger than themselves. This means paying attention to institutions and organizations, history, social inequality, and culture alongside individual biography and psychology, and tracking whether people's actions change those surrounding contexts. If we want to improve this country's care systems, the first step is to understand them. And if, as the adage goes, the measure of a civilization is how it treats its most vulnerable, we can learn a great deal about contemporary American society by observing how it manages serious mental illness—or fails to.

Examining these men's stories side by side primes us for a set of sociological rather than psychiatric or psychological questions. For instance, What explains Rick's and Joshua's very different life experiences despite similarities in their age, race, and delusions of impending death? What explains how the clinical teams process these men, interpret the significance of their beliefs, and arrive at divergent meanings of *treatment* and *care*?

It's not so surprising that poor and rich people live differently, but a closer look at some of the consequences may give readers pause. Consider the commonsense notion that poverty leads to constraint, while wealth means autonomy and choice. Why, then, does the DMH help get Rick a subsidized apartment, no strings attached, and respect his freedom to drink or refuse treatment, while Joshua feels scrutinized, surveilled, and controlled by his wealthy family and the Actualization Clinic—perhaps the very resources that keep him from the most precarious parts of Rick's situation? And looking at the strange state of American mental health care: How did we even get here?

THE LONG SHADOW OF THE ASYLUM

The United States once had a straightforward tool for managing serious mental illness.[4] If a person was deemed to be a threat to society, whether dangerous or merely disruptive, local officials and families could have them locked away for years at a time. Warehoused in public asylums or tended to in upscale private hospitals, the "problem" was made invisible.

From the beginning, critics questioned the effectiveness of asylum treatment and the ethics of forced care. In egregious cases, people who were merely unconventional or rebellious were labeled mentally ill and sent away. Investigators and ex-patients repeatedly reported abuse and gross neglect inside the asylums, and even expensive private facilities deprived people of their fundamental rights. Yet from a social problem–solving perspective, ready access to psychiatric confinement made the era a sort of golden age.

Then, within the space of a generation, the asylum was gone. In the mid-twentieth century, confinement gave way to deinstitutionalization. Rather than detaining people with mental illness in hospitals, the idea was that they would live in communities offering robust outpatient services. New social security programs would offer the material means for them to thrive, and new legislation would protect their rights to freedom and bodily integrity. Former hospital "patients" who passively received care would instead become empowered "clients" able to choose their own treatment regimen from the new effective medications. That, at least, was the vision.

In practice, the community care movement made good on the civil liberties while offering only a weak social safety net. Little of the promised investment came through to replace the hospitals, leaving a gaping hole in patient services. New medications proved useful for many but not all, and the side effects could be disabling. Without consistent support, a lot of people living with mental illness ended up in the ER. Emergency hospitalization meant brief episodes of care and control, perhaps seventy-two hours on a psych ward, but little in the way of sustained treatment. In deinstitutionalization's wake, the responsibility for managing patients shifted from the states to local governments and families.

In this country of stark inequality, that often meant no services at all. Where even the most awful asylums had guaranteed food and shelter, the outside world guaranteed neither. Some ex-patients thrived, but others—especially those who lacked resources or social

support—were at increased risk of homelessness, jail, and brief emergency holds that neither stabilized them nor connected them to
ongoing services. Today, recent government statistics paint a dismal
picture: of the country's approximately 582,500 people experiencing
homelessness in 2022 (and some argue that this is a significant under-
count), research suggests that around 20 percent—well over one hundred thousand people—are severely mentally ill.[5] A 2017 report found
that 33 percent of prisoners and 44 percent of jail inmates had at least
some "history of a mental health problem."[6] The few state hospital beds
left—less than 10 percent of the capacity at midcentury—are reserved
primarily for people caught up in the criminal justice system.[7]

This book explores two treatment approaches that emerged to
address problems once "solved" by the asylum. It compares intensive
outpatient services located in the same urban center but existing in
two social worlds. Fifty years after the turn to community care, people
diagnosed with serious psychiatric disabilities spend most of their
time outside hospital walls. What *community care* means, however,
can shift drastically with context. Moving between the city streets and
exclusive care facilities for the rich, I will introduce people who are
"free" but not treated as well as those who are treated but do not feel
free. At stake are the kinds of futures we think people deserve, along
with the meaning of *freedom* itself. All this tells a story of madness,
urban politics, and family, and of how American inequality shapes
what it means to be a human being.

STUDYING INEQUALITY IN PSYCHIATRIC CARE

My research involved ethnographic fieldwork conducted in public
safety net and elite private treatment centers in Los Angeles, a city
known for both its Downtown social service ghetto and its private
beachside facilities dotting Malibu. The Downtown Skid Row area
is infamous as "America's homeless capital"—a dumping ground for
people with mental illness, ex-prisoners, addicts, and others who have
been pushed to the social margins. Every street corner has public and
nonprofit social service providers situated alongside people living

in tents. Depending on the daily machinations of the city's battle with homeless rights advocates, police may aggressively break down encampments and open-air drug markets. Other times, officers may ignore them. Across town, in West LA and in Southern California's beach cities, wealthy people diagnosed as having serious mental illness and/or addiction attend luxurious treatment centers, from outpatient day clinics to residential facilities by the ocean. Programs may offer yoga, holistic care, and farm-to-table organic meals alongside therapeutic treatments and university-affiliated psychiatrists.

To understand these unequal forms of psychiatric care, I embedded myself in two organizational worlds across a five-year period.[8] A participant-observer, I became a volunteer at the Los Angeles County Department of Mental Health, where I observed weekly team meetings, client-provider interactions at the clinic, home visits, and therapeutic groups between 2013 and 2015. In the first year, I additionally volunteered with a homeless outreach project, which brought me into contact with potential DMH clients and other social service and law enforcement agencies engaged in street work. Outside clinical settings, I shared meals with subjects, attended social events with DMH employees, spent nights in homeless encampments, marched with activists fighting street sweeps of unhoused people, participated in the US government's annual "homeless count," drove people to appointments or other engagements, and otherwise tried to participate broadly. The observations helped me see how treatment and everyday dilemmas presented themselves in practice, how context shaped possible actions, and how different organizations interacted as a loose system.

And at the Actualization Clinic between 2015 and 2017, I observed weekly case conferences in which care workers discussed clients, attended some group therapies and social activities, and participated in events for private agencies in a referral network. Yet there was a veil of secrecy in this world—part of what the affluent pay for—so immersion was far more difficult. Owing to privacy concerns, I was rarely able to accompany therapists on home visits, and Actualization limited my access to those clientele selected by the clinic and those I had met in therapy groups.

To round out my study, I also visited collaborating residential programs, rehab facilities, and sober living homes. There I engaged in activities like meals with staff and clients, celebrated birthdays and achievements, and played as a doubles partner for a psychologist who used tennis as therapy. These experiences allowed me to get to know clinicians and patients beyond what was discussed at treatment meetings as well as observe the rhythm of daily life. Supplementing my field observation, I conducted fifty-five recorded interviews across the public and private settings. These allowed me to probe deeper into how people interpreted their experiences, to document their pasts, and learn from their expertise. For a more detailed account of my investigation, including my access, my research tools, the impact of my identity, and the logic of comparison, see the research appendix.

The treatment worlds were in some ways similar. Both the poor and the privileged approaches had evolved in part as a response to the deinstitutionalization movement and its failures. All the infrastructures of care, from public clinics, psychiatric group homes, and supportive housing to private centers and residential therapy programs, address needs once taken care of by the asylum. At first blush, the clients in both places look similar; their shared primary diagnoses include schizophrenia, bipolar disorder, and major depression. And because of their shared roots in the 1970s movement to create "hospitals without walls," the DMH treatment team and the Actualization Clinic share an organizational structure, using case managers to meet people outside the clinic and deliver whole-person, biopsychosocial care.

But there are also profound differences between these two client groups. These reflect the fact that community care takes place in different kinds of communities. The DMH serves people who might have been hospitalized long term in the past as well as those who do not seem seriously mentally ill—like those who are possibly "just homeless." Actualization, on the other hand, serves the severely mentally ill alongside rich college-age drug users who appear to have only minor psychiatric needs. These divergences clued me in to the broader forces shaping the treatment of mental illness. Each world has developed its own form of community treatment based on the practical problems and resources at hand as well as the needs of powerful actors beyond the identified patient: city elites concerned with urban disorder and homelessness, and families who can afford to pay for private services.

Yet unlike an omnipotent local government that can simply lock up the street person, or the affluent family that can dictate its adult child's future, strong patients' rights laws mean authorities must get peoples' consent. For both the DMH and the Actualization Clinic, the central dilemma is how to engage people's free choices rather than coerce their compliance. Behavior is leveraged, induced, rehabilitated to some norm, tolerated, or excused, all while more explicit forms of power like arrest, eviction, abandonment, or hospitalization lurk as threats in the background.

The sociologist Nikolas Rose has described the management of individual choice and responsibility as a hallmark of rich liberal democracies, terming it "governing through freedom."[9] Unlike authoritarian control that restricts freedom, this approach works with people through incentives, mind-sets, and nudges toward "proper" choices. In a society that purports to celebrate free-market principles, for instance, government is supposed to encourage individual entrepreneurial action rather than impose economic plans from above. The complication in the case at hand is that psychiatric providers must govern patients through freedom, even when they suspect that a person's free will is compromised by mental illness or could become destructive.

The United States is arguably unique among wealthy nations for prioritizing what the philosopher Isaiah Berlin called "negative liberty"—*freedom from* big government intervention.[10] We see this in the libertarian cultural emphasis on freedom of speech, the individual's right to bear arms, and states' rights. Such priorities contrast with those of centralized European governments, which emphasize "positive liberty"—guaranteed resources like education, health care, and housing that shape people and give them *freedom to* pursue their life goals.

We can read asylum closure in the United States as a striking case of negative liberty's triumph over positive liberty—*freedom from* wins over *freedom to*. The patients' rights achievement was substantial, and no doubt it served to protect people from abuse. But without a positive right to resources and care, many people with serious mental illness only became free to be homeless or free to be held responsible in criminal court.[11] This is the legacy, for better or worse, of psychiatric deinstitutionalization, and it manifests in highly unequal ways.

UNEQUAL ILLNESSES AND THE MEANING OF FREEDOM

My argument throughout this book is twofold.

First is that the experiences of mental illness, treatment, and recovery are all profoundly shaped by social inequality and in ways not always obvious. Researchers who study rates and severity of illness have long known that serious mental illness and poverty tend to go together statistically. This is because hardship exacerbates distress, and people with disabilities often struggle economically if not given proper supports.[12] But my comparison of the DMH and the Actualization Clinic reveals something else: social class shapes how people can live with and recover from those illnesses. Patients that have similar psychiatric diagnoses and medical prognoses (in terms of predicted course of illness) can have radically different *social prognoses* (in terms of possible lives and identities).[13] In effect, I show how the meaning of recovery itself may be transformed by context.

My second contention is that these unequal visions of recovery can lead to surprising differences in the meaning of client choice—namely, an unexpected freedom for poor patients and constraint for the privileged. Public safety net providers tolerate it when clients don't take their prescriptions (medication "noncompliance"), when they use illegal drugs, or when they behave badly—so long as these actions are limited to certain places. In understaffed clinics for the poor, workers put most of their effort into simply reducing patient arrest and homelessness. Here recovery is defined as keeping people housed, out of jail, and from triggering too many 911 calls. The DMH doesn't have the capacity to rehabilitate most people, and it doesn't want to involve harsh police treatment, so it focuses on generalized harm reduction and spatial containment: keeping people alive and out of the way. This *tolerant containment* ironically bestows a kind of freedom within the material limits of poverty.

In elite private treatment, where clinics are accountable to affluent families, recovery is defined as generating class-appropriate futures—for instance, returning to college or work, developing hobbies, or reconnecting with friends. These providers engage in a concerted effort to change behavior and therapeutically rehabilitate wayward adult children. No doubt there are behaviors tolerated as "eccentric" rather than "crazy" up to a point, but many affluent families intervene when such behaviors go too far. Precisely because care and control go hand in hand, privilege may mean constraint rather than choice. This *concerted constraint* restricts some freedom in the moment but promises a better future.

I'm aware that these findings contradict received wisdom. Scholars who study social control and class typically predict what the philosopher Michel Foucault called a "disciplinary" approach to managing poor social deviants.[14] A disciplinary model attempts to reform these individuals through heavy surveillance and micromanagement of their everyday lives until they become responsible actors. Others expect that the city will simply arrest or banish troublesome poor people who fail to act responsibly, while privileged social deviants will be indulged with maximum choice.[15] No one would predict that state social service agencies will tolerate the formerly homeless person's otherwise illegal behavior in subsidized housing, or that elite treatment providers will be the ones doing the micromanaging.

Yet the surprise makes sense once we combine theories of social control with research on inequality and parenting. In a study comparing working-class and upper-middle-class child rearing, the sociologist Annette Lareau found that poorer families take a "natural-growth" approach.[16] Lacking time and money, they provide love and safety, giving kids room to learn through trial and error. More privileged families, however, engage in a "concerted cultivation" of their children. This includes highly structured activities, surveillance, and intensive socialization practices that the poorer families simply can't afford. Working-class children have the benefit of more free time and self-direction at the cost of their expected future, but the upper-middle-class child learns skills and dispositions for navigating the adult world.

We can see the tolerant containment of deviance as akin to a cash-strapped city's version of natural-growth parenting, and concerted constraint as elite treatment providers' way to cultivate and control privileged futures. This viewpoint helps make sense of the surprising "inverted" regimes of tolerance and control. But different ethical tensions arise when addressing adults with psychiatric disabilities. Unlike natural growth with a healthy child, tolerant containment and its freedom may look suspiciously like government neglect of a person in need of care. And unlike cultivation of a privileged youngster, concerted constraint and its intensive rehabilitation may resemble overbearing paternalism.

To see the logics and tensions in action, let's return to the two men introduced earlier. Rick and Joshua both may be hospitalized briefly when their delusions of death create emergencies, but in the contemporary era, this only defers the problem to another point in time. Legally speaking, neither man exhibits consistently "dangerous" behavior or "grave disability" in procuring food, clothes, and shelter—factors that might lead to a court appointing a conservator (legal guardian) to control them. Nor does either treatment program wish to simply lock these men up—the whole point is to help them thrive in the community.

Absent long-term hospitalization or forced medication, what can each program do? To keep Rick from the streets or jail, the DMH sought to contain him in a place where he could be tolerated and avoid arrest. It worked with the tools at its disposal and moved him around. That week he stayed in the motel room, after which he moved to a sober living home. This was not to his liking, because Rick was a drinker, so the case management team looked for other temporary living situations. Eventually, it did the bureaucratic work to repurpose his housing voucher, and he moved into a new apartment.[17] There he felt safe. This was a success of sorts, but the workers feared he would soon believe that his "stalker" had tracked him to the new neighborhood.

To cultivate a life for Joshua beyond his delusions, the Actualization

Clinic first worked to constrain his behavior. It suggested that his family *leverage* him into treatment engagement—the clinic's term for withholding money or affection. In the Buddhist psychologist's words, clinic staff "got really existential" with Joshua about the meaning of life and death and discussed homosexual contact as a legitimate form of human connection. In an act of literal paternalism, the semiretired owner of Actualization joined the case as an older male "replacement father figure" who might be useful, given Joshua's mourning of his father's death. Finally, the team intervened on what the psychoanalyst saw as Joshua's fear of being unsuccessful by encouraging him to play piano at a senior center. They asked him, "What do you have to give, in the time you have left [before death from AIDS]?" Between family social pressure and the relationship building, Joshua resumed psychotherapy and agreed to an increased dosage of an antipsychotic drug. He said he accepted that he was HIV negative. This, too, was deemed a success, although Joshua suddenly declined to engage in further psychotherapy. The team was unsure whether his delusion would return.

Notice that "success" is relative. That's because the problems themselves are relative. Keeping someone housed and out of jail is a fundamentally different goal from making that person "actualized" and respectable. It involves a different relationship to personhood and choice. Hypothetically, the DMH might have psychoanalyzed Rick's made-for-Freud masturbation delusion, mobilized relatives to leverage him with money or love, and encouraged taking up a hobby en route to restarting medication. Yet those therapeutic and social network resources weren't available, nor were they particularly urgent for the goal of keeping Rick housed and out of jail. Hypothetically, the Actualization Clinic could simply have let Joshua hole up and drink, stewing over his phantom AIDS until the next emergency, but that wouldn't satisfy his family's need to heal their relationship or get him back to a respectable life.

During the asylum era, each of these situations could have been "resolved" by placing Rick and Joshua into locked facilities for extended periods. Instead, without asylums or a legal way of constraining people, psychiatric providers have had to develop different tools. They must manage behaviors that are perhaps troubling and dangerous if not officially "dangerous" by the legal standard, as well as clientele who accept some interventions while resisting others. Each clinic must navigate clients' freedom in a terrain that has developed haphazardly over a half century of resource gaps, bureaucratic irrationalities, and ethical contradictions.

EMBODIED SOCIAL PROBLEMS AND VALUED CHILDREN

Those of us who have spent any time in major urban environments like Los Angeles, San Francisco, or New York City already know, or at least think we know, a little about some of the other people in this book. Rather than know these people personally, however, we are more likely to know them as part of a nameless, faceless mass. Even the most caring souls develop strategies to avoid interacting with the people that the sociologist Andrew Scull once dubbed "sidewalk psychotics."[18] They may have bothered us with their strange mutterings or interrupted our walks through the neighborhood by sleeping on the curb. Often we ignore or overlook these anonymous street denizens until they interrupt the smooth functioning of our days.

Such people are an embodied social problem in two senses. First, their presence—their physical bodies—in otherwise gentrified urban spaces is often the most visible reminder of social and policy failures. Second, those societal failures and the suffering they cause can leave literal marks on the flesh, visible in people's damaged bodies and less visibly in their fractured psyches. Sometimes these people get arrested or hospitalized, sometimes they get resources for community living, and sometimes they get nothing at all. In any case, it's likely they remain an object of fear or annoyance to the average passerby.

Or perhaps we know someone more intimately—a sibling or child, a treasured friend we lost track of, or ourselves during a crisis. Maybe that person has cobbled a life together, succeeded beyond everyone's expectations. This is a loved one with a still-possible future of recovery. Or maybe that individual has come close to the zone of nonpersonhood among those on the streets. This is a loved one who rejects family "care" outright as a form of control and threatens to wreak havoc for relatives. They are sources of heartbreak, of embarrassment, and of dread for what the next day holds.

This brings us to the deep ethical tension running through these chapters. Critical scholars and activists have shown how psychiatry can become abusive, as when people's rights are taken away, they are traumatized by physical restraint in emergency hospitalization, or they are forcibly medicated with powerful drugs.[19] But what about the subtler dilemmas of power in everyday voluntary treatment? In some cases, ethical questions that seem obvious in one setting may suddenly look different, depending on the available resources and our relationship to the person in question.

If a patient is psychotic and using drugs but safely housed, should that count as success, or is it failure? Is mandatory physical labor exploitation in a welfare program but therapy at an exclusive residential treatment farm? Is choice better understood as a person's stated desire to be left alone, or the cultivated ability to control impulses and pursue more elaborate life projects? And how do our answers change for strangers, our loved ones, and ourselves?

The title of this book, *Sons, Daughters, and Sidewalk Psychotics*, is supposed to be jarring. If "sons and daughters" indicates both a loving and a possibly condescending paternalism, and Scull's phrase "sidewalk psychotics" sounds like a stigmatizing label for people scorned by mainstream society, it's because this is how contrasting treatment systems often process people. At stake is a question of personhood and belonging. A patient can be seen as an embodied social problem that needs to be moved from a gentrifying neighborhood, or the treasured child/sibling/parent of a paying relative who needs to be "fixed." Of course, any given person may be *both* a nuisance to a local business owner and somebody's beloved kin. Yet there are very different resources, expectations, and dreams allocated for people, depending on the social position they occupy.

To illustrate these differences, the book is organized around three points of comparison. In part 1, "Community Care for Different Communities," we see that although the two mental health-care systems share diagnoses, symptoms, and dilemmas about freedom, they are engaged in separate projects. One is addressing urban poverty and the problems of homelessness and incarceration, and the other is managing strained family dynamics. In part 2, "Unequal Treatments, Unequal Recoveries," we see how "success" is understood and what kind of future a person can expect. For the public treatment provider serving clients long abandoned, the goal is helping a person remain "not homeless, not in jail, not in the hospital." For the elite private provider, the hope is to equip patients with a robust and class-respectable identity. Finally, part 3, "The Paradox of Client Choice," shows how these contrasting recoveries are achieved: the low-surveillance and harm-reduction approach of tolerant containment for the poor patient, and an intensive form of care and control— concerted constraint—for the privileged adult child.

•   •   •

Three notes to readers: first, the book describes different kinds of treatment institutions and possibilities rather than different types of families. Every family member I talked with, regardless of how rich or poor they were, saw their relative as beloved kin, not a sidewalk psychotic. But they didn't all have the same means. Without the time and resources to know how to navigate between insurance systems, for instance, it is hard to access quality early treatment. People are often surprised to learn that private insurance may lack services that Medicaid, public health insurance for the poor, covers, like intensive case management. This leaves middle-class people to choose between two imperfect options. Relatives may also have to choose between working for pay outside the home and caring for a loved one themselves, unpaid, in the home. Without enough space, it can be near impossible to live with a person who is in an extreme state. These are just a few of the ways resources impact who can be a "good family member." And sometimes even the wealthy can struggle to secure appropriate services.

Second is a note on terminology. The vocabulary surrounding

mental health remains fraught with debates over rights, roles, and the nature of unusual psychic states. Even today, despite billions spent on the latest genetic and neuroscientific research, *serious mental illness* (e.g., conditions like schizophrenia, bipolar disorder, or major depression that "substantially interferes with or limits one or more major life activities"[20]) remains scientifically mysterious. We lack solid explanations of cause or biological tests for accurate diagnosis,[21] and some people prefer to think of their experiences in spiritual or political rather than medical terms. For this reason, I also use language like *psychiatric disability* and *madness* to honor competing perspectives, including historical researchers skeptical of projecting contemporary diagnoses across time and place and ex-patient activists who celebrate "mad pride" rather than consider themselves sick.[22] Instead of relying on one set of terms, I rotate usage where appropriate and work to acknowledge both the contested nature of psychiatric science and the undeniable profundity of some peoples' disabilities.

Finally, in line with university human subject protections and medical privacy protocols, the names of nearly all individuals and private treatment organizations are pseudonyms. My research secured approval from the Los Angeles County Department of Mental Health's Human Subjects Research Committee, and I obscure identifying health information in accordance with the committee's procedures and federal requirements. Public organizations like the DMH are named, as are some leadership figures, but the workers themselves are given pseudonyms. Upon request, I occasionally obscured information such as a person's place of origin, and I have limited identifying characteristics if a person was engaged in legally compromising behavior. There are, however, no composite characters. Informed by ongoing discussions of the ethics of researching vulnerable populations, I took cues from treatment providers and clients to minimize potential harms.[23]

PART I

COMMUNITY CARE FOR DIFFERENT COMMUNITIES

CHAPTER 1

DILEMMAS OF THE STREET
AND OF THE HOME

The mid-twentieth-century closing of the United States' mental hospitals simultaneously advanced patient civil liberties and eroded a major part of the social safety net. Today, after sixty years of *community care*, the term's significance remains an open question. For whom is mental illness a problem? What type of problem is it? And what could constitute a solution? This first section of the book will show how the unequal community contexts of contemporary Los Angeles shape both the meaning of serious mental illness and the possible ways of managing it.

Throughout, I will argue that despite some shared history and dilemmas, public safety net and elite private psychiatric providers are engaged in different *projects*. In a public project to manage crises of urban poverty, mental illness is bound up with homelessness and the general suffering on city streets. Treatment takes place in shelters, jails, ERs, and supportive housing, all of which serve to spatially contain visible disorder. When elite providers manage crises in family systems, on the other hand, mental illness is a problem of love, heartache, and fear of downward social mobility. For those affluent few who can afford to try to keep private crises private, care proceeds in the family home, boutique clinics or hospitals, elite sober living centers, and specialized residential treatment facilities.

To introduce these unequal contexts and projects, this chapter contrasts two meetings with a shared problem: how to manage people who are out of place and won't go where directed. We first join the Spring Street Task Force in Downtown as city officials and business leaders debate how to address a homeless encampment when civil liberties lawsuits have made it difficult to simply "sweep" the area of the unhoused. Mental health outreach workers engage Jack Marshall, a homeless, middle-aged Black man. Arguably sick enough to qualify for housing subsidies, Jack refuses the outreach workers' overtures and stays on the street. We then visit NAMI (National Alliance on Mental Illness) Westside Los Angeles, where we hear privileged patients tell their stories of successful treatment. Yet one desperate Japanese American mother says it's not enough: despite the enormous sums she has spent on private care, her son George Tanaka refuses medication and threatens to run away.

The contexts in which these problems are posed shape the solutions seen as possible. Where the city's goal of clearing the streets makes housing the solution to many problems, privileged families' dreams of a respectable future require myriad, individualized, and sometimes last-ditch treatments that may yet fail. To understand these dilemmas of the street and of the home, we will shift our gaze from the present to the past; from the "identified patient" to the organizational context; and finally, from local problems to the broader structures of American society.

CLEARING STREETS WITH THE SPRING STREET TASK FORCE

On a cool afternoon in the winter of 2013, I sat with representatives from an assortment of Los Angeles city and county agencies in a damp church basement. We gathered for the latest meeting of what some had dubbed the Spring Street Task Force, dedicated to removing a homeless encampment near the historic Olvera Street district in Downtown. Under pressure from a coalition of Chinatown business and political leaders, whose patrons and constituents had reportedly been harassed by homeless people near a bus stop, the Los Angeles

County Board of Supervisors had requested that law enforcement and social service providers work together to clear out the tent city.

Standard practices, however, were under attack, so the task force would need a new approach to policing encampments. A group of activists and Skid Row residents had secured a court order—known as the *Lavan* injunction—that would prevent the Los Angeles Police Department (LAPD) and the city from confiscating and destroying property. An earlier case, *Jones v. City of Los Angeles*, had declared it unconstitutional to punish people for being homeless if the government could not provide adequate shelter, and indeed, the city lacked the requisite shelter beds relative to the large homeless population.[1]

A woman from the City Attorney's Office explained the consequences of the city's failed legal appeal. "The latest ruling from the Ninth Circuit, which will apply to all of the West Coast, is that unattended property is covered by the Fourth and Fourteenth Amendments." This meant that the Spring Street Task Force would need to respect people's possessions even if the objects looked to be trash.

"That's crazy," exclaimed Howard Glass, an elder African American supervisor from the Los Angeles County Department of Mental Health. Tapping his temples, he looked around to see others nod in agreement. The city attorney's representative assured the assembly that the office would continue to appeal, but in the meantime it had to pull the police back. In fact, the city wanted the task force to invert the order of contact. She explained, "We're trying to put social, public health, and mental health services and sanitation as the leadership. We're telling LAPD, 'You are not the lead, you are the helper in case someone gets out of hand.' . . . This is a hard pill to swallow, but this is the right lens through which this needs to happen."

With the *Lavan* injunction in place, the City of Los Angeles would have to manage street populations when its primary tools for doing so—policing and property confiscation—were restricted.

For activists and homeless citizens in Downtown Los Angeles, the court order was a significant victory. As the sociologist Forrest Stuart has shown, Skid Row residents had been subjected to a radical

experiment in hyperpolicing that pushed them into bare-bones programs and confiscated their belongings in the name of tough love.
Few of the purported benefits of this approach—what Stuart termed
"therapeutic policing"—ever materialized.[2] The flood of officers never
significantly lowered crime rates, and few people remained in mega-
shelter addiction programs when directed there by law enforcement.
Critics contend that such policing-first approaches to homelessness
tend to compound poverty and prevent people from getting back on
their feet—a ticket and small fine, for instance, can be a huge setback
for a person who is already struggling. That's why, in LA and elsewhere, they have advocated for a Housing First approach: the first
order of business should be securing housing and making attached
services fully voluntary.

Stuart's fieldwork ended with the advocates' triumph. Mine began
in the aftermath. I saw firsthand how the injunction might temporarily protect people from police contact, but it could not magically
conjure resources to end homelessness. Los Angeles still had a drastic deficit in affordable housing stock, stretched social services, and
ever-increasing populations getting by in tent cities. The court orders
left everyone unsure what would replace heavy-handed policing in the
management of homelessness Downtown.

The city's and the county's eventual response, Operation Healthy
Streets in Skid Row and the collaboration with the task force on
Spring Street, would justify encampment clearance in the name not
of law enforcement but of mental and public health. Rather than
send police to clear the tents, the city would identify an area for street
cleaning, deploy mental health and public health workers to engage
people, then bag, tag, and store nonhazardous belongings on the day
of the power washing. Police removal was now to be the backstop, a
third step rather than a first.

The city attorney's representative acknowledged that this approach
would be deeply inefficient and that the encampments might come
right back, but it was the only option after the court ruling. Then
she noted, "You all know that the more connection, the more inter-
ference, repetition, the better chance we have." Where the business

owners wanted "police sweeps," a solution featuring the metaphor of a broom to trash, she offered a less satisfying one: "In the city, we call it a funnel." Here agencies would hem in and clean out and generally narrow options for the homeless until these individuals were persuaded to accept service offers or, at the very least, go somewhere else.

And what would "motivate" people to accept existing services, acknowledged by many in the room as inadequate or undesirable, without police pressure? The majority on the street clamored for the subsidized apartments of the Housing First approach, but amid a housing crisis and a prioritization system that focused on the most "vulnerable," the housing vouchers were reserved for the estimated 20 percent of unhoused people with serious psychiatric disabilities. On the other hand, outreach workers believed that many of the "truly ill" would reject offers of help.

The chair of the Spring Street Task Force meeting, a woman representing a county supervisor, stated that the group could not ignore the "criminal element" imported to Spring Street from Skid Row. Others were stuck in a policing mind-set as well. A supervisor from the Los Angeles Homeless Services Authority (LAHSA) recommended a Connect Day on which the task force would display every available resource to justify a sweep. "Take it or leave it," she said. "This is the last day before law enforcement comes in."

The task force members decided, however, that they could no longer legally authorize policing in this way. Nor could they initiate property clearance without a documented safety or public health hazard. The city did not want to risk the fines or legal action if police arrested the wrong people or wantonly destroyed property. Howard from the DMH added that outreach workers and law enforcement had yet to figure out who was part of the "criminal element," who was mentally ill, or whether, as some had speculated, a loan shark credit system had been imported from Skid Row.

The city attorney's rep agreed. "The 'homeless' is not a monolithic population. There are mentally ill people, felons, rockers, all kinds of people." Until the task force better understood the situation, it couldn't simply threaten encampment dwellers with the police. The plan was to continue to survey the area, sort people into categories, and link them to appropriate resources.

Howard whispered to me that this approach would resolve neither the legal dispute nor the resource limitations. The DMH couldn't force the nondangerous or non-gravely disabled into care, and most other people wouldn't be so profoundly disabled as to qualify for the housing linked to intensive mental health services. Further, DMH and LAHSA outreach workers were unsure what it would mean to become the new front line of contact without the police.

Chinatown leaders still wanted the camp displaced, but they seemed to become more interested in helping the seriously mentally ill. This logic of exceptional treatment for the disabled held appeal for the Spring Street Task Force more broadly, and it meant substantial attention paid to a small handful of people. A Chinese American businessman, corpulent in his dress shirt and wearing an expression of concern that struck me as genuine, asked the DMH to find Jack Marshall, a middle-aged African American man he'd seen setting up camp outside a Vietnamese sandwich shop.

JACK MARSHALL'S "POOR JUDGMENT"

Later that week, I accompanied DMH Homeless Outreach Mobile Engagement (HOME) workers. We found Jack wrapped in a fraying brown coat, just where the businessman said he'd be. That edge of the neighborhood is slightly industrial and feels rougher than the Oakland Chinatown I had frequented as a child, but I felt at ease amid the smells of dim sum and fishy water. Jack seemed at ease too, telling me he liked staying in the area because he was part Chinese.

When the HOME workers asked whether he wanted food, Jack said he liked donuts and hot chocolate, but he hadn't had a meal in a while. Mona, a Filipina nurse and outreach worker, took the moment to point out that Jack could go to a Board and Care home that offered three meals a day and wouldn't expect much of him (this housing is funded by residents' Supplemental Security Income checks and minor subsidies from the county). "If you want to stay indoors, you can just lay there." However, while stroking his thick black beard, Jack said he wasn't interested.

Mona asked whether he'd prefer an apartment. "I ain't got no money," Jack replied dismissively.

"Let's say you could just *magically* move into an apartment," Mona said, smiling. "What would it look like?"

Jack was incredulous. "I don't believe in that." The other outreach worker laughed, and Jack added, "Not these days and times, and not for a Black man."

Just then, in a flurry, a woman threw open the doors of the sandwich shop, hurriedly greeted Jack good morning, and handed him a Vietnamese sandwich before rushing back inside.

Beaming with pleasure, Mona exclaimed, "You want food, and there it is! Like, maybe if you *really* wish for a place, it will happen . . ."

"Maybe," Jack squinted skeptically. "I'm blind, so I can't really appreciate no apartment right now."

Undeterred, Mona made one more attempt at persuasion. "When you talk about 'not for a Black man,' but you know our president is half Black. So, it's changing times."

As we walked back to the main Spring Street encampment, the DMH HOME workers agreed that Jack's claims seemed off (specifically, those about being part Chinese and blind). It struck me that his wariness of social service offers could be grounded in experiences of real racism and broken promises. Still, Mona thought that the ultimate issue was serious mental illness. That's why she'd gone for a playful approach—discussing the "magic" of food and apartments manifesting out of thin air—that she used to engage nonrational people. It was a kind exchange, and it might pay dividends later.

Either way, Jack was surviving and accessing food on his own, and he was therefore not "gravely disabled" or a threat to himself or others, so the workers agreed that there were no legal grounds for putting him on a psychiatric hold. The HOME team had made its offers of medical treatment and housing and established that Jack didn't meet criteria for a 5150, so the next steps were up to him.

At the following meeting of the Spring Street Task Force, Howard from the DMH reported that it had found Jack, and he appeared to have no mental health or substance needs. The corpulent business-man was shocked. "I don't mean to be ignorant, but what exactly does 'mental illness' mean, then? He's sleeping out on the street for a very long time and doesn't use drugs."

"Poor judgment," assessed Laura, the leader of the DMH intensive treatment team. Other outreach workers had purportedly visited Jack over the years, and he continually refused their offers. He fit a street outreach agency truism to a t: those people most appropriate for the housing were always most likely to refuse it.

"It's a sad sight to see," the businessman said. Howard agreed, then added, "He can refuse medical treatment." As if looking for a way around the rights Jack retained, the county Board of Supervisor's representative asked whether the DMH could seek a conservatorship and become Jack's legal guardian. Howard explained that in California, such a conservatorship would only be possible after a hospitalization and a designation of "grave disability." Both were unlikely for someone like Jack, who was adequately surviving on the street.

"The city and we, as a society, refuse to force people into treatment. It's a balance between peoples' rights and recognizing that they need help," Howard offered. "There's a gap between what people *need* and what they're willing to do," Laura explained.

Given new legal scrutiny of the policing of homeless encampments, restrictions on coercive psychiatric care, and grossly inadequate social services, the task force's prospects for helping people like Jack—or even just clearing the Spring Street space—looked grim.

RESTORING HOPE AT THE NATIONAL ALLIANCE ON MENTAL ILLNESS

Three years later and ten miles west, I was a world away at the National Alliance on Mental Illness's (NAMI's) monthly speaker series. In this setting, psychiatric disability was associated not with urban disorder and street sweeps but with crises of the family.

I'd come to hear testimonies of service users who were in recovery from serious mental illness and living fulfilling lives. The setting was a cheery if bland multipurpose room in a local nonprofit community center. I helped set up the chairs and introduced myself to families as we passed food and chatted. One of the speakers whom I'd already met, Leonard, waved and introduced me to his mother. Joseph, the family services coordinator at the elite private Actualization Clinic, connected me to others while he, too, made the rounds. As audience members trickled in, featured guests began to take the stage.

Zara, the local NAMI president, began by speaking of her own struggle with a profoundly ill child. "One in four families in my neighborhood has a member with a mental illness, with anxiety, depression, schizophrenia, bipolar, so many ways that the brain goes awry." From her experience, she learned that "people need therapy, medications, and an educated, supportive family." Education was where NAMI came in, providing families with training courses on the biology of mental illness and connecting them with general support groups. After this preamble, Zara introduced the night's speakers as "four heroes and a heroine," each of whom had managed serious mental illness and was now giving back to the community.

Leonard was up first, sharing his life's story of dashed then transformed dreams. Still boyish in his early thirties, he cracked a wide smile as he began his account. While a successful student at a prestigious university who was planning a career in investment banking, he had experienced a psychotic break—typical timing, as most symptoms like this emerge during the late teens and early twenties. Eventually, he'd endure more than twenty hospitalizations and unsuccessful outpatient programs. His mother always stood by him, even when the family dynamics grew heated at home. Then a "special place," the Actualization Clinic, finally put an end to the cycle.

Today, Leonard could proudly say that since attending the clinic's Intensive Outpatient Program, he hadn't been hospitalized a single time. He closed by saying he was now pursuing a master's degree in psychology and hoped to help the elderly and others experiencing mental illness. "I lost my mind," he explained. "But I gained my heart."

The next speaker was Geraldine, a white woman in her late thirties who struggled with bipolar disorder. After her independent life at college, she found moving back in with her family demoralizing. She drank heavily, and her medication seemed to have stopped working. When she was hospitalized after a suicide attempt, she realized that others shared her struggle but lacked the family resources that she had. Rectifying this inequality became her new goal, and she decided to volunteer with social service agencies while she resumed her studies.

As she worked toward master's degrees in public policy and social work, Geraldine began an unpaid job as a creative writing teacher at Step Up on Second, a nonprofit mental health agency serving low-income patients. The work gave her purpose and a whole social network that she had lacked. Moreover, it gave her an answer to what she called the "what do you do [for work]" question—a painful query for those spending their days on the family couch. From there, she moved on to paid employment in mental health.

Two other speakers then described their private treatment experiences, one in an intensive drug rehabilitation facility in Utah and the other in a dual-diagnosis (mental illness and addiction) sober living home in LA that featured meditation, self-help, and organic healthy eating. The latter had been attended by a young Black man with tightly cropped hair who smiled exuberantly as he described the clean eating and juice cleanses, and how he'd been able to titrate off his antipsychotic medication with the intensive holistic regimen. It was all very Southern California: nine integrative health steps to transform the mind and body, and daily affirmations to remain positive.

The final hero was Dev, a middle-aged South Asian man who rose to a great height when he stood to address the audience. He, too, had a successful college career until he began to experience strange thoughts, was admitted to a psychiatric hospital, and was diagnosed with a psychotic disorder. Even after he became stable, he found he could no longer think clearly. A neuropsychological test revealed profound cognitive deficits, and his doctor explained that no medication could fix those. Coming as he had from a family of high achievers, Dev was distraught. "In Indian culture," he said, "your whole self-worth is tied to education." His family hired the Actualization Clinic to get him back on track.

Dev echoed Leonard's claim that Actualization was different from the rest of the mental health system. "Meeting Joseph was the first time a person cared more about me than just a job, really cared about me getting better," he declared. Actualization focused on "abilities rather than disabilities," so it sought out what people like Dev could contribute to the world. Learning that Dev had played college tennis, for instance, Joseph took him to the local courts. Dev recalled thinking, "What good is tennis if I can't have a real life?" He didn't want to leave the house, but Joseph pushed him into a routine, not accepting Dev's protests that he wasn't ready. "Readiness," Dev said, "is in hindsight." With Actualization's assistance, he returned to college, then pursued a master's in social work, and today runs a business as a peer coach for people with mental health struggles similar to his own.

"Leonard and Dev got their lives back," Zara said proudly. She told the audience about Actualization's case management approach that not only coordinated treatment but also filled in gaps in life activities. Dev added, "The research tells us that the key is one special relationship, and for me it was Joseph." Waving his hands, Joseph accepted the compliment before deftly directing attention back to the speakers. "They're the ones who did the work," he said.

This room felt full of promise, up until audience members raised a problem that elite mental health-care providers and a Southern California lifestyle might be unable to resolve. Marsha Tanaka had paid for Actualization services and a private dual-diagnosis sober home, but she was still struggling with her twenty-five-year-old son. Diagnosed with a psychotic disorder, George had experienced legal troubles, multiple hospitalizations, and a brief disappearance to the streets. What was a family to do when, given access to high-end treatment, its loved one rejected it?

Marsha and another mother framed the problem as "impaired insight," or the idea that some people's mental illness prevents them from understanding that they are mentally ill. To them, all five speakers "had insight" into their conditions, meaning they agreed that they were sick. Marsha's son did not, and he intermittently refused to take medication. Dev acknowledged that this situation was a real challenge. "You can't go with the 'medical model' approach, telling someone they have an illness and providing psycho-education. They'll just say, 'Fuck you!'"

The impaired insight or anosognosia concept remains controversial, with critics suggesting that it both silences patients' legitimate disagreements with diagnosis or treatment and lacks an objective scientific basis.[3] As a practical shorthand, however, it summarized Marsha Tanaka's frustration with patients' rights laws that limit forced care to emergency situations. Did it even make sense to offer George choices about treatment if he seemed too ill to know he needed the help?

GEORGE TANAKA'S "ANOSOGNOSIA AND AFFLUENZA"

Arnie and Marsha Tanaka invited me to their home in West LA. A single-story, brown and white three-bedroom house in a quiet neighborhood, it was a modest place that, given LA's housing shortage, nonetheless came with a price tag well over $1 million. The Tanakas greeted me with warm smiles and solid handshakes, and we began with small talk about our respective connections to Japanese American communities in California. Then we pivoted to our real purpose: talking about George.

His parents explained that he had become hyperreligious in college and made increasingly strange statements. He decided to leave school to tend to his elderly grandmother, but he soon became preoccupied with God and banging on the walls of his room with tools. Arnie and Marsha had no idea what to do, but a friend suggested they call 911.

This friend said that a police initiation of a 5150 psychiatric hold would be discreet, but Marsha remembered that "they sent six cop cars, all lights, sirens coming down the block, and I'm thinking, 'I thought this was supposed to be quiet?'" Ironically, the 5150 was dead in the water. Like many unfamiliar with California's mental health laws, the Tanakas were shocked when the police determined that George was neither dangerous nor gravely disabled. He was entitled to his right to refuse care.

"They said, 'There's nothing we could do, because he's not harmful to himself, to others,' all that criteria," Marsha recalled. "I said, 'There's eight cop cars out here, and you can't do one thing? You can't take . . .' [They said,] 'No, ma'am, I'm sorry, we can't do that.' I just said, 'This is ridiculous.' I just walked back into the house." "That's when you feel like you're hopeless," Arnie said. "It's, like, my God, you can't do *anything*?"

The police eventually got George to leave, but his parents found they couldn't "hold the line" and keep him out of the house. They weren't prepared to let him fend for himself on the streets. The call to 911 "was like a Thursday night," Marsha said. "Then Friday night he came back, and we let him back in the house, because we didn't know what else to do."

The Tanakas couldn't ignore the situation any longer when they hosted a party at their home, and George began to bang a hammer on the wall of his room. Arnie described it as a surreal cinematic comedy of errors as he tried to keep his guests in the yard and unaware of the drama inside, entertaining them while monitoring his psychotic son. When he called 911 this time, a sympathetic law enforcement officer defined George's behavior as dangerous, claiming that the damaged wall might fall on someone. This officer initiated a 5150 hold and took George to the hospital. After a brief time in a public ER, George was transferred to a private hospital for two weeks.

The Tanakas found the hospital system equally frustrating, because its representatives wouldn't disclose information to them because of privacy regulations. They were financially responsible for their son's care, since he was on their insurance policy, and for thousands of dollars in deductible payments, but they had no right to information about how the hospitalization was working, whether George was taking medication, or anything else, really. That meant they were particularly taken aback when he was released and directed to a clinic in

Skid Row. As Arnie put it in describing George's brief homeless forays Downtown and on Venice Beach, "I mean, it's close—you know, you think that it's so far away. But it's, like, here we are, I have a son that actually thought about [being homeless]."

Marsha said that the Actualization Clinic became invaluable when her son disappeared. He had sold his car and flown to Puerto Rico, where he purportedly believed that the Tanakas were royalty. Richard, the owner of Actualization, calmly coached the parents on when to send George money and when to withhold it—what Actualization calls leveraging—and what to say on the phone until he decided to return. Unlike the hospital, Richard worked collaboratively with Marsha and Arnie and kept them in the loop, so when the next crisis arose, they turned to him again. This time, he helped talk George into going for a brief meeting at a private hospital, where he was committed against his will. When George called his parents and pleaded for them to get him out, Richard helped them be resilient and follow the plan.

The Actualization Clinic honed its expertise in engaging clients who lacked insight, managing parental anxiety, and creating systems of behavioral incentives through years of trial and error. In Richard's terms, George Tanaka was an "anosognosia and affluenza" case. Not only did he lack insight into his illness, but he also came from a class-privileged background that, without appropriate boundaries and expectations, had left him spoiled. The sense of entitlement that can be a marker of upper-middle-class distinction became a problem, in Richard's eyes, when a person would not minimally conform to expectations. Richard pointed out that George simply assumed that if he sold his car, his parents would buy him a new one. Unlike some older psychoanalytic theories of the "schizophregenic mother," Richard didn't believe that family dysfunction *caused* psychosis. Instead, the families had created situations in which children never learned responsibility; this became disastrous for those who grew into adults with serious mental illness.

Having the means to pay for elite private care at least temporarily, the Tanakas held out hope for their son's recovery. The Actualization Clinic had been responsive to Arnie and Marsha's wishes and helped establish a promising treatment plan. George moved into a dual-diagnosis mental health and sober home, and soon he was playing on a sports team, resuming his old hobbies, and attending community college. Still, the Tanakas confided in me that they couldn't sustain the expensive regimen. They had run through their savings and were borrowing from relatives. Furthermore, George hadn't gotten on board with his treatment plan: despite his successes there, he purportedly likened the expensive treatment residence to a "prison."

·   ·   ·

Rather than finding either a local government's domination of the disconnected street person or a privileged family's ability to force its member to go where told, we see that both city and family must work with an individual's choices in the community. The struggle to cope with the urban sidewalk psychotic and the disruptive adult child might seem like an inevitable or even a natural feature of human existence. Bizarre strangers or relatives descending into madness can no doubt be found in literature and family lore across time and place. Yet these dilemmas of the street and the family home are historically specific, and from another cultural vantage point they might not seem natural at all. Let's take a step back and consider these meetings again.

Why are these seemingly authoritative actors—government workers at the Spring Street Task Force meeting and parents at the NAMI meeting—actively managing "problem" people in the community rather than simply placing them out of sight and out of mind? Why is Jack Marshall "free" to be untreated and sleep on the street, drawing the ire and sympathy of passersby? Why is George Tanaka roaming around LA or disappearing to Puerto Rico, and why does Marsha struggle over whether to keep her son at home, in an expensive private facility she can't afford, or kick him to the streets? Where, in other words, do these situations come from?

The answer is psychiatric deinstitutionalization. Jack Marshall and George Tanaka have become problems of the city streets and of the family home because the United States never created a community care system that could replace the asylum. Not all the patients or potential patients we meet in this book would have been candidates for confinement, but their options today are nonetheless circumscribed by the history of the asylum and the haphazard infrastructure developed in its wake.

MANAGING MENTAL ILLNESS IN MODERNITY

Care for serious mental illness in Western societies has gone through a series of overlapping, nonlinear reforms.[4] Strikingly, the past three hundred years have brought movements to transfer people with psychiatric disabilities from the community to asylum confinement, then out again; today, some advocates have undertaken a renewed effort to "bring back the asylum."[5] In the United States, the asylum was the way to manage disruption from the mid-nineteenth century to the mid-twentieth, and a vast infrastructure was in place to lock people up in hospitals. Often brutal and ineffective at treatment, it was nonetheless an effective social problem–solving tool.

Where did the asylum come from? The physical confinement of "madness" has a prehistory in Western countries dating to the fourteenth century, though broad-based social policy, like a state hospital system, was a modern development.[6] Well into the eighteenth century, people with serious mental disabilities lived among others and were considered a local problem. The "town fool," as some were regarded, might be left alone, but he or she had no rights per se. Those who became too bothersome might be confined in the home or in a jail, living under the dominion of relatives or officials. The collapse of feudalism as a social system and the rise of industrialization brought droves of country folk to the cities looking for work. This left the disabled unmoored from local social relations and care. Urbanization created a new, highly visible problem: a mass of out-of-work peasants, paupers, and petty criminals, the mad among them, thronging newly industrial cities.

A paternalistic attitude toward the insane person was considered natural. For classical liberal philosophers, madness was a clear limit case in the expansion of individual rights. As John Locke put it in

1690, "lunaticks and ideots are never set free from the governance of their parents."[7] Two centuries later, John Stuart Mill similarly argued that liberty was "to apply only to human beings in the maturity of their faculties" and that "good despots" remained necessary for those who could not be educated into responsible freedom.[8] It was obvious, indeed axiomatic, that people who experienced delusion or other profound disability could not self-govern. As medical and social thinkers grappled with precise definitions of madness and debated the question of agency and freedom, the practical solution took hold: building places to lock people away.

Within the new institutions, caretakers deployed strategies from brute restraint to kind persuasion to manage and normalize the mad. The philosopher Michel Foucault called the rounding up of all manner of problem people "the Great Confinement."[9] From small-scale private operations where privileged families could send difficult members to large-scale state-sponsored institutions for the poor, orphaned, insane, or otherwise nonproductive masses, the houses of confinement proliferated as an alternative to simple imprisonment or indigence. Over time, patients were separated from other inmates and psychiatry emerged as its own medical discipline in the asylums. This cemented the semantic change from *madness* into *mental illness*. Institutional confinement's various forms were in some sense always tied to dilemmas of urban poverty and "problem" relatives, but the large public asylum scaled it up and made it broadly available.

In the United States, the nineteenth-century campaign to build asylums was seen as a major social reform. Dorothea Dix famously fought to rescue the disabled from jail or neglectful families, comparing American policy unfavorably with Europe's "civilized" hospital system.[10] Yet Dix's campaign was in some sense *too* successful—the more asylum beds made available, the more people were sent to fill them, and the dream of humanistic care was short lived. As the hospital censuses rose, individualized treatment became impossible. By the beginning of the twentieth century, public asylums in the United States had become warehouses, some holding up to four thousand patients at any given time. In such massive institutions, the sheer "numbers render the inmates mere automatons, acted on in this or that fashion according to the rules governing the great machine."[11] In the 1950s, at the peak of the American psychiatric hospital system, more than six hundred thousand people were so confined.

It was during this period that critiques of psychiatric care found an eager public. Journalistic exposés such as Albert Deutsch's 1948 *The Shame of the States* documented a massive gap between the rhetoric of humane asylum conditions and, well, reality.[12] In their pioneering 1958 study *Social Class and Mental Illness*, the sociologist-psychiatrist team of August Hollingshead and Frederick Redlich found that wealthier patients received various somatic and talk therapeutics, while many poor people were relegated to custodial care, absent treatment.[13] Other critics aimed at not only public dungeons but the high-end private hospitals that worked to the same end: depriving people of their liberty. Famous and egregious cases included husbands declaring wives insane and having them locked away as an alternative to divorce; these and other cases led to particularly strong feminist condemnation of the system.

Riding the wave of 1960s counterculture, the psychiatrist R. D. Laing suggested that the people called mentally ill were actually the sane ones in a crazy world, with much to teach mainstream society.[14] Sociologists like Erving Goffman described the parallels between mental hospitals and other "total institutions" such as prisons, army barracks, and even concentration camps.[15] Drawing on a year of observation inside an asylum, Goffman argued that the treatment "mortified the self" and merely socialized people into being patients. In popular culture, Ken Kesey's *One Flew over the Cuckoo's Nest* offered a similarly powerful indictment of the hospital's assault on individuality.[16] All pointed out that psychiatrists couldn't reliably diagnose illness, as competing physicians frequently described the same patient as suffering from different diseases. Indeed, given that no biological tests existed for diagnosing the major disorders, the dissident psychiatrist Thomas Szasz went so far as proclaiming mental illness a "myth" used to control noncriminal social deviance.[17] The psychiatric hospital's reputation was in tatters.

FROM ASYLUM TO COMMUNITY

Then came deinstitutionalization. It was a product of powerful economic forces, social movement pressure, genuine belief in reforms, and premature faith in new treatments, and it came with heaps of unintended consequences. Rather than a single moment, it was a decades-long undoing of an archipelago of state and private hospitals and legal statutes facilitating confinement. It begat a community system that was funded piecemeal and relied largely on voluntary participation, with inadequate treatment available even for those who wanted it. Deinstitutionalization both resulted from and generated highly polarized debates around whether people should be allowed to live in the community or hospitalized against their will. And it moved responsibility for the management of mental illness from state governments to cities and counties, on the one hand, and to families, on the other.

Ideological, technological, and economic factors all played a part.[18] The ideological critique was the province of radical civil libertarian intellectuals and iconoclastic artists, like Goffman, Laing, Szasz, and Kesey—but also mainstream policy makers. President John F. Kennedy's Community Mental Health Act of 1962, for instance, eagerly and optimistically aimed to move half the institutionalized population to local care within a planned two thousand community mental health centers. Kennedy's zeal was likely influenced by his observations of his own sister's plight. Rosemary Kennedy, who seemingly suffered from psychiatric and intellectual disabilities, had been lobotomized and hidden away from the world, not in some public "snake pit" but in elite treatment facilities for the wealthy. Kennedy had seen firsthand the risks of psychiatric abuses in the name of care.

The discovery of chlorpromazine (marketed under the brand name Thorazine and others), the first antipsychotic, in the 1950s coincided with calls to close the asylum, and it helped some patients function well enough to be discharged. Medication enabled a new approach to patient care that would rely not on coercion and confinement but on individuals' compliance with a drug regimen that would putatively

restore their reason. Even the earliest research showed that the medication worked only for some people, and many found the side effects
intolerable, yet a naïve enthusiasm that it would facilitate community
independence was hard to repress.

Meanwhile, a third driver of deinstitutionalization rose in the form
of financial projections; without substantial tax increases, the hospital system was quickly becoming financially unsustainable (recall
that some six hundred thousand people were so confined in the mid-
1950s). As the sociologist Andrew Scull argued in 1977, the "fiscal crisis of the state" created a strong structural pull alongside the cultural
forces of the 1960s.[19] Right-leaning politicians saw an opportunity for
massive savings in a move from state-based custodial to local management. During the rollout of Great Society programs, some argued that
the federal government should not pay for both community-based and
institutional settings for the disabled. If the government established
community living options, so the logic went, it need not fund the asylums as well.

The Social Security Amendments of 1965, which established
Medicaid public health insurance for poor Americans, also played a
significant role by disincentivizing long-term hospitalization in favor
of in-community services. Federal Medicaid funds would be made
available for community-based care but not for Institutions of Mental
Disease (IMD) (those housing sixteen or more people with mental illness).[20] The measure was a way to incentivize state governments to
invest in municipal programs and give up the state hospital model,
which they would have to self-fund if it were to be sustained. In practice, however, this Medicaid IMD exclusion meant neither the state
nor the federal government would pay for long-term indigent care—
and the emergent community system was woefully inadequate to
replace all the functions of the asylum.

With hindsight, the triumph of deinstitutionalization looks more
like a tragic irony: an unlikely coalition of civil libertarian liberals
and fiscal conservatives pushed for the destruction of an abusive and
neglectful system that had nonetheless housed, fed, and organized the
lives of over half a million people.[21]

THE DOUBLY FREED PSYCHIATRIC PATIENT

It is hard to overstate how radical this transformation was. Even the most ideologically individualistic thinkers saw mentally ill people as the exception to freedom and responsibility. In 1962, the libertarian economist Milton Friedman echoed Locke and Mill when he wrote, "Paternalism is inescapable for those whom we designate as not responsible. The clearest case, perhaps, is that of madmen. We are willing neither to permit them freedom nor to shoot them. It would be nice if we could rely on voluntary activities of individuals to house and care for the madmen. But . . . we may be willing to arrange for their care through government."[22]

Perhaps the paradigmatic proponent of unfettered freedom and a bare-bones government, Friedman drew the line at the mentally ill. In his characteristic contrarian tone, he at least recognized that murder was not socially acceptable. But because he believed that the private sector would never see a clear profit motive to care for indigent disabled people, he conceded that there might be a need for a government welfare function.

Only a decade after he wrote, however, the conventional wisdom had changed. Patients were free but without those guarantees of government assistance. And unlike in the past, where neighbors or family members might simply exert control over them at the local level, the mentally ill now had the formal right to be left alone. A series of new civil libertarian laws added to the confusion by making it far more difficult to hospitalize people, force them to comply with therapies, or make them take the new medications.

To invoke one of Friedman's ideological opponents, we can think of this as the double-sided nature of freedom. Karl Marx once wrote that the transition from feudalism to capitalism doubly freed the serfs.[23] No longer bound to the land owned by a lord, former serfs were indeed free to leave and sell their labor power elsewhere. Yet they were also "freed" from the guarantee of subsistence and protection that the feudal system offered, as they were suddenly forced to either work in poor factory conditions or starve. Deinstitutionalization doubly freed the psychiatric patient, who became free to live on the outside and act in bizarre ways but also free to be homeless or held criminally responsible for his or her actions.

DILEMMAS OF THE STREET AND OF THE HOME

Critics of the new regime coined a phrase to describe this paradoxical freedom and abandonment: people were "dying with their rights on."[24] The period of hospital closures of the 1960s–80s occurred at the same time as a number of so-called neoliberal transformations to American society. Deindustrialization and the outsourcing of industry to poorer countries meant that it became far harder for Americans with modest educations to find well-paying work like factory jobs. Disinvestment in public housing and the destruction of low-income settings like single-room-occupancy hotels made urban homelessness far more common. In the critical geographer Ruth Wilson Gilmore's terms, the twin disinvestment by both industry and government constituted an "organized abandonment" of entire regions.[25] As is common during times of social upheaval, both property and violent crime rose.[26]

The government's general response was not to increase benefits or pursue root-cause solutions but rather to punish. Ex-patients were collateral damage in what the sociologist Loïc Wacquant has identified as a major reorientation of state priorities: economic deregulation to benefit the rich, the weakening of the social safety net through disinvestment in public goods, and the expansion of police and prisons to sweep up the resulting social problems.[27] For thinkers like Wacquant and Gilmore, punishment and poverty were functionally interconnected—the more communities experienced job loss and social need without a strong safety net, the more government used police and incarceration to manage the fallout.

Broken windows policing and the war on drugs devastated poor, and especially Black and Brown, communities.[28] People with psychiatric disabilities were often caught up, increasingly jailed for minor disturbances that might have previously been handled informally or landed them in hospitals. Downtown Skid Rows and marginal urban areas would become what the scholars Dear and Wolch have called "service dependent ghettos," wherein large numbers of ex-patients were either relegated to halfway houses or left to languish on the streets.[29] In less technical terms, those authors would label places like Los Angeles's Skid Row "landscapes of despair." Rotating in an "institutional circuit" of short emergency hospitalizations, shelters, and jail cells, many received brief bursts of biopsychiatric treatment alongside punishment and abandonment.[30]

Many people with serious psychiatric disabilities lacked social connections, and so they faced all this alone. Others experienced the new system alongside their loved ones, because beyond the city, the major social institution tasked with management of madness was the family. Yet as confinement gave way to community care, families were often unsure of what to do. They found that they couldn't secure their loved ones adequate voluntary treatment, housing, and benefits, nor could they confine them and force care like they might have in the past. Most turned to the poorly funded public system, where they might be cut out when patients rejected their involvement. Families possessing greater resources, however, might have recourse to an alternative system in which *they* are the clients.[31] Either way, families were suddenly tasked with a care and control role that would have seemed unthinkable a generation before.

Most ethnographic literature on mental health care in the United States is an account of public and nonprofit services for the poor. Socially connected, privileged patients have received less social scientific attention, perhaps because they aren't a publicly visible social problem like the homeless sidewalk psychotic.[32] But understanding the aftermath of deinstitutionalization is impossible without considering the families—whether they're of modest means navigating public systems or those with more money navigating private ones.

Consider, for instance, that at the same time patients' rights movements for self-determination gained political clout, a burgeoning family member social movement sought greater influence in civil commitment procedure and treatment planning.[33] Perhaps the first major California family support group, Parents of Adult Schizophrenics, began in 1974. Uniting with other similar grassroots chapters, it eventually formed the California Association of Families of the Mentally Disabled, which then joined with fifty-eight other groups nationwide to form the National Alliance on Mental Illness.[34] From the start, a fundamental ambiguity was embedded in NAMI—was it an organization dedicated to the patient's perspective, or did it focus on the family's perception of what was needed?[35] Sometimes these aims aligned, and sometimes they did not. Today, as then, families sought a variety of ways to "deal with" the problem of mental illness, some of which directly contradicted the patient's wishes.

GOVERNANCE PROJECTS AND ECOLOGIES

In my analytic framework, we can best understand these worlds of community care by breaking them into two dimensions: governance projects and ecologies. By *governance,* I mean the broad shaping of human action via rule setting, incentives, and the cultivation of people's dispositions and desires. Consider both the governor of a state, who enforces laws to ensure the smooth functioning of society, and the governess, typically a woman hired to train the children of wealthy families through inducement and leading by example. Governance projects, then, are enterprises that shape behavior toward a shared goal—in this case, addressing visible disorder for the city versus managing unruly relatives for the family.

By *ecology,* I follow other sociologists in borrowing a biological term for describing the relationship between organisms and the environments that sustain them—in this case, I mean people and the set of organizations, physical locations, and cultural institutions in which they live their lives. Empirically, I map out care ecologies by seeing which organizations and actors collaborate and recognize each other as part of a shared orbit—for instance, two programs that routinely refer clients to each other are likely part of the same ecology. We can think of community care first as tied to distinct schemes to manage behavior and locally defined problems, and second as made materially possible in physical spaces and organizations with contrasting resources.

With all this in mind, we can return to the Spring Street Task Force and the NAMI Stories of Recovery event with a better idea of how the dilemmas and responses in each arose. During the asylum era, both Jack Marshall and George Tanaka might have been hospitalized long term. Today, both are treated (or not treated) in the community. Each man is designated seriously mentally ill, each disagrees with such a diagnosis, and each hampers the plans of seemingly more powerful actors by refusing to engage in treatment. The business owners at Spring Street, for instance, are baffled when the DMH claims there is nothing to be done about Jack Marshall. At NAMI, Marsha Tanaka struggles to deal with her son's sometimes bizarre actions.

These difficulties surrounding the legal and cultural empowerment of seemingly irrational people bridge the massive social chasm between service dependent ghettos like Downtown Skid Row and the privileged households of West LA. Yet despite shared histories and overlapping dilemmas, the two groups are engaged in different projects within different social worlds.

The Spring Street Task Force is part of a project of *urban poverty governance.* Here mental illness is one more problem amid the city's need to combat physical urban blight and police crime, replace or rezone shantytowns, promote gentrification, house homeless people, improve public transportation, and so forth. These governance processes occur in a specific ecology of public safety net organizations and spaces. The NAMI meeting, on the other hand, is part of a project of *family systems governance.* The Actualization Clinic has been hired by Marsha Tanaka to guide George back to the expected life of an upper-middle-class family, within a different organizational ecology.

This framework helps us move beyond general questions such as How does the community shape psychiatric care? Or What are the politics and economics of managing mental illness? Such questions

can't be answered in the singular, since much depends on *which* community we are talking about as well as the political economy of its
relevant infrastructure and market.

.   .   .

In the following chapters, we will encounter local puzzles that tie back
to the question of governance projects and ecologies. For instance,
you will learn why public outreach workers try to secure diagnoses
of serious mental illness for people who are arguably just homeless;
why DMH workers worry that they are only there to justify police
sweeps; and why the state has not only left people on the street but
also given them "the right" to be there. You will also learn why some
elite private psychiatric providers believe that the rich can cause more
"damage" than the poor; why diagnostic specificity actually matters
in private care; and why there aren't more "nice" Board and Care
homes for the wealthy. Finally, you will learn about paradoxical cross-
over between these ecologies: why some upper-middle-class families
choose Medicaid over private insurance, for example, and why Black
and Brown families at another NAMI branch view their project as
inseparable from urban governance dynamics.

CHAPTER 2

SORTING OUT THE DOWN AND OUT

For a moment, the sounds of laughter and small pleasures obscured the low hum of suffering and boredom on San Julian Street. Belle Sharon of the Los Angeles Homeless Services Authority (LAHSA) took a breath and approached a circle of African American men, interrupting their spirited conversation. She explained that the group would have to temporarily break down their camps for the upcoming Operation Healthy Streets power washings. Still, they would retain rights to their property, and she could direct them to services in the meantime. One man shrugged and said he'd already seen a posted announcement.

The soon-to-retire outreach worker then revealed her secret to getting off the street. "If you want housing, you have to get evaluated at DMH [Department of Mental Health]."

"I'm not crazy," replied a white-haired gentleman.

"You know you gotta be crazy to be out here," she countered.

Away from the crowd, Belle reflected on the outreach projects and street cleanings. As a Black woman who had struggled in her youth, she empathized with people who had the odds stacked against them. Poverty and homelessness could be outside individual control, she insisted. And she saw the city's response as more political than humanitarian, aimed mostly at appeasing local business owners and recent transplants. "We all know what this is about," she said coolly. "Gentrification."

At that moment, LAHSA could only offer most homeless people shelter beds and occasional hotel vouchers. Nearly everyone wanted permanent housing, but prioritization was based on disability and shifting definitions of vulnerability. In the previous chapter, we met Jack Marshall, who had serious psychiatric needs and was offered— but refused—housing. Belle was working with those who didn't qualify. What could she do? Well, if access to housing required a mental illness diagnosis, she would make people look mentally ill. Thus, for several months of 2013, I'd watch her take seemingly healthy people to the DMH to create bureaucratic records of treatment and evaluation.

•   •   •

On the streets of Downtown Los Angeles, mental illness and homelessness blur together in the project of urban poverty governance. Macro-level processes of capital investment and disinvestment, constraints on housing supply, budget crises at multiple levels of government, and changes in both criminal and mental health law shape interactions between workers and potential clients. Care and control take place in a public safety net ecology of shelters, public hospitals, jails, and treatment programs that constitute the "frontline dams of social disorders in the city."[1] Given the difficulties of managing social problems in public space, care provision is inexorably tied to the politics of street clearance.

Rather than a story of the local state's power to dominate the poor, however, outreach interactions reveal how a lack of resources combines with civil liberties to generate spaces of precarious and dubious freedom. Hard-won rights mean that homeless people and psychiatric patients have a "freedom from" state intervention like arrest or hospitalization yet no social rights *to* housing or care. The city accepts encampments, drugs, and bizarre behaviors so long as they stay in the right zones—namely, away from more powerful, affluent people. Given enough pressure from business owners, some areas may eventually be cleared. Yet once those displaced people become a problem for other well-connected actors, complaints will start again. Ironically, through this process, some of the city's most powerful people have come to believe that they are stymied by the rights of the weakest.

We last encountered the Spring Street Task Force when the legal scrutiny of policing, restrictions on coercive psychiatric care, and grossly inadequate social services made street clearance unlikely. Thus, the plan was to survey the area and separate those who might qualify for the services from those who might eventually be dispersed with policing. To *sort out the down and out*, homeless outreach workers must try to identify people who fit narrow criteria for resource qualification, create crises to drive qualified but seemingly uninterested people toward services, generate psychiatric histories for the nondisabled to become qualified, and ultimately provide enough service to justify police sweeps.

By triangulating between multiagency meetings, street outreach interactions, clinical care, and the perspectives of potential clients on the street, I paint a picture of a system at war with itself. Where did this service ecology and its strange rules of the game come from? Why did Skid Row become the treatment hub and human dumping ground it is today? The best place to start is with a brief history of Downtown Los Angeles, the growth of the housing crisis, and the local manifestation of the deinstitutionalization movement.

THE DOWNTOWN SKID ROW ECOLOGY

Given its location near the Los Angeles River, Skid Row originated in eastern Downtown LA as a home to the packing and shipping industry of the late nineteenth and early twentieth centuries. To accommodate workers, often migrants, it offered affordable if ramshackle housing stock such as single-room-occupancy hotels.[2] As industry receded, those rooms began to be filled with a primary population of elderly white men dealing with disabilities and alcoholism. Then in the 1960s, industrial zoning changes brought major new investment to the Downtown area. At a time when many American cities were destroying their Skid Rows, Los Angeles took a different approach: activists compromised with developers and city officials and created the 1976 "containment plan." This protected Skid Row's low-income housing stock and aimed to keep poor, disabled, or addicted people and relevant services concentrated within Skid Row—and away from development zones.

In the late 1970s, deindustrialization meant that a larger population of men, disproportionately men of color, were out of work and housing insecure. By the 1980s, the "new homelessness" had become visible in Los Angeles. Reagan-era cuts to public housing and the privatization of welfare services meant major changes in the availability of aid, leading to the development of service dependent ghettos comprising many charities rather than robust public programs. Police directed the down and out to the containment area of Skid Row. Yet business owners in surrounding areas hoped for further development, complained about the tent cities, and began to demand "sweeps."

In the 1990s and 2000s, three "megashelters" married to intensive policing were sited in Skid Row. Under the Safer Cities Initiative, hundreds of new police officers entered the area, using the threat of arrest to direct people into the shelter programs. This is what the sociologist Forrest Stuart calls therapeutic policing. It is also a response to the force that Belle identified: gentrification. That project has been remarkably successful, from a developer's perspective, in Downtown LA—Skid Row has shrunk by half, with some parts replaced with market-rate artists' lofts and hipster bars. But the city's actions also generated considerable resistance. Today, legal decisions have made it impossible to simply clear away the homeless, while resource inadequacies make it just as impossible to house them.

Contemporary encampments are no longer contained to areas like Downtown. They're cropping up throughout Los Angeles County and across large swaths of California. In 2022, an estimated 170,000 Californians were unhoused, emblematic of a complex series of interlocking problems. Some of the homelessness can be attributed to simple supply and demand: California communities are famous for "not in my backyard" (NIMBY) politics and exclusionary zoning; people have fought against the development of multifamily and affordable housing. Combined with the state's strong environmental protections, which delay construction, housing production proceeds glacially here. Yet industries such as tech import more and more people willing and able to pay high rents. This drives up prices overall—often well past the means of large portions of the population. In the absence of other housing options or a robust social safety net, even employed people are at risk of homelessness.[3] Notably, this is not unheard of in other places, but cities like New York have extensive shelter systems (mandated, in that case, by the New York state constitution) and are better able to hide their unhoused populations. What ultimately characterizes California cities' crisis, then, is *mass homelessness outdoors*.

Writ large, homelessness has been shown by scholars to be a housing market and policy problem rather than an individual-level problem created by mental illness and addiction.[4] To wit: US cities with more abundant and cheaper housing stock have their own crises of psychiatric disability and problem drug use but lower rates of homelessness than cities like San Francisco, with its legendarily high cost of living and insufficient units. In Detroit, for instance, there is no shortage of people with psychiatric and addiction needs, yet those people are sick or addicted *indoors*. Housing advocates focused on economic inequality are, in other words, correct that mental illness is not the primary cause of homelessness. Even so, if around 20 percent of Los Angeles County's more than fifty thousand homeless people have serious mental illness, then that is a crisis in its own right.

BIRTH OF THE DEPARTMENT OF MENTAL HEALTH

The Los Angeles County Department of Mental Health was born of optimism during the early deinstitutionalization period. Grand plans, however, gave way to false starts and betrayal.

In 1957, California's Short-Doyle Act incentivized its counties to invest in "preventive services," and the Los Angeles County Board of Supervisors voted to create the DMH in 1960. Amid genuine hope for community-based care and the potential cost savings of transitioning away from state mental hospitals, the DMH was supposed to develop a vast community network. But in 1967, the then governor Ronald Reagan signed the Lanterman-Petris-Short Act to end inappropriate involuntary hospitalization, and things began to go awry. The DMH's director at the time, Harry Brickman, recalled being blindsided by the speed of the process: "I had a conference with Ronald Reagan . . . and the handshake was that they would not close down the State Hospitals until we in the community had an opportunity to develop halfway houses and transitional facilities for those with major mental illness. We shook hands, and, I think within a month, he began to close down the State Hospitals. . . . The result of it is that they began to dump them on the streets."[5]

Notably, at this point there were more low-cost living options than there are today, and mental patients released during the early deinstitutionalization period did not automatically become homeless. Yet these ex-patients were among the most vulnerable to the ill effects of structural changes like the rising cost of living, the lack of low-skilled labor opportunities, and the destruction of low-income housing stock. Soon a patient homelessness crisis emerged from within the larger housing crisis affecting the precarious poor. Brickman and the DMH, without the time needed to develop a vast preventive care network, were left to contend with a mass of indigent patients in need of basic survival resources as well as psychiatric care. And they simply didn't have the means to help them.

URBAN POVERTY GOVERNANCE AND THE RIGHTS OF THE MARGINAL PATIENT

From its very origins, LA County's Department of Mental Health was dealing with urban poverty, housing insecurity, and the unintended consequences of new civil liberties. People like the DMH supervisor Howard Glass began their careers in this milieu. Leaning back in his office chair, Howard explained his personal history as a social worker and then an administrator, and he offered his interpretations of the historical forces that had brought him and his agency to this moment.

"We try to play Solomon with the problem of homelessness—and this has been a struggle ever since—when I first got into this profession, we were dealing with state hospitals and indeterminate commitments," he noted. "Some people would be in the state hospitals, commitments that were initiated forty, fifty years prior. . . . It's always been this kind of fine balancing act between patients' rights and the rights of the individual . . . balancing that against the needs or desires of the community and the population at large." Tolerance and enforcement had tugged social service agencies this way and that since the closing of the asylums, manifesting in a series of strange compromise policies meant to attend to a street population that could be neither effectively serviced nor made to disappear. Where homelessness and serious mental illness overlapped in a series of civil liberties dilemmas, officials like Howard felt forced to split the proverbial baby in two.

Howard believed that the balance had been shifting toward patients' rights and homeless people's ability to live on the street, to the point that the city had lost its tools to create order.

So, when I grew up, someone was loitering, sleeping on the street. Police take their nightstick. "Hey, get moving," you know, "no loitering." Well, we have taken that to a whole new level today, and it's completely—The legal pendulum has swung completely in the other way . . .

So, with outreach and [Operation] Healthy Streets, that's how the service community, including DMH, got brought into it. They say, "Okay. We can go and police and make sure we're following the protocol, et cetera, handed down by the courts to warn people and not throw their belongings away, whatever they might be." Then you bring in public health, because that's a loophole in this [*Lavan*] injunction . . . if there's human waste or whatever, vermin . . . that can empower government a little more to take certain actions.

That the government needed public health crises to be "empowered" shows just how strange the politics of street clearance had become. A disenfranchised population now had a right to exist in public space, much to the chagrin of business and political elites. Since the police were delayed until the city offered real assistance, the social service providers had a new role: justifying law enforcement. By classifying homelessness as a health problem, separating the sick from the merely poor, offering appropriate provisions, and recoding an encampment as a public health threat, the city could potentially skirt the injunction. They just needed agencies like the DMH to play along.

Note the tricky meaning of *rights* here: given that the city and the county lacked the resources to house or otherwise serve the thousands of people in need in the Downtown area alone, there was no "positive" right to shelter or care. But there was a "negative" right to avoid police harassment, at least at certain times of the day and in certain zones. If in the past the homeless were largely relegated to "marginal space," the new court decisions made it difficult to displace them from even "prime space" of political or economic value.[6] As Howard sighed, "You're left there with your toy pail, trying to empty the oceans."

NAVIGATING THE INJUNCTION

The Spring Street Task Force we met in chapter 1 had been initiated at the behest of a Chinatown business group. Homeless people, they complained, were harassing senior citizens at a bus stop. The business owners said they wanted municipal officials to "fully address" the Spring Street encampment of tents and tarps that had come to line both sides of the street, with still more people sleeping near a local church. Unlike Operation Healthy Streets in Skid Row, which no one expected to truly "succeed," the Spring Street Task Force hoped to remove its targeted encampment.

The Chinatown entrepreneurs repeatedly asked city police and county sheriffs to investigate the encampment for criminal activity and confiscate unattended property. Ongoing lawsuits, however, made officials wary to agree to direct police sweeps without first working toward adequate service provision. At task force meetings, the supervisor from LAHSA continually pitched her idea for a Connect Day, in which all the various social service agencies would set up booths and inform the Spring Street homeless of available assistance before a police sweep.

But others wanted the sweep to happen right away. "Haven't we done enough outreach?" asked a Chinatown representative. "The ones who are idiots have got to go."

"No, we *haven't* done enough outreach," responded an older county official, invoking people's rights and the court ruling. How, he asked, would they even begin to distinguish the "idiots" and criminals from those who were just homeless or disabled? "The problem," he insisted, "is way bigger than Spring Street."

Others murmured agreement, but the practical problems remained.

The county Board of Supervisors' representative stated that the task force would proceed with the Connect Day. "For those who need—"

A Chinatown businessman interjected, "And those who are *eligible* . . ."

This, of course, was a key distinction. Many people *needed* resources, but that didn't necessarily mean that they would qualify for services.

Finally, the Chinatown group demanded that the representative confirm her boss's position. "Does the county supervisor want a cleared-out Spring Street, or a permanent encampment with services?"

"No, she wants it gone. It's a quality-of-life issue."

To my left, I heard Howard the DMH supervisor whisper to another official that for some Spring Street denizens, displacement would be "the end of the world."

The task force decided that the DMH could continue focusing on the "truly sick." As in the case of Jack Marshall, the businessmen at the meeting expressed sympathy for those they perceived as not being troublemakers, and they asked what providers planned to do with, say, undocumented immigrants who could not qualify for housing and other resources. A LAHSA worker responded that people could enter rehab facilities or Spanish AA, and Howard explained that the DMH, as a mental health provider, had some leeway to accommodate people lacking valid immigration documentation.

For the mental health outreach workers, there was a possibility that if the project processed people quickly enough, they might be able to make a case for accessing more housing. Political attention meant potential liability for their organizations, so they needed to document and account for the obvious cases of severe mental illness. Such scrutiny on the area also meant more resources at the workers' disposal. As the leader of the DMH homeless outreach team told me, the ugly politics of street clearance and gentrification might just give them the opportunity to really help.

THE SCIENCE OF STREET DIAGNOSIS

So how did outreach workers sort out who was appropriate for rapid housing and mental health services and who was a candidate for detox or shelter? As they saw it, there was mental illness, and there was *mental illness.* One had to learn to ignore everyday suffering and hunt for clear psychopathology. Street diagnoses could be murky, but outreach workers pointed out clear cases, like "Mr. Plastics," who wrapped himself in black trash bags, or the woman who bid workers, "May your cars never be without fuel!" Sometimes people stood out from the chaos among the dozens of Skid Row denizens on San Julian alone, but it took something special.

Leticia, an experienced Black psychiatric nurse in her fifties, offered hygiene kits to most people without giving them a second glance. She had spent much of her career conducting 5150 calls with the DMH's Psychiatric Emergency Team; to her, low-level issues didn't register. Leticia got excited, however, when we encountered a dark-skinned elderly man sprawled on the concrete, unmoved by the yelling and the people passing by before his eyes. Gaunt, with flies perched on his dreadlocks, he didn't react when she approached. For the clinician seeking "true madness," his demeanor looked less like another junkie on a nod and more like catatonic depression or schizophrenia. It took several encounters before he told us his name—Darryl—and claimed that he had been homeless since 1987.

"This is where I am," she said, handing him a card with the intensive case management team's office location. "Darryl, I'm Leticia . . .

come down here to see me so we can help you out. When you gonna come?"

Darryl's gaze remained resolutely fixed on the pavement.

As she tried to make eye contact with him, Leticia asked, "You want me to come pick you up? Sometime today? Later today? Well, we'll try, what's your last name?"

Later, I would drive the county car, helping Leticia take Darryl to the office. The case management team got him placed at the LAMP Community (formerly the Los Angeles Men's Place), a nonprofit homeless center known for its progressive, high-tolerance approach. As the team began preparing his Section 8 (referring to Section 8 of the Housing Act of 1937) housing voucher paperwork, they were astonished to get zero hits on his name in their information management system. Darryl wasn't a "high-service utilizer" who cost the county lots of money, but he was a different kind of outreach gem. He was an obviously disabled person who had slipped through the cracks, experienced years of homelessness, and was *willing* to go into apartment living when offered. Darryl would eventually be housed in an independent unit in Northeast LA.

Compared with my observations of Operation Healthy Streets in Skid Row, the Spring Street outreach seemed promising. There were fewer people, and the workers had twenty housing vouchers specifically assigned to the block. I drove with Carlos, a sixty-year-old Mexican American DMH housing specialist, to meet up with a pair of homeless men who might qualify for a voucher. Like Howard, Carlos was an old leftist who liked to rail against the system. His ponytail and casual dress distinguished him from clinicians, and he proudly considered himself a working-class man of the people. He made a point to tell me how he'd worked in a factory in Milwaukee and still had friends back there who had never emotionally recovered after the region outsourced its industry to other countries. For him, going to Skid Row and doing "the work," as he called it with reverence, was bound up in a broader rage at American social inequality.

Carlos explained that the DMH could potentially enroll people to help get them into housing (as Belle tried to do), then move them down to a lower level of services. This offered a way to engage those who might not normally qualify but wanted the assistance. I noticed someone already waiting on the sidewalk. With a hunched back, white hair down to his shoulders, and a long gray beard touching his chest, he resembled a miniature Gandalf from *The Lord of the Rings*. As we neared, the man squinted at us skeptically through wire-rimmed glasses.

Abe was his name, and his companion, Dave, had collapsed earlier while clutching his head. The DMH team arranged for Dave to be taken to the hospital. Carlos said perhaps that facility would document sufficient disability for the housing vouchers, but Dave was released that afternoon, diagnosed as having experienced a cluster headache. Now sitting in his wheelchair, Dave mumbled words that only Abe could understand. The pair had moved from Colorado Springs, preferring temperate Los Angeles to the cold winters of their former city.

Carlos explained that Abe and Dave would have to come to the mental health clinic to be screened by a social worker. Gesturing with his hands, he indicated that he knew this might be a big deal for them. As an ethnographer in training, I marveled at his ability to connect with these men, who looked askance at others on the street. It was already a big deal, Carlos said, that they had trusted us with Dave's wheelchair and bag during the hospitalization.

As he squatted down to someone's eye level or talked about his on-the-road hippie days, when he'd seemingly visited every single person's hometown, Carlos demonstrated an enviable ability to establish a quick rapport. He schooled me in the art of outreach and scolded me when I once finished a to-go meal in front of people camped on the sidewalk.

Despite Carlos's ease at interpersonal connection, however, bureaucratic hurdles complicated things. Abe received Supplemental Security Income (SSI) for some sort of disability, but he didn't have serious psychiatric needs, and Dave's hospitalizations were more likely neurological than psychiatric. But upon learning that the men had been homeless on Spring Street for two years and for stretches in Colorado besides, Carlos seemed buoyed—it was enough "homeless history" to meet one dimension of the voucher criteria. When a DMH nurse asked whether the guys could pay for a hotel with their disability incomes, Carlos rushed to say that a record of this could render them "housed" and start the "homeless clock" over at zero. Though the DMH team stayed in touch with the men in the coming months, ultimately they would not qualify for housing assistance; Dave's neurological condition wasn't enough to secure a voucher prioritized for people with mental illness.

Even when the team found people who qualified, they ran into other problems. A Latino man in his fifties living on Spring Street told of his record in the psychiatric information system for his ten-plus years of prison mental health care. Indeed, he'd been medicated when he heard voices while incarcerated, which would be enough to authorize services. But once Carlos learned that the man was a registered sex offender, he had to recalibrate.

When I asked what the team could do in terms of housing, Carlos sighed. "If you have to register [as a sex offender] we can't even start, not even an outside chance."

"Aren't these 'shelter plus cares'?" I asked, referencing the specialized type of housing vouchers the DMH could use. These obviated criminal background checks, so the hiccup surprised me.

"No," he replied. "These are 'regular homeless Section 8.' If there's any kind of background check, you're done."

"But you guys are gonna enroll him?"

"We already enrolled him," Carlos spat, revealing an animosity he'd kept hidden from potential clients. He said they had been pressured to accept the man, who didn't even seem all that mentally ill.

When I asked what the DMH could do, Carlos shut me down: "[He's] lucky as a child rapist to not have been killed out there."

If stories like Darryl's show the success of compassionate outreach and rapid housing, stories like Abe's and Dave's point to the far more common difficulty of securing resources for even those with documented disabilities. People may meet some criteria but not all, putting outreach workers in the awkward position of making promises they can't keep and potentially undermining trust on the street. Others meet the criteria, but like the man who was a registered sex offender, they get disqualified on the back end. And all these people at least wanted what the DMH could offer. Workers had to deal with another problem: the people most appropriate in terms of severe disability often seemed the most likely to refuse resources.

CREATING A CRISIS

The DMH could not force a person into a hospital or shelter simply because of mental illness or homelessness. The anthropologist Arline Mathieu observed such an attempt to remove homeless populations through psychiatric commitment in 1980s New York City.[7] Police and emergency crews had pushed homeless people into hospitals and shelters, leading to a civil liberties suit. In an embarrassing turn of events for NYC, a judge concluded that the activities were illegal. Even that was a far cry from the asylum era, when local authorities could simply hospitalize people with little oversight. In contemporary California, known for its especially strong psychiatric patient civil liberties, DMH workers had to convince, not coerce.

What could be done if people did not accept what was on offer? The case of an elderly Mexican woman who lived beside the church near Spring Street is instructive. She'd been targeted for the county Older Adult mental health program. Despite qualifying for subsidized housing and case management, she told workers that God had commanded her to stay near his house.

So, a few weeks after the City Attorney's Office explained the new protocol, LAPD officers passed through Spring Street accompanied by a sanitation truck to haul away property, in preparation for a later street cleaning. Whether it was due to compassion or the legal injunction, an officer slowed the process and tried to ensure that everyone had an opportunity to claim their belongings. As the officer poked through the unattended property, a stocky guy named Matt approached. Part of a group of homeless drinkers, he asked the cop for leniency.

"That's the old lady's stuff," he said, referencing God's neighbor. "Can I go look for her?"

The policeman replied that he didn't want to destroy anyone's things. He could wait for a bit.

A friendly drunk, Matt had always been welcoming to me and the outreach team, and I could see he wanted to help. So the two of us teamed up, running down to the church office to look for her. No one in the office had seen the old woman, but they agreed to store her things until the evening. As Matt and I crossed the street to tell the police officer, a DMH outreach worker and a case manager from the Older Adult Program said that they were looking for her too. They frowned when I said that Matt was trying to help claim the property before it was taken. It would be better, they thought, to let the officer confiscate her items.

The case manager said, "This could be a motivation for getting her to come with us. . . . I hate to create a crisis, but it will help. We can get all the other stuff back." Then, directly contradicting the officer's stated offer of storage, he added, "You can't stop the police from doing this."

He most likely said this because of the leverage therapeutic policing provides. Maybe having her property destroyed by the cops would be the tough love needed to get the old woman to come into their program. Then the officer called us over to show us rat droppings in her sleeping area. This arguably constituted a public health hazard, so her things were taken to the dump rather than into the church storage.

A week later, the Older Adult Program worker was out on Spring Street again, still unable to locate the woman he hoped would become a client. When I asked about his previous tactic of creating a crisis, he admitted that he must have looked "really insensitive." But he explained that the program hadn't gotten any engagement from her thus far, and it didn't look to be forthcoming, so the confiscation of her property represented another strategy. "But I still don't know if we've done the right thing. I mean, here we are a week later, looking for her. Who knows what will happen?"

In fact, the woman refused to engage with the mental health program. Matt, her Spring Street neighbor, said he had never noticed

she was mentally ill until the Older Adult Program workers pointed
it out to him. Then it was confirmed when he invited her into his tent
one cold night—she tried to fight him, and Matt kicked her out, calling her "cuckoo." Now he believed that the old lady was too sick to
have civil liberties and needed "to be in Camarillo," a state psychiatric hospital that, as I told Matt, had closed more than a decade prior.
Matt responded with a layperson's account of deinstitutionalization:
"Ronald Reagan is the one who threw all the crazy people out of the
hospitals, then started building prisons . . . to get more DAs [district
attorneys], more public defenders, more cops, more COs [corrections
officers], so they'd get a lot more jobs by treating people like sheep."

More conspiracy theory than history, Matt's account was nonetheless partially shared by the outreach workers, who agreed that the old
woman probably belonged in a hospital. She was precisely the kind
of "deserving" crazy homeless person who should be protected, and
perhaps creating a crisis could alter her desires and make her choose
"correctly," in their sense. It did not, so she remained on the street,
next to God's house without a blanket.

SOMETHING LIKE AN ASYLUM

After a morning round of outreach in Skid Row, I stood in the DMH
clinic with a nurse from the Psychiatric Mobile Response Team.
Bald and so muscular as to strain his dress shirt, the nurse had been
assigned to morning outreach alongside the DMH team during
Operation Healthy Streets. It certainly wasn't his first choice, as evidenced by his John Varvatos boots (a designer brand more appropriate to Melrose Place than San Julian). When I pointed out his stylish
footwear, he chuckled and said that he'd need to clean them when he
got home that night.

Frustrated with people's refusal to accept offers of housing accompanied by mental health services, this nurse was convinced that homelessness was largely a matter of individual choice, not circumstance.
"The thing is, [officials are] gonna realize that there is more housing
than there are people. But people don't want to go inside. This woman

[today] told me she doesn't want to go inside because there are too many rules."

After years of placing people with mental illness on 5150 holds and seeing them returned to the streets, he had become disillusioned. Allowing for such choices was a problem, he thought, right up there with the problem of madness itself. In fact, he claimed, homelessness was not an issue of resources at all, for plenty of units were available.

On a factual level, that was simply untrue. There were tens of thousands more homeless people in Los Angeles County than there were housing vouchers or affordable units. When I pushed back, the psychiatric nurse countered that the Skid Row Housing Trust (a nonprofit Housing First agency) had opened plenty of new apartments, but people weren't going inside. Again, I knew he was wrong. I'd recently been with people trying to get on the trust's waiting lists.

Scholars of homelessness challenge the idea that the apparent "choice" to be on the street is straightforward. As the sociologist Mitchell Duneier wrote of homeless men in New York City, it's easy to misread when they say, "Fuck it!" and claim to have chosen the hand they were dealt. As Duneier put it, "Although giving up was a choice of sorts—no one forced them to do it—it was not a choice they made at a time of rational stability; it was not a choice that a person wanted to make."[8] And as the sociologists David Snow and Leon Anderson have found, many homeless people distrust social service agencies because of bad experiences with providers in the past; they can feel safer with the community of friends they've made on the street. Further, moving homes is among the most stressful life events for people of all backgrounds. Sometimes the homeless, too, find the prospect overwhelming.[9] Regarding even severely mentally ill homeless people, the anthropologist Tanya Luhrmann argues that housing refusal also relates to a street culture that prizes toughness and survival: to accept housing from a mental health program is to be marked "crazy" and weak, two of the worst things one can be.[10] People may have quite understandable explanations for rejecting assistance.

For our purposes, the muscled nurse needn't be right or wrong—instead, his beliefs reflect his experience. Working with a particularly disruptive subset of the homeless population, he continually engaged people who, for whatever reason, turned down services that appeared to be in their best interests. Or they secured housing and then lost it. Once, the nurse told me, he'd evaluated a man who had won a six-figure lawsuit after being struck by a county car. After renting a beautiful loft and paying for six months' rent up front, the man soon refused to leave the apartment, clean it, or use its air-conditioning. When the police wouldn't take him, someone called the Psychiatric Mobile Response Team. The team discovered that the man had been hoarding bags of feces throughout his apartment—he was about to be evicted. For this nurse, the ultimate proof of futility was seeing people get access to resources, then continue to live as though they were homeless until they ended up back on the streets.

Relaying his exasperation, the nurse echoed the public health concerns of Operation Healthy Streets and articulated a solution that he knew others might find distasteful. He bashfully looked to Leticia, his partner, then to me. His idea? "It could be like animal shelters. And hear me out, I know it sounds inhumane, but you could have people in concrete rooms that drain to the center, and people could come in and hose people down. You can't force these people on meds, and the thing you have to think about is sanitation."

The animal shelter analogy was idiosyncratic, but the sentiment was not uncommon. Other DMH workers would tell me that California needed a return to the old state hospital model, or at least some way to stop disease from spreading. Like the nurse, they indicated that their work could feel as though it amounted to nothing most days, and that made them long for "solutions" like asylums.

It would be a mistake, however, to suggest that the DMH wasn't doing anything to deal with homelessness simply because it wasn't forcing people into housing or hospitals. The limits of coercive psychiatric power enabled a different kind of interactional and classificatory work that we turn to next: outreaching relatively healthy people to transform them into official clients and get them goods normally reserved for the "truly ill."

MAKING PSYCHIATRIC HISTORIES

The Spring Street Task Force finally hosted its Connect Day. Various agencies met in the church to set up booths and hawk their services to the Spring Street homeless. Howard of the DMH and I walked from the church to inform people of the event. He gestured and said to me, "You get a front-row view of the inadequacy of our safety net." Echoing what he'd said at the meetings, he told me that the county needed lower thresholds for civil commitment of the severely disabled, along with significantly more resources for the rest of the population. Rather than universal benefits, as he'd advocate, our system had decided that only some people were worthy of them, which galled him. "I tell young social work students, it's the Poor Laws of Elizabethan England. Separating people into the deserving and undeserving poor, and not a damn thing has changed."

I could see what Howard meant. Yet from my observations, some things *had* changed. Now the "deserving poor" weren't those who wanted to work or get clean or give their hearts to God. Now the official criteria were "seriously mentally ill" and "chronically homeless," with the most disruptive sometimes receiving priority. Howard told me that the California Mental Health Services Act (a special fund created by taxing millionaires' incomes) meant that the DMH programs had weathered the storm of the Great Recession while many other services were slashed. As a result, the DMH took on a greater presence than it might otherwise have for people who weren't seriously ill. With resources ostensibly available, yet only for this designated group, DMH workers were officially assigned to find people who passed diagnostic criteria and service utilization thresholds. However, since many of those people refused care, the slots were occasionally left open.

It seemed, then, that there was an opportunity to help others— those who might not ordinarily qualify for disability-linked housing vouchers.

Given the lack of precision in psychiatric classification, outreach workers could plausibly refer both those whom they assessed as "truly ill" and those whom they could *bureaucratically construct* as such. The street clearance project and the specially allotted Section 8 housing vouchers further bolstered the resources they had at hand.

For the DMH homeless outreach team, the goal was typically to place people into one of the department's intensive case management programs. After observing the nurse Mona refer a person who seemed only mildly disabled, I asked how she makes decisions. Like other street-level bureaucrats, she possessed a great deal of discretion and the perspective to anticipate the discretionary practices of other social service agencies.[11]

Mona and her partner explained that the gatekeepers' motives are often mysterious, leading outreach workers to abandon strict criteria and refer frequently. The homeless outreach team members themselves had no housing resources, so referrals were their best tool.

"For me," Mona said, "sometimes I'll just give it a try."

Her partner elaborated, "They might kick back the referral if it's not a serious enough mental illness . . . the agencies are choosy sometimes and not so choosy sometimes."

"What do you mean?" I asked.

He shrugged. Choosiness varied by "individual workers," he said, "or they have other criteria that's not on the books. We don't know."

Given that the agencies were "not so choosy" sometimes, the outreach workers came to see labeling large numbers of people and referring them up the DMH chain as a reasonable strategy.

During Operation Healthy Streets, I shadowed LAHSA outreach workers as they informed people of the upcoming street cleanings. Belle, from the start of the chapter, explained to me that access to housing vouchers was controlled by the Department of Mental Health. This was true both because the DMH had a line on special vouchers at that time, and because it offered the diagnoses useful for accessing the other resources controlled by nonprofits in the area. If the DMH homeless outreach team usually sought the seriously mentally ill before turning to the moderately disabled, Belle believed that the DMH's resource monopoly justified referring lots of people there.

Social scientists have long argued that psychiatric diagnosis can cause stigma and negatively impact a person's identity, but Belle worked to convince people they could use it to their advantage. Far from being a "degradation ceremony" that separated out the crazy from the dignified homeless person, her suggestion that people get a DMH evaluation was offered so matter-of-factly and so broadly that it seemed *de*-stigmatizing.[12] Furthermore, policy changes had already incentivized people to seek other benefits through mental illness. As welfare scholars have pointed out, applications for disability benefits based on psychiatric disorders spiked after welfare reform in 1996 made it harder for able-bodied people to access basic survival incomes.[13]

At least some portion of people who might have simply used welfare in the past now try to use psychiatric diagnoses to access SSI. This is not to say that all people who followed Belle's lead were intentionally "faking it" per se, since many *were* experiencing mental health struggles of some sort if not serious mental illness. Belle believed this off-the-books tactic was the best way she could help people, since her agency lacked adequate resources to do otherwise.

LAHSA had access to hotel vouchers, for instance, but these only lasted a few days and did not necessarily come with follow-up assistance. Once it took an older woman from Spring Street to a hotel in Gardena but did not assist her afterward. When I saw her back at the encampment, she approached a group of outreach workers and yelled, "Are you guys LAHSA? Screw all of you. Make me walk back from Gardena with all of my stuff." The hotel vouchers could temporarily clear people out but did nothing to stop them from moving back—and when they returned, they'd likely have a less sanguine view of services than they had in the first place.

Abe and Dave, the homeless men from Colorado, also became fed up. The LAHSA team found a Craigslist ad for a place in Kern County that the men could afford with their combined SSI, but the apartment had stairs that Dave couldn't navigate in his wheelchair. Abe told me that he felt jerked around by the different social service agencies and didn't think LAHSA could do anything. "What we really want is that

Section 8 from DMH," he said. If being mentally ill got you permanent housing, Abe and Dave would try to be mentally ill. It didn't
work, and instead they left the area for a while to trim cannabis on a
marijuana farm.

Several months into Operation Healthy Streets, however, Belle
proudly told me that she had taken more than forty people to the
DMH to get processed. She recognized that few wanted what her
homeless services agency could offer, so she selectively drove clients to
the DMH and coached them on what to tell the clinicians. Unlike the
group of men whom she simply told to go to the clinic, Belle chose to
shepherd special people through the process.

One morning, I accompanied Belle to pick up a young African
American woman and coach her on DMH procedure. Before the
woman went in for her appointment, she claimed not to have any
mental health problems. Belle recounted, "Well, I told her, 'You're
homeless. Aren't you upset?' And she said yeah, she's angry and down.
And I told her 'that's mental health, that's signs of depression.'" Yet
Belle was still worried that the DMH outpatient clinic would not think
her severe enough. "But let me tell you, I bet you that here they're
going to tell her that she's fine, she doesn't have any mental health
problems. Unless you're schizophrenic and talking stupid, they're not
gonna do anything." Whether or not Belle's interpretation was accurate regarding the woman's "depression," she was almost certainly correct that it wasn't enough to qualify for specialty services or housing.

Sometimes Belle believed that people truly had unrecognized mental health needs, and sometimes she used diagnoses in a purely stra-
tegic way. One morning, I shadowed her and her outreach partner as
they took a homeless African American man to a Burger King. He had
a profound palsy, and his entire body periodically shook. Belle wanted
to help him save face, so she told the fast-food workers that he had a
neurological disorder, not a drug problem. Although his speech was
interrupted by his shakes, the man engaged us in friendly conversation
as we drove to a motel, telling us about his youth before moving to LA.

Upon transporting him to the hospital for his violent trem-
ors, Belle learned that he had been hospitalized for schizophrenia

many years before. She and I were both surprised, as his condition appeared to solely impact motor function. But she smiled and told me, "I don't see it [schizophrenia], but I'm going to use it for FSP [the Full Service Partnership, an intensive case management program]!" *Schizophrenia* was key; less severe diagnoses rarely gained traction. In the end, the man lost control of his ability to walk, so he was reclassified and consequently qualified for a skilled nursing facility rather than psychiatric care.

Tasked with serving the general homeless population and understanding that the DMH could facilitate housing, Belle and her partner were convinced that using diagnoses was necessary to open resource avenues. It was what the local ecology of their work required. Viewed in this way, sending people of ambiguous psychiatric disability up the DMH chain was logical and even moral.

How did psychiatrists at the DMH regard such fast-and-loose approaches to diagnosing mental illness? I assumed they would defend the scientific nature of their medical specialty and insist on the sanctity of diagnostic decisions, but this wasn't always true. Differently positioned doctors had different viewpoints. Sitting in his office, Dr. Wong of the Full Service Partnership program told me he wasn't interested in his profession's "academic distinctions." He said that the *DSM V*, the American Psychiatric Association's latest diagnostic manual of mental disorders, contained too many categories. Having worked hospital and prison wings before coming to community care, Wong saw himself as a pragmatist. He ignored highly specific differential diagnosis because it didn't matter clinically.

In his experience, the medication response became more important than the diagnosis. He surprised me by saying next that he could essentially treat every seriously ill patient with the same medication. "Does the person have bipolar, schizophrenia, or depression? Give someone Abilify [a second-generation antipsychotic], and it will help for everything. Just depends on the dosage." Since Wong worked at the most intensive outpatient care setting, those having primarily social service needs had presumably been filtered out by the time they reached him.

A younger psychiatrist I shadowed, on the other hand, had a much less relaxed relationship with diagnostic messiness. This was because he was the one filtering and misdiagnosing patients. Temporarily at the FSP case management program, just filling in, he usually worked at the walk-in clinic. Between patients, he remarked that he much preferred this intensive treatment program to evaluating people who had come in off the street. When I asked why, he stated that half the clients at the walk-in clinic were not mentally ill at all—they needed things like housing and welfare. He often diagnosed them as having a mental illness, sometimes with an NOS (Not Otherwise Specified) designation, and then prescribed an antipsychotic or mood stabilizer.

The use of "workaround diagnoses" to access benefits made sense to me, but I was confused as to why he was also prescribing people such heavy drugs.[14] Given the side effects, it seemed strange and even dangerous. The doctor said he was aiming to calm potentially violent people. With an air of derision, he told me, "There is no medication for anger," but the drugs were necessary "so they don't hurt anybody."

For reasons different from those given by the LAHSA workers, this young psychiatrist was collaborating to bring all sorts of people into the DMH's orbit. Truth be told, those clients were unlikely to get housing with an NOS diagnosis. And the medications might stifle anger, but they also just might lead to bad side effects, be thrown away, or get sold on the street. Still, I came to see that beyond what happened to any individual, there were consequences for the system.

Despite the young doctor's misgivings, he had become a cog in a classification machine specializing in misdiagnosis. I would repeatedly hear other clinicians complain about treating or evaluating someone who appeared to suffer primarily from poverty. But the workers sometimes second-guessed themselves because these patients already had records indicating serious mental illness (diagnosis or medication history) in the information management system. None wanted to reject a truly disabled person who needed mental health care. Neither solving homelessness nor leading to proper treatment, then, the game of making psychiatric histories had taken on a life of its own, and clinicians now found it that much harder to evaluate people in earnest.

BALANCING BUDGET CUTS AND PUBLIC SAFETY

Back at the Spring Street Task Force, the Chinatown representatives were livid. Connect Day had come and gone, but the city had decided it was not enough to justify a police sweep. The encampment remained, and outreach workers were tired of explaining that the remaining "truly ill" didn't want services, and those who wanted housing wouldn't qualify for it and refused temporary help such as winter shelter (a temporary expansion of beds during the cold months). Many people still chose to stay outdoors, citing poor shelter conditions and rules that felt infantilizing. The Department of Public and Social Service coordinator said he had helped people apply for SSI benefits, but these could take months to process—it was no quick fix for clearing the encampment. After what one task force member estimated as $2 million spent for outreach and street cleaning, they still could not justify the business owners' desired police sweep of the Spring Street encampment.

What's more, the plan for housing the people who did qualify for the twenty specialized vouchers was in jeopardy. In March, the Federal Budget Sequester of 2013 effectively froze the processing of Section 8 housing vouchers that had not yet been initiated. If the plan had been to shift from policing to mental health outreach tied to housing, it was out the window. Until national austerity measures were lifted, they'd need a new local plan—just like municipalities around the country. As an official said, the problem was far bigger than Spring Street.

"We need a change in national policy where we say that no one can be homeless," Howard told the task force. Given the budget cuts, they would have to be more efficient and creative in addressing the problem. "Without a national social policy commitment," he added, "there's not much that can be done."

The Board of Supervisors' representative responded, "Yeah, but this is about public safety."

By way of rebuttal, Howard pointed out that law enforcement "can't handle social problems—they have a judge telling them and clarifying what they can and can't do."

A county sheriff's deputy concurred. "We're bound by *Jones v. City* and the *Lavan* case. *Jones* says you can't do anything without a place for the person to go, and *Lavan* says you can't touch their property."

A psychologist who worked with the sheriff's department then spoke up. "I don't want to offend anybody, but I believe agencies are pushing the homeless onto each other." She'd even met people who were being displaced to LA from other cities and states. Furthermore, the county psychiatric hospitals were "flooded." "What," she asked the room, "does it say about us as a society?"

Such grand rhetorical questions were unanswerable at a political meeting. Eventually, a representative from a city councilman's office got down to brass tacks. "What is our goal? We won't solve homelessness, but the one thing we can do is improve public safety. Let's clean and have the [police] officer come through."

The new plan, then, was to increase the frequency of sidewalk cleanings on Spring Street. A representative from La Plaza, a Mexican American cultural center, said that she needed the area cleared out soon, because she had a major fundraiser. At this point, however, outreach workers became upset at being party to a simple street clearance project. A DMH homeless outreach worker told me bitterly, "We're just here to justify the police."

I asked whether he felt used, and he nodded.

"Yeah, but if you're gonna use us, at least give us some resources." Without those vouchers or other material goods, the workers were outreaching people empty-handed. Yet what else could they, or the Spring Street Task Force, do? Outreach workers turned their efforts toward constructing a highly detailed contact log demonstrating that they had referred people to the Department of Public and Social Service, the DMH clinic, or another agency. Without the resources for housing people, there was a significant organizational goal displacement—not treating the mentally ill, nor housing the homeless, but merely documenting contacts.

The concern for public safety was echoed on Spring Street, where it took on a more conspiratorial tone. An older white man living there claimed that the police weren't enforcing any basic rules. Although he had moved to Spring because the police bothered him less there than they had in Skid Row, he was now convinced they were deliberately allowing the area to become dangerous to eventually justify a large sweep. He said he had complained to an officer about a group of drinkers down the block, with the officer responding that he was unable to do anything.

"Where do I go?" he asked me and a DMH outreach worker. "This was a nice, sweet spot, if the cops would do their job. . . . We want to get away from Skid Row . . ."

The worker replied, "Well, not here."

This response might seem callous, but he saw Spring Street's "regular" homeless people as a distraction from his chief mission: finding the mentally ill and securing them treatment. This had become clear when he and his colleagues arrived to find that some people had apparently moved around the corner. I asked whether we would look for them—we'd spent months developing rapport—but Mona the nurse said to look only for the ones who were severely mentally ill. Otherwise, we were assigned to Spring Street *the place*, not the people on it.

One day, I arrived to discover that the police had cleared the encampment at last. This was due to neither securing people housing and treatment through the DMH, nor persuading them to leave on their own, nor acting on some change in the law at the court of appeals. Spring Street had finally become a public safety concern.

Whatever the truth of the old man's conspiracy theory, the lack of police intervention seemed to precede new levels of violence. One of the LAHSA workers claimed that she had called the county sheriff's office when a large homeless man threatened her, and it never responded. There had been a report of a stabbing, and then finally the street was cleared.

A pair of LAPD officers were parked in their squad car on the corner. They said that they were assigned to sit there the whole day, but nothing had happened on the street since the reported stabbing. The homeless people on Spring Street, both the "truly ill" who refused service-linked housing and the nonqualifying, had moved their tents around the corner to a neighboring park. Soon after that, the Spring Street outreach team members returned to their regular duties.

A NOTE ON FAMILY

Upon reading the outreach interactions described above, you may have noticed that relatives are conspicuously absent from the narrative. I often wondered about homeless clients' families but came to realize why outreach workers didn't immediately inquire. It was a touchy subject (family histories often were littered with burned bridges, abuse, and abandonment) and not usually actionable (a relative who *could* and *wanted to* help would have already tried). So how did someone fall through both the family and the social safety nets and end up with the "rights" to be psychotic and homeless in Skid Row? Roberto, a DMH worker, told me his life story to teach me about the cracks in the system. His biography gives us a more personal take on the history of deinstitutionalization in Los Angeles and how social inequality shapes who can even try to be a "good family member."

Born in the late 1950s to a single mother, a farm laborer, Roberto began to hear voices and act strangely in his late teens. He was sent to Patton State Hospital and diagnosed as having schizophrenia; this, however, was the 1970s rather than the asylum era. He soon came home and received his high school diploma—signs of deinstitutionalization's promise—but he was still struggling, and then his alcoholic mother died of cirrhosis of the liver. By that time, Roberto's older siblings had started families of their own and lacked the resources to assist, so he became homeless.

During the 1980s, Roberto lived Downtown, drinking heavily while hearing his mother's voice telling him not to give up. When I asked whether he'd ever been 5150'd during that time, he explained that as a person who didn't cause trouble, he was left alone. He didn't *fight* treatment per se—he was simply not enough of a problem to register as someone whose rights should be violated so that he could be helped. Eventually, a street outreach team got him into mental health services, and Roberto was lucky to receive a Section 8 apartment. He resumed taking antipsychotics and began to volunteer with a peer group, which eventually led to a job as a community worker for the DMH. From there, he reconnected with friends and family.

This story shows us how various forms of inequality and disadvantage can make it much harder for some families to help a seriously disabled loved one. For a low-income single mother with her own addiction struggles, a hallucinating son is a major burden. Roberto's mother likely lacked the educational and cultural knowledge to navigate social service systems, which were thin to begin with, and his siblings cared but couldn't help. When the pain of losing his mother pushed him over the edge, there was neither a family safety net nor a social safety net to catch him. Like so many others, all he had left was his "right" to descend into madness on the sidewalk.

· · ·

In Downtown LA, public psychiatric care is tied to a project of urban poverty governance. The Department of Mental Health, born of deinstitutionalization, is tasked with managing homelessness as much as it is with providing treatment. Given historical developments around constrained housing supply, the retrenchment of welfare services, repeated bouts of austerity, and the civil liberties of both homeless people and psychiatric patients, the crises of homelessness and mental illness become intertwined or even conflated.

Government actors can't repeat the asylum-era tactic of mass institutionalization, for this is neither legally acceptable nor materially feasible without the hospital infrastructure. Instead, social service providers channel people into and out of resource pathways, which are dependent on *voluntary* action on the client's part. If this means that psychiatric power is less concentrated and potent, it is also surprisingly dispersed: all sorts of people who might not have used psychiatric services end up at the DMH in search of housing and SSI. Mental illness is thus revealed as a social construction—not because it is somehow a "myth," but because everyone knows that the designation is slippery and manipulable for a variety of interests.

Laboring in these strange and trying conditions, workers can come to see clients in a highly circumscribed light. Think again of Roberto, whose family was unable to help him. When finally outreached in Skid Row, his social network connections were invisible: he likely appeared to be a socially isolated, legally empowered adult who managed to secure food for himself and therefore not be "gravely disabled." From the outside, he was not a beloved family member but an embodied urban social problem. As we will see in the next chapter, this is very different from how clients are understood in elite settings, when wealthy families are the paying customers for their relative's mental health care.

CHAPTER 3

REMAKING RELATIVES, REMAKING RELATIONS

Elite private providers of mental health care are tasked with managing family dynamics as much as psychiatric illness. They work to treat both the "identified patient" and the dysfunctional family unit, intervene in emotionally charged kin relations rather than the local politics of urban space, and address individuals rather than manage a problem population. Care and control take place in an elite private ecology of boutique clinics, residential programs, sober living homes, and a whole infrastructure separate from public institutions. In this project of family systems governance, providers view clients as like obstinate children, threats to reputation, and people with unfulfilled potential.

In the past, families might have had greater authority to dictate behavior or simply send relatives to asylums. Today, however, patient civil liberties mean that parents and clinicians—even the best-resourced ones—must work with people in primarily voluntary ways. At the limits of the law and existing care infrastructure, families and providers work in parallel with state actors to negotiate the fractured legacy of deinstitutionalization.

In the first part of the chapter, we will learn what money buys and how treatment can be tailored not just to symptoms but to family needs. Much of the clinical work is impressively thorough and shows real possibilities of care. Still, as we'll learn in the second half, the private mental health market contains certain dysfunctions. In some cases, middle-class parents are baffled to learn that private insurance doesn't cover options that might be available on Medicaid, and even the affluent find that some crucial resources simply don't exist.

Money can open treatment pathways, but it can't do everything. Sometimes that's because there's not enough of it—thus, we see middle-class families struggling with out-of-pocket costs and making tough choices about forgoing the private path of mental health care for the public one. And sometimes it's because patients' rights laws empower privileged clients just enough for them to run away or get arrested, leaving even the wealthiest parents to fear that their beloved adult children will become sidewalk psychotics.

THE ACTUALIZATION CLINIC IN ITS ECOLOGY

The Actualization Clinic served as my entry point into this world. Occupying a nondescript building in West LA, its walls were lined with photographs of mountains and ocean vistas. Fruit bowls and flowers projected an image of healthy living. A young receptionist greeted clients in the waiting area, where they could read various California lifestyle magazines. Upstairs, there were offices available for individual meetings as well as an expansive set of rooms for the Intensive Outpatient Program's therapy groups. The décor was subtle—an intentional contrast, I learned, with luxurious "spa" conditions at some Malibu centers that Actualization workers deemed inappropriate.

This clinic is one part of a broader system and history of elite health care in Los Angeles. Beginning in the 1850s, private sanatoriums emerged to serve rich tuberculosis patients who flocked to Southern California for the weather and the promise of healing. Regional boosters sought to market the climate and institutions to draw tourists and develop the area. As one nineteenth-century brochure put it, "Invalids come here by the hundreds, and in every case, where they are not past all hope, they speedily find that precious boon which they have sought in vain in every other clime."[1] In 1904, a doctor named McBride founded the Southern California Sanitarium for Nervous Diseases, marketing it with the motto Not Just to Live, but to Enjoy Living.[2] Today, it is the private Las Encinas Hospital, which offers both psychiatric and addiction treatment.

Actualization founder Richard came of age in the 1970s, and like many of his generation believed that large psychiatric institutions could not heal people. When an elite doctor sought his help with tending to a patient leaving long-term hospitalization for community life, Richard saw the possibility for a new business model in the era of deinstitutionalization. He, a former psychiatric technician, and his wife, a psychiatric nurse, started the Actualization Clinic to offer hospital discharge assistance for wealthy patients. Later, they brought on Joseph, a PhD psychologist who had directed a locked psychiatric facility, to provide therapeutic expertise.

Together, the trio built a case management team akin to the model used in the public sector but consisting primarily of master's-level marriage and family therapists. With echoes of Dr. McBride's motto, the team focused on psychosocial rehabilitation and helping people "get a life." They also acted as a referral service, connecting privileged families to the wide variety of private psychiatrists and therapeutic providers in the area.

I first met with Richard at his office, where he offered a startling reframing of poverty and privilege. A sixty-something white man with a thick beard, slight belly, and jovial gleam in his eye, he asked rhetorically whether it was harder to work with rich or with poor psychiatric patients. From his perspective, wealthy people presented different problems related to social capital and reputation. He said to think of it in terms of who or what was being impacted—beyond the patient.

"Who can do the most damage? The homeless person [can], to themselves. But it's gonna be one on one. A manic or psychotic person with resources and connections can do so much damage, you wouldn't believe it. To their family business, to their community . . ."

Rather than a disturbing sight on a gentrifying street corner, the well-resourced patient might be a liability to the family's material standing and community reputation. The challenge to the social order is different for the wealthy because patients are recognizable, socially connected, and financially able to make things happen. The damage the Actualization Clinic attends to is *relational*.

Although poorer families at the National Alliance on Mental Illness (NAMI) no doubt try to work the public system for their relatives, and even the homeless clients of Downtown have occasional family involvement, the family play an outsize role in elite private care. They, not the state, are the paying customer, and Actualization and other private clinics must ultimately satisfy their needs over the patient's. Once, when I asked whether the county, the state, or insurance companies audited Richard's clinic, he explained that he was "audited" by the families every billing cycle. "Every few weeks, I've got to send a millionaire dad running a major company a bill for a few thousand bucks, and he wants to know why is he paying it," Richard began. "The reason he's paying it is 'cause he's talked to me several times. He's talked to the doctor. He's talked to the son, and he feels really lucky to be able to pay the bill. I get audited every two weeks by everybody."

Believing the wealthy to be good stewards of their fortunes—at least savvy enough to seek a good return on their investment—Richard suggested that families' satisfaction and willingness to foot the bill were the ultimate arbiters of his clinic's success. If they were satisfied, he was clearly offering a good product.

PRIORITIZING THE FAMILY SYSTEM

Zara, the leader of the NAMI Westside Los Angeles group we met in chapter 1, told me that the mental health system mistreated families as much as it did patients. When we met for tea in the downstairs office of her grand home in West Los Angeles, she began by referencing the neurologist Oliver Sacks's book *The Man Who Mistook His Wife for a Hat*. Describing the chaos that serious mental illness could bring to a family system, she riffed on Sacks: "Ask not what disease your relative has. Ask what disease had kidnapped your relative's brain and thereby kidnapped the entire family."

This phrasing might draw the ire of some patients, as it implies that the person has been abducted and controlled by a foreign, hostile entity. For those psychiatric service users who see their unusual experiences as part of their identity and their behaviors as freely chosen rather than signs of illness, this indeed could be offensive. Yet for Zara, this formulation captured the powerlessness of even well-off families. Trying to help a relative whose brain had been "kidnapped" was hardly an illegitimate exercise of control, but families were being told that they had to abide by the strange choices of a seemingly sick loved one.

A therapist by profession, Zara had encountered mental illness during her career, but she came to focus on the family dimensions after her daughter had a psychotic break while away at university. She and her husband were upset at the way doctors cut them, the parents, out of treatment decisions. Since her daughter was an adult, the family was not entitled to information. Furthermore, there was no one to guide them through the process. "My only daughter became acutely mentally ill when she went back East to college—with depression, with psychosis, with anorexia and bulimia, carving on herself with knives, completely psychotic. . . . At [the hospital], there was nothing for us as a family," Zara recalled. "There was no family group. The psychiatrists were not inclusive because, of course, our daughter said, 'You can't talk to my parents.' And one psychiatrist was very mean to us and very narcissistic, and we were so appalled at the neglect of the whole family unit."

This experience led Zara to help teach families about how to engage with loved ones who "lacked insight" into their illness by using the LEAP method. The Listen Empathize Align and Partner approach teaches caregivers to realize that they can't reason with a person whose brain has been "kidnapped." Instead, one has to "align" with the loved one and their strange beliefs until it becomes possible to persuade them to try medicine. "When some person, like a parent, says, 'You know you have schizophrenia. You have to take meds. You're really crazy,' they never stay on their meds," Zara explained. "But if a parent says, 'I love you. I respect you. I respect your point of view. Wow, I understand you feel the FBI is persecuting you and there's cameras in your bedroom. That must be so hard for you . . .'" Such respect for the person's experience, even if feigned, could start a conversation about treatment.

Zara also taught families about conservatorships, facilitating workshops on the legal components and the emotional difficulties of maintaining guardianship powers. Since most conservatorship efforts failed, however, care would typically proceed without formal control. At the very least, Zara could refer people to private places like the Actualization Clinic, where their needs as the paying customer could be kept front and center.

WHAT MONEY BUYS

When I first began studying elite mental health-care settings, I was surprised by what could be considered a priority. Since there were rarely baseline material survival issues to cope with here—little risk, for instance, of imminent homelessness—a well-off family could direct clinicians' attention to behavior that might not even register by public safety net standards. Take, for instance, a client who wrote strange and embarrassing things on social media, whose mother insisted that the Actualization Clinic control his internet usage.

Adonis was a white man in his early thirties who came to case management after a series of hospitalizations. His private insurance covered some services, and his wealthy family could afford further out-of-pocket specialty attention. Diagnosed as having delusional disorder, he was convinced that celebrities were discussing his sex acts online and plotting to foil his career in the entertainment industry. According to his case manager, Norah, "He thought all of these Hollywood people were in cahoots to stop him from being a famous actor because of his sexual deviance. When he started tagging the FBI and famous people and people he went to high school with, like, 'Help me, they're trying to destroy me!'—it was going all up and down Facebook to the point his mom got his access code and was trying to delete stuff."

The Actualization Clinic staff visited Adonis five days a week in his apartment, and Norah followed his mother's requests. She spent considerable time "reality checking" and keeping Adonis off social media, and she responded to his text messages late at night or met him on weekends. Norah—the only Black worker at Actualization—told me she was shocked by the privileged lives of rich white people. She also complained about what she saw as the mother's unhealthy obsession with keeping up appearances. But this was her job.

I understood her frustration, but I'm loathe to trivialize the situation, for Adonis was in pain and his mother was at her wits' end. He continued to be treated for significant delusions at Actualization's Intensive Outpatient Program and then a university-affiliated Thought Disorders Intensive Outpatient Program, and the parental concern here is understandable. Rather than accept Norah's judgment, I simply want to highlight the family's ability to direct attention to something that wouldn't be a focus in a public clinic concerned with baseline needs.

Consider how a homeless person's online ranting from a public library computer terminal might elicit raised eyebrows but also might simply be ignored. Similarly, a family at a public clinic might be deeply worried about a member's online behavior yet struggle to persuade a clinician to make it a daily priority.

Adonis's case also illustrates another benefit of family money: the ability to keep loved ones in an alternate circuit of social control institutions than those catering to the lower and middle classes. Norah reported that Adonis's family had used its vast means to get him out of trouble as a youth. Sometimes he was merely humiliating his parents, but on at least one occasion he had seriously harmed someone.

> So, he would be doing all these behaviors, and the whole town would just be, like, "Ooh," aghast at his behavior, and he was embarrassing [his family]. And so he got sent away a lot. I mean, when he was younger, he was like a big, meathead football player, he got mad at his girlfriend, I guess she was cheating on him. And busted the window of her car and beat up the other dude. And they sent him to a school in Costa Rica. And he should have gone to jail. He almost killed the kid.

Where another person might have been incarcerated, wealth helped the family keep Adonis in the alternate system of international boarding schools and elite private psychiatric care. This can be challenging once the person is an adult, as that individual can more easily say no to being sent away or hospitalized, and the criminal justice system might be less amenable to diversion. But at least sometimes, wealth buys the possibility of escaping legal responsibility. Ironically, this might instead mean a parallel system of surveillance and constraint: rather than the state control or jail warehousing that might attend a criminal charge, the privileged patient is heavily surveilled and therapeutically micromanaged by private mental health-care providers who, for instance, constantly monitor internet behaviors (we'll return to these systems of control in chapter 9).

Such dynamics—prioritizing relatively minor things, protecting family reputation, and avoiding legal consequences—might make care for the rich sound indulgent or nefarious. Perhaps it can be. But money also buys expertise, time and attention, and care that can transform both the family member and family relations, so that people who initially resist treatment and parental control become poised to fulfill their own and their family's dreams.

BRINGING OUT THE "REAL" CLIENT

Bradley, a thirty-six-year-old white man diagnosed as having bipolar disorder, helped me understand the complex negotiations over treatment refusal. He recalled his first visit to the Actualization Clinic when he was in his mid-twenties and in a manic state. He had rejected his psychiatrist's recommendations and felt that his parents were trying to dictate his life from afar, but for some reason Actualization was different. Richard put him at ease and told him he had choices. Their first encounter was still fresh in Bradley's mind.

> I felt very controlled and felt like everyone's against me, and I shouldn't be here. . . . [Richard] was, like, "We don't want you to be here unless you wanna be here. And I think that there's something going on with you, something that we can try to figure out."

He really partnered, I don't know if you're familiar with that
LEAP method? It's, like, Listen, Empathize, Agree, and Partner. . . .
I don't know how they got through to me, but they somehow were
able to reason with me when I was super irrational . . . and not having any family here, they're like my second family now.

Here we see an illustration of that LEAP method for what Richard
has called "anosognosia and affluenza" cases. Richard's first move was
to put Bradley in the proverbial driver's seat of his recovery. Rather
than addressing his "impaired insight" head-on or informing Bradley
he was mentally ill, Richard acknowledged uncertainty ("I think that
there's something going on") and partnered with Bradley ("something that *we* can try to figure out"), allowing for reasoning even when
Bradley was "super irrational."

For loved ones living out of town, the "second family" support and
surveillance offered by the Actualization Clinic were effective in that
they came without the charged dynamics of long-standing parent-
child fights. When Bradley had a crisis, the case management team
was there to guide him through legal troubles, facilitate inpatient and
residential treatment placements, and keep his family in the loop. For
instance, Bradley had tried to go off medication several times, interrupting his life and career. The "lowest point" of his life, he said, was
when he'd stopped medication, become manic again, and left a stable
job to become an actor. After heavily drinking one day, he got into a
car accident and was arrested for driving while under the influence.

Although this might have started a cascade of problems—an out-
burst in jail that led to a longer incarceration, job loss, eviction—
Bradley was caught by the family safety net, now expanded to include
his clinicians. Richard met him at jail and arranged his transfer to
a private psychiatric hospital, then to Transitions, a private dual-
diagnosis residential program for bipolar disorder and addiction.
There Bradley learned more about his diagnosis and new coping
skills. Actualization, he explained, had helped him return to independent living in a moment of crisis. Now he saw a psychiatrist he liked,
in part because she provided psychotherapy in addition to medication

management. The team corresponded frequently with Bradley's parents, who were excited about his growth.

Richard told me that the family had recently visited Los Angeles, and Bradley's mother reported that he'd managed it beautifully. He'd picked them up at the airport and took care of all the details, like paying for the parking meters. Then he took them for a meeting with his psychiatrist to discuss a "breakthrough"—he'd been able to track his own signs of mood elevation signaling the onset of mania and wanted to work with the doctor and the Actualization team to control it. Bradley's father echoed his wife's satisfaction with their son's progress, telling Richard that Bradley was becoming who he was meant to be. He thanked Richard profusely for helping "bring out" "the 'real' Bradley."

Note what the Actualization Clinic did in this case: beyond averting crisis and getting a "noncompliant" patient into treatment, it brought the man and his family's once-divergent goals into alignment—a "real" version of the client who seemingly satisfies everyone involved.

DIAGNOSTIC SPECIFICITY

The next thing money buys is a quasi-scientific approach to care. Gerald, an Actualization therapist who had formerly worked on a DMH-funded community treatment team, explained how diagnostic workups and a client "profile" helped specify treatment plans. He noted that beyond fewer layers of red tape, the private world could offer highly tailored services.

> [Actualization] is probably the closest to the FSP [Full Service Partnership—California's case management teams] model I've seen [in the private sector]. But way less clients, way less bureaucracy, way less oversight. . . . The other thing we've done really well is we have a really good network of providers. . . . If we need trauma specialty . . . I'm gonna send you to a trauma expert. I'm gonna send you to an expert who's good at diagnostics to make sure we get the right kinds of differential diagnosis. I know the best place to treat somebody with your profile.

The Actualization Clinic collaborated with a psychologist who could administer cognitive testing and a well-known psychiatrist named Dr. Myrdal for overall diagnostics and medication adjustments. Affiliated with a university and respected for his research on differentiating schizoaffective and bipolar disorders, Dr. Myrdal was the go-to when clients were struggling with medication. His $750 diagnostic evaluation was a multihour affair, including various psychological scales, a thorough medical history, and neurological workups. The team members were especially impressed with his use of genetics, which they believed was "where the field is going."

When I met with Dr. Myrdal at his office, however, he insisted he was simply practicing thorough psychiatry. This included physical testing to rule out an organic cause of mental symptoms, and psychological evaluation forms to measure dimensions of need and suggest proper psychotherapy. Further, he said, the Actualization workers had misinterpreted his use of genetic testing; he did not—and could not, given the state of the science—use it diagnostically. Primarily, he used genetics to get a sense of patients' metabolisms, allowing him to plan appropriate medication dosage.

In fact, Dr. Myrdal echoed what I'd heard from DMH clinicians regarding the imprecision of psychiatric science. Like Dr. Wong from the previous chapter, who said he could essentially treat every seriously ill patient with the antipsychotic Abilify, Dr. Myrdal said that medication treatment was a "shotgun" approach, not one targeted to specific diagnoses. "These [different illnesses] all sort of feed on one another," he said. "Our medicines are really a shotgun approach, 'cause they affect the whole brain and they go everywhere in the brain. It explains why a medication like Quetiapine, which is Seroquel, or [inaudible], why they might work for psychosis, why they might work for mania, why they might work for depression . . . and we don't probably even know why the same drug works for all three conditions."

Although he had devoted part of his career to diagnostic research and was far more committed to it than someone like Dr. Wong (who scoffed at "academic distinctions" made between diagnoses, which weren't helpful for running a prison wing or public clinic), Myrdal nonetheless agreed that the science was in its infancy and not always clinically useful. At one point, we discussed speculation in the psychiatric community that future genetic research might render categories such as schizophrenia and bipolar disorder obsolete, for each might overlap or in fact be twenty different conditions that are currently being lumped together.

And yet, differential diagnosis mattered in this ecosystem in a way that it simply didn't in the public safety net. Specificity gave a sense of scientific assurance and illuminated treatment pathways forward. Rather than a bureaucratic tool used to access cash benefits and housing like at the DMH, a proper diagnostic workup here might lead rich clients to targeted interventions and programs.

"THE SWAT TEAM IS HERE"

In treating Stellan, a man in his early thirties who performed bizarre rituals that seemed to indicate both obsessive-compulsive disorder (OCD) and psychotic illness, the Actualization team turned to Dr. Myrdal. The aim was to clarify a treatment plan and then move the man into specialized care, as outlined in a treatment conference.

"Connectedness is an important issue," the case manager Zach explained. "Stellan hasn't touched anyone in years."

Stellan's mother contacted the Actualization Clinic because he had experienced strange bodily sensations like tingling in his fingers, which he related to "an entity," and he refused to be touched. His inability to tolerate physical contact had gotten so bad that he was avoiding water droplets and had stopped bathing. The family employed a psychiatrist, a therapist, and a shaman.

"What's the problem?" asked Joseph, the psychologist. In the team's parlance, this was a way to understand symptoms within the context of the patient's life. Deirdre, the clinical director, scoffed and jumped in with what she saw as the obvious pathology at hand.

"He is floridly psychotic."

"He has severe OCD and is delusional," Zach followed.

Deirdre returned to the connectedness issue. It wasn't that the relational or psychodynamic dimensions had caused the illness, but that the illness had impacted the family in a negative way. Stellan's inability to touch had started before his father's recent death, and that caused a powerful regret. "He feels remorse he couldn't hug his dad before he died."

Someone asked, "Does he have the right diagnosis?"

Deirdre shook her head.

A case manager who had spoken with Stellan's doctor added, "The psychiatrist needs some help here. He doesn't see it as classic OCD."

"I have classic OCD," Deirdre offered, "and the difference is I know it is irrational. But for him there's not even . . . it's delusional. He's not medicated properly."

Joseph echoed her sentiment. "We asked the doc to increase the antipsychotic, and he's considering it."

Deirdre expanded on the family dynamic. "Mom hugs the air around him. She says, 'I know it's his illness, but sometimes I still feel rejected.'"

"It's just so typical that the family doesn't know what to do," said Joseph. "They go with what the doctor says, year after year."

"The SWAT Team is here," someone called out with a laugh.

Deirdre concluded, "He needs to go to Dr. Myrdal. We're not gonna be able to help him without the right meds."

Several pieces of the governance project are apparent here—as is the slate of possibilities opened by money. Governing for the family system involves a broader ecology of psychiatric services, a set of connections and referrals typically nonexistent for poorer people. In this case, notice how the Actualization team orients to its client's needs. First is the emphasis on the relational dynamic: the framing is in terms of connectedness and Stellan's inability to hug his father or his mother. Yet the family systems formulation is entangled with a psychiatric one: Deirdre says that the case management team can't help him without the right medication, and thus the first task is to take him to Dr. Myrdal for an evaluation and a medication switch.

The "SWAT Team" analogy fits with the team's vision of itself. Like a special police unit, the team believed it was equipped when standard mental health care failed. The therapeutic plan that emerged from this treatment meeting was to get the new psychiatric evaluation and then connect Stellan with focused psychological care. Zach began to meet the man in the community and pull him from his routine. Before long, he excitedly announced to the team, "Stellan wants to try something different." Deirdre replied. "That will be major when it happens. And it will. 'Cause *that's what we do.*"

Dr. Myrdal prescribed Clozaril, often considered the antipsychotic of last resort. If not monitored closely with consistent blood work, elevated levels of the drug in the bloodstream can compromise the individual's immune system and potentially be deadly. In fact, many DMH psychiatrists Downtown wouldn't prescribe it, because poor clients' lives were too chaotic to maintain the lab work needed to ensure safe use of the medication. (Between this and the fact that some medications may not be covered by a person's insurance, I began to see how prescribing practice was also tied to social circumstances and inequality.)

Next, Actualization developed a plan for Stellan to attend a residential OCD center in the LA area where he could address his rituals and fixations. This program, which cost approximately $40,000 a month and did not accept insurance, involved four hours of psychotherapy a day: three hours of individual cognitive therapy and exposure and response prevention therapy, plus one hour in group.

I visited the center, and while I couldn't observe Stellan's treatment, I spoke with a clinical psychologist and read over the facility's materials. The center's therapy exposes patients to a stimulus that would normally trigger them, such as crowds or contamination, and then supports the patients in refraining from the compulsive behavior. It also engages in family systems work, not because families *caused* the distress, but because of what it terms the behavioral accommodation of family networks that enabled the problem to continue. According to the clinic, the whole family home dynamic would need to change for a patient to improve, no matter how many hours of individual therapy that person attended.

The Actualization Clinic continued with weekly visits during the months Stellan was in residential treatment, collaborating with the other program by undertaking "in vivo" expansions of its exposure therapy in the broader neighborhood. Thus, over the period of one year, Stellan's "SWAT Team" had rearranged his care system, switched him to a new psychiatrist and new medication, and enrolled him in specialist residential therapy.

THE HYPER-UNEQUAL MARKET

Most families can't afford a treatment approach like that taken for Stellan. Zara from NAMI often referred people to the Actualization Clinic, but she understood that insurance rarely covered such services, and private pay was exorbitant—"You could spend a fortune at the Actualization Clinic!" she marveled. Indeed, it was a luxury good, costing roughly $5,000 for twelve home visits a month, and that was before the cost of private psychiatrists, psychotherapists, and other services. The market for mental health care is profoundly bifurcated: some public services available for the poor, elite services provided for the rich, and a huge gap in the middle.

When their daughter became psychotic, Zara and her husband managed to put together the money for an extended residential treatment stay. "We put our daughter in a place for a year. It was $1,000 a day," she noted. "We took out a huge mortgage on our home to pay for that, and it was onerous. And a lot of parents wouldn't do that, to risk losing their home."

I admired her commitment to her loved one. But beyond the question of *willingness* to risk the house was the fact of economic inequality: unlike most families, the couple owned a home that could be used to finance hundreds of thousands of dollars of private treatment.

Zara went on to contrast the real therapy and activities of private long-term residential centers with the equivalent for poor people, the county-contracted Institutes of Mental Disease. "[Elite residential programs] have cooking classes, they have art classes. They take [patients] hiking, and they're all schizophrenic or bipolar disorder and they live in separate houses right near this community center, very expensive but they do things with people to help them get well, and the public Institutes of Mental Health [*sic*] don't do anything to help them get well." Though she lacked personal experience with the DMH and most of the people she worked with used private services, Zara was convinced that public mental health-care providers did not work closely with families. She distinguished between public case managers, who helped with accessing benefits, and private therapists, whom she believed could approach the "nuances and difficulties" of mental illness.

Places like Actualization and high-end specialty therapy programs tend not to take insurance, because the administrative work involved is a hassle. Focusing on clients and families who pay directly means a lot less paperwork and not having to continually justify treatments to an insurance company that tries to deny care-related claims. Private insurers, on the other hand, don't want to cover expensive boutique treatments that are either not medical per se (e.g., field trips) or have ambiguous outcomes (as with some psychotherapies), hence difficult to justify in cost-benefit terms.

During my fieldwork, however, a private behavioral health insurer I'll call Breyer Insurance reached out to Actualization to conduct a pilot program. Occasionally, insurers initiate "single-case agreements" and cover case management or other specialty services, but they typically treat places like Actualization as an out-of-pocket expense. But after the 2010 Affordable Care Act (also known as Obamacare) went into effect, people who might have previously been excluded by private insurance providers for preexisting conditions were suddenly buying private insurance. Between this and parity requirements that expect insurers to cover behavioral health services as much as physical health, Breyer was now on the hook. At a meeting in the Actualization conference room, the insurance company's representatives explained that they were serving patients with serious mental illness who had been untreated for years; now these folks were insured and running up high hospitalization bills.

Much as the public case management teams were funded to keep people out of emergency services, Breyer wondered whether intensive case management like the Actualization Clinic might help it save money. The Actualization team was excited, as this might mean the ability both to serve a wider population and to have a steadier patient pool when its private-pay clientele dipped. These insurance changes meant that at least some middle-class people might be able to access places like Actualization or high-quality residential centers. In the end, however, Breyer concluded that Actualization was too expensive to justify. The hyper-unequal market would remain bifurcated.

From the client perspective, the difference in level of care could be shocking. Leonard, one of the speakers at NAMI's event from chapter 1, was in a unique position to discuss different treatment systems. Unlike many of the privileged clients, he had weathered dozens of hospitalizations and hellish medication transitions in both elite private and public-serving treatment settings. At Actualization, where he felt safe, he learned techniques to stabilize himself—a situation he contrasted with the clinics for the poor, which he remembered as intimidating, and the horror he felt when visiting a Board and Care home.

Now, no longer in need of an intensive therapeutic program, Leonard had moved his care to a DMH-contracted nonprofit center, where he saw a psychiatrist and a therapist. Although this facility wasn't scary, he nonetheless believed that its patients were merely "surviving" and not "thriving" as they might have been at Actualization. "It's safe and clean, but it's not really a rehabilitation place," he remarked. "It's really a place to have a day program and check in with your doctor and a psychologist, which is sad, because a lot of people who have mental illness have brilliance. And a lot of people who have mental illness have something to share in society. But maybe because they don't have the support, family or a loved one, they're preoccupied with surviving instead of thriving, and that's sad." Leonard was certain that the Actualization program's therapeutic tools and mind-set toward patients had kept him out of the hospital. Something as simple as the clinic's fresh fruit basket, for instance, made the place *feel* like a healthy environment. Regarding the nonprofit clinic, he said, "Even if they would just go to Trader Joe's and buy a little orchid, like a little green plant, it would symbolically mean that people are looking at you from a different perspective."

THE PROVIDERS NETWORK

On a late fall morning in Marina Del Rey, I arrived at an exclusive waterfront hotel for the Providers Network Luncheon. The breeze off the water perfectly tempered the Los Angeles sun, and a photographer took group pictures against a backdrop emblazoned with treatment center logos. I posed with Geoffrey, a dual-diagnosis sober home operator wearing a man bun, and we laughed at how the photo session felt like a Hollywood red carpet event.

Geoffrey was a no-nonsense guy, a martial arts instructor and former addict who thought that many of the high-end mental health treatment centers were scams. Rather than charge excessively for luxury, he kept his mental health and sober living home nice but modest (for this side of town), emphasizing the discipline, physical activity, and Twelve Step treatment model that had saved his own life. Another attendee, one of his business partners, ran a wilderness camp, taking young people to Utah to escape the outside world before transitioning to community living in a place like Geoffrey's Namaste Gardens. The two shared clients whose trajectory through the private treatment ecology might consist of stops in a psychiatric hospital or monthlong stints at rehabs in Malibu or throughout the western states.

Richard from Actualization opened the event with a speech describing the origin of his agency and the Providers Network. He told the assembled mental health providers that in the 1970s, he would struggle to coordinate discharge and planning when patients ended up in the hospital. Not yet knowing the hospital staff, he began cultivating relationships among these professionals by hosting lunches, slowly acquiring the contact info and rapport necessary to make a smooth connection between treatment facilities. Today, with more than forty service providers in the room, the event had blossomed into a meeting place for referrals and community connection—a safety net for the well-to-do.

We sat in a large circle and listened to providers hawk their services. Directors from single-illness specialty clinics explained their psychotherapeutic approaches for conditions including borderline personality disorder, eating disorders, and sex addiction. Also represented were a range of residential addiction centers at different price points, from around $10,000 a month in Arizona to $60,000 in Malibu. For psychosis, there were partial-hospitalization program and Intensive Outpatient Program options. A clinic of highly credentialed private psychiatrists explained they would take insurance, unlike those doctors who only took cash. For legal troubles, a mental health lawyer told us of her expertise in criminal diversion cases and helping families secure conservatorships.

Some providers avoided announcing their dollar prices out loud during their presentation by saying their services cost *market rate*—which elicited laughter from the audience. The luncheon attendees understood that it often meant "more than you'd like to spend." The majority seemed to know that the costs of care were shocking, and jokes like these served to alleviate the awkwardness. But aside from the psychiatrists who emphasized that they accepted insurance, nobody seemed concerned about their services' accessibility to the general public.

WHAT THE MARKET DOESN'T PROVIDE

And yet for all the many treatment options, a gaping hole exists in the elite care ecology. At a smaller networking event, clinicians complained that there were no good long-term, monitored housing options for the privileged client with serious mental illness. Board and Care homes for low-income people had scant staffing and activities, so where were the quality ones? There were sober living homes geared toward addiction that had rebranded themselves "dual diagnosis" to include serious mental illness, but that, too, created problems. Deirdre of the Actualization Clinic described a young woman who lived in a sober living facility but had no addiction. Recently, the client had begun picking up the language of Twelve Step and *calling* herself an addict. Other providers echoed that they needed a better discharge option for the seriously mentally ill.

Over the course of four Providers Network meetings, I only saw one long-term housing option for chronic mental patients: an upscale

Board and Care home further down the coast. As the representative explained to me, it was difficult to operate in a housing market like Los Angeles. Actualization occasionally referred people to a program in an adjacent county, but there was little within LA itself.

Ultimately, much of the Providers Network catered to "launch clients," or younger people trying to meet the expectations of adulthood (thus *failing to launch*). Often these agencies only worked with people for a few months at a time and at earlier stages of illness and addiction. I was puzzled by the lack of long-term housing with care for those well-off people who needed extra support. There had to be *something* between becoming a success story like Leonard or Geraldine at the NAMI Recovery speaker series and having to live with the poor in Los Angeles's Board and Care homes. If nothing else, this seemed like an obvious service gap and a prime market opportunity for some entrepreneur.

Mr. Daniels, a Board and Care operator whom I first encountered in the public safety net ecology, helped me understand. Given his twenty years in the mental health business, he had begun consulting for elite private treatment centers that needed to pass government licensing and inspection. His role positioned him to explain the political economy of this market, wherein the intersection of zoning and treatment regulation, neighborhood objection, price point relative to investment, and elite expectations conspired to prevent the establishment of high-end Board and Care facilities.

> The first problem is, Where do you build it? If you're going to have it in a nice residential neighborhood, a nice home in Hancock Park [genteel midcity area] that has roughly five bedrooms—so, you'll use three of them [as bedrooms], the others for [therapeutic] sessions. You bought the house in Hancock Park, $3, 4, 5 million, [you charge] at $6, 7, 8,000 a month. You can't get it licensed for more than 6 [residents]—well, if you need 10, you can't build it. It's more than NIMBY [not in my backyard]. You'd get a BANANA [build absolutely nothing anywhere near anybody] situation.

If someone's paying $6,000–7,000 a month, they want it nice. Well, there's no grounds. [Want] big grounds? Maybe do it in the Valley [outside the city]? Big backyard, you can get it for a little cheaper. Still, are you going to be able to build it in a commercially zoned area for 10, 15, 30 people? Then you have turnover. Here [in a poor Board and Care] I have people for 5, 6, 20 years. You're not going to get it over there. . . . They're not gonna stay for 5 years.

Factors ranging from rich families' preferences for care in certain neighborhoods to those neighborhoods' costs, zoning restrictions, and reticent neighbors combined with patient-resident turnover to severely handicap what would seem like a major opportunity for profit. Further, Mr. Daniels told me, the other players in the private mental health industry fought the development of high-end long-term care, because they would lose *their* business to on-site providers.

Still, I was unsatisfied by an explanation purely based on economics. Couldn't someone figure out how to build a nice care home outside the LA housing market, close enough for families to visit but far enough away to cut costs, located in, say, an unincorporated area with lax zoning laws, that might therefore be profitable? And why would wealthy people be willing to spend $30,000–$50,000 a month on intensive treatment but not $6,000–$7,000 a month on high-end custodial community care? Mr. Daniels didn't have a strong answer—he just insisted they wouldn't do it.

My take on the situation, after having spent more time in this world, is that Mr. Daniels's claim only made sense if I considered the *future orientation* of the families and the elite clinicians. They envisioned the creation of a respectable, middle- or upper-class life for the patient, not a life of safety and basic management.

Imagine a wealthy, property-owning family with an adult child who has experienced an initial manic episode or drug-induced psychotic break. It utilizes a place like Transitions, investing $60,000–$100,000 in the residential program in the hope that it will "work"—that their son or daughter will find the right medication, experience therapeutic breakthroughs, and develop coping skills for recovery. This was Bradley's experience. But perhaps a year later, the person is in crisis again, and this time the family takes out a second mortgage on its home to fund another round of treatment, for a longer period.

But what if the loved one isn't self-managing nor on the cusp of getting a job? It's not clear that another round of intensive treatment will "fix" the person. It's one thing to spend $250,000 on treatment that could lead to recovery. A family might deplete its savings or risk its home on the belief that three months of intensive treatment could turn the child's life around—a $100,000 investment in the future. But twenty years at $6,000–$7,000 a month for safety and for staff to coordinate daily activities? That doesn't align with the hope that privileged families (and many mental health-care providers) hold on to.

This dynamic also helps clarify what they're selling at places like Actualization, Transitions, and the various elite centers: a vision of the future. Board and Care homes are not treatment centers. They do not purport to fix people. All they can offer in terms of a future is twenty more years in the Board and Care. At the intersection of the privileged family's dream of full recovery and the mental health industry's need for profitability, a market gap remains unfilled.

THE PRIVATE VERSUS PUBLIC INSURANCE TRAP

Paying out of pocket is not viable for most middle-class families. The more educated and culturally savvy may find success working their insurance system, but the hyper-unequal market structure means that those in the middle class must more often make tough choices between what the private and the public social service streams provide. Families are hesitant to give up private insurance and place their adult children on public services, which would open access to some resources (such as case management teams) while closing access to others (such as top hospitals that won't take Medicaid, for instance). Recall also that the DMH wraparound programs prioritize people with jail and homelessness in their histories, so it could be hard for middle-class families to qualify for those intensive services unless their loved one's crisis had already become a public problem.

Mary, a Latina university professor, was in that spot. She speculated that during the asylum era, her son Alex probably would have been hospitalized for his whole life. Instead, he was facing institutionalization in prison.

In the living room of her West Los Angeles home, Mary told me she'd spent years working every system she could. Alex had exhibited behavioral difficulties and aggression that she'd initially attributed to environmental stressors—he was among the only Black children in a mostly white school, and Mary's husband had died young. But she soon suspected that something more medical in nature was the source of her son's issues. She got Alex connected with the Regional Center, which arranges services for people with developmental disabilities. This was a coup and a testament to Mary's cultural savvy—Alex was higher functioning with his particular developmental needs that otherwise wouldn't be typically accepted at the center, and the center helped channel federal benefits unavailable for Alex's treatment with a psychiatric diagnosis alone. Throughout her son's youth, Mary juggled her private insurance, the Regional Center, and the school district to put together an array of services to help him.

But Mary's savvy eventually reached its limit. Now a young adult, Alex was hospitalized after starting a fistfight with a neighbor. There he was diagnosed as having paranoid schizophrenia. His mother tried to get him into the Actualization Clinic to give him structure, but her insurance wouldn't pay for the Intensive Outpatient Program day therapy. Life at home rapidly deteriorated. After Mary's nephew suggested that the schizophrenia diagnosis (which would later be revoked) meant that Alex was too disabled to control his own destiny, the cousins got into a physical altercation. In what the family would later argue was a grossly excessive charge, the police booked Alex on attempted murder.

Mary hired a private attorney and asked a sympathetic prosecutor to consider alternatives to incarceration for her son. She learned about the Department of Mental Health's diversion program, but she heard that clients had low prospects for recovery and would receive very little attention. Instead, she worked with her insurance company to cover a long-term residential treatment program. Yet what she had wanted from the beginning was the private therapeutic community-based care of Actualization. Switching to public services *might* provide a less therapeutic level of community care with social support, but she didn't want Alex to lose access to the private resources he *did* have by going into the public system. Caught between the gaps in both public and private insurance coverage for mental health care, Mary chose the devil she knew.

WHEN THE COUNTY BECOMES THE BEST OPTION

Other middle-class families make a different choice. To be clear, it's usually one or the other—they are generally told to give up their private insurance if they want to access the intensive case management teams or county-funded Institutes of Mental Disease. Indeed, most people diagnosed as having schizophrenia will eventually end up on public insurance.[3]

Jessica Chavez, a law student, reached out to me concerning a policy brief about conservatorship reform that I had coauthored. Interning at a mental-health-focused public interest law firm, Jessica had come to law school after working in prison abolitionist nonprofit and activist groups. Her experiences with her sister, thirty years old at the time, had pushed her to reconsider her formerly civil libertarian opinions on both mental health and criminal legal systems. After I answered her questions about California's civil commitment changes, she agreed to an interview.

Jessica's sister, Rita, had dropped out of college, moved home, and begun to enter altered states in which she became aggressive and cruel. The Chavezes needed help, but they did not trust the police. The mother had once called 911 when her son was high and behaving erratically, and the responding police officer became combative and told her, "I was *this close* to shooting him." Consequently, the family did not believe in dialing 911. Yet there was no other option when Rita became psychotic; the Psychiatric Emergency Team and other mental-health-focused first responders were rarely available.

The Chavez family was middle class and well-educated. After Rita's first hospitalization, Jessica mobilized her cultural knowledge to do what seemed to be the most logical thing: the family bought the best private insurance package possible. This backfired, however, when Rita found private psychiatrists who would simply give her the prescriptions she wanted. Taking large amounts of doctor-prescribed Adderall, she would become psychotic and start the hospitalization cycle all over again. Some benefits of the expensive insurance, like access to good private therapists or specialized treatment, didn't do much, because she was either unwilling or too mentally disorganized to navigate the appointments.

Rita spiraled and began stealing alcohol from grocery stores, leading to run-ins with the law that exhausted her family. Then her parents learned of the county's Full Service Partnership program at a NAMI meeting. The ideal situation would be to keep their private insurance and start the case management at the same time. But when Jessica consulted with the county, she was told that Rita's private coverage must be canceled if the family wanted Full Service Partnership. This arrangement would mean fewer therapeutic resources but the kinds of stabilizing social work interventions that the family desperately needed.

The Chavezes chose the public route, and the case management program did what the private-insurance-covered services had not: they visited Rita at home and helped her make it to appointments with the doctor, navigate criminal justice issues, and resume some semblance of a routine. But what would seem to be the best of both worlds—opportunities for high-quality care with private therapists, psychiatrists, or specialist programs alongside case management for psychosocial care and help navigating the community—remained only for the rich.

WHEN GOVERNANCE PROJECTS COLLIDE

To close this section, I want to return to NAMI, but a different chapter—NAMI Urban Los Angeles. Unlike the overwhelmingly white and privileged demographic of the Westside Los Angeles chapter (and indeed NAMI more generally), the Urban group is composed primarily of Latino and Black families who have far less wealth. Moreover, they must navigate a racially unequal—or even racist—public mental health system. Here managing family members necessarily means engaging urban poverty governance issues. For the leadership of NAMI Urban Los Angeles, working on mental health was inseparable from advocacy work in criminal justice and homelessness policy.

Jerry Washington is an African American man whose jet-black eyebrows contrast sharply with his snow-white soul patch. Like many NAMI parents, he had no idea what to do when his daughter experienced a psychotic break in college. NAMI Urban Los Angeles was instrumental in helping his family navigate the mental health system and his daughter's encounters with the criminal justice system, and he felt greatly indebted to the organization. As he approached retirement, he agreed to take a leadership role in it.

For Jerry, the separation between the worlds of mental health care reflected a more general feature of living in the region: "I tell you, I was born and raised in Mississippi, and I still haven't seen many places as segregated as Los Angeles." The massive social inequality between wealthy white families and more modestly resourced Black and Brown families meant significant differences in the experience of mental illness. The person of color's risk of being criminalized and arrested rather than receiving mental health care meant learning a different mental health system. Jerry explained, "I believe our NAMI affiliate is the only one who offers a particular support group for criminal-justice-involved families. That's a whole 'nother—the mental health system has enough challenges on its own, but the criminal justice system has even more. When you reach that intersection between the two, it's very difficult for families to navigate by themselves." That intersection, combined with the fact that few families at

Urban could afford services out of pocket, meant that a mental health crisis would nearly always involve the state. Private issues would not remain private.

Jerry knew some of the Westside people and was appreciative of their work, since their group had helped "incubate" the Urban chapter. Yet they couldn't help with many of the issues that Urban was working on. "[Westside] is pretty financially well off, which is good, and good people, that—things just are what they are. They just don't have that experience. I went to a few meetings with people, and the levels of care, the things they talk about, are not the things that I'm most concerned about. Because I'm really focused on improving the public system." When I asked him to elaborate, he said that Westside families mostly kept their relatives in private services and away from the DMH. Furthermore, they seemed unconcerned with the second major issue facing the Urban chapter—advocating for affordable housing development and keeping their loved ones from homelessness.

> I went with a group of ladies talking about types of housings you need, to cover the whole thing, the shortage in Board and Cares and the nuances between Board and Cares and sober living facilities and all of that. They [Westside families] were more concerned about the financial sustainability, I guess would be it, because many of them were already paying what would be in my opinion . . . exorbitant amounts of money to provide basic needs, like housing . . . they were, like, "How do I keep the cost down to $3,000 a month?"
>
> I don't need that. I need public housing. I need money to be invested.

Between the fact of the special criminal justice support group and advocacy for public housing, Jerry seemed to suggest important distinctions between Urban and Westside that aligned with my sense of two distinct governance projects. It seemed to me that for families of color who lacked the money for private services, their family care was inseparable from the dynamics of urban social problems. I wanted to know whether this sounded correct.

NEIL: Tell me if I'm sort of getting this right. For your family and your community, it's not just focused directly on mental health. Like, you are also trying to work around the politics of housing and homelessness, criminal justice system, all these kinds of things in addition to what folks on the West Side have to deal with.

JERRY: Absolutely. Yeah, no, no question about it . . . I was just in a meeting yesterday . . . when we were talking about the criminal justice system. I'm thinking about very different things, and they were talking about how to work *with* the police. All good stuff, you wouldn't be against it, but it's kind of hard for you to do if you got forty-seven bullets in your back. . . . You know [police] training can only take you so far, but I don't think you can train people out of the racism that they grew up with.

For Jerry and his group, criminalization, homelessness, and police brutality are never far away. Calling 911 is different if you fear that your Black or Brown loved one will be shot (or when the police tell you they narrowly avoided shooting him or her).[4] Here place, race, and resources meant that the family systems governance and urban governance projects could not be disentangled.

•   •   •

In the project of family systems governance and the elite private care ecology, mental illness manifests as a relational problem of love, protecting futures, and reputation management. The responsible actors are family members and paid agents like private psychiatrists and case managers, and the goal is some sort of rehabilitation aimed toward an acceptable life. The Actualization Clinic, itself born of deinstitutionalization, aims to cope with a very different problem from that of the street client. It deals with the entitled wealthy person whose connections and money mean that this individual can be destructive to social networks and the family name.

For those with substantial funds, there is the promise of diagnostic specificity and tailored care. Diagnostic categories remain scientifically murky, but money creates exciting possibilities for mixing and matching treatments—for instance, OCD exposure therapy in residential treatment for a person who is being medicated for a psychotic disorder. But surprisingly, this ecology lacks a key component—long-term housing for the profoundly disabled adult. Since the most profit to be made is in residential rehabs or psychiatric facilities, and hope is a key product to be sold, the system is set up for short-term treatment that imagines robust futures, not long-term custodial care.

Importantly, not all families are even able to pursue this project. Even when relatives are willing to go to treatment, middle-class parents must choose between public and private insurance routes that offer very different things. And as the leader from NAMI Urban Los Angeles confirms, mental health advocacy *is* advocacy for housing and criminal justice reform for many families of color. Some of these families might dream of graduate school and a career, but they often become focused instead on keeping loved ones out of jail and off the street.

PART II

UNEQUAL TREATMENTS, UNEQUAL RECOVERIES

CHAPTER 4

SOCIAL PROGNOSIS

During the asylum era, a psychiatrically disabled person's future might have meant a life of long-term confinement. Even during the post-deinstitutionalization period, most doctors gave devastating prognoses of continued mental illness, with little hope for long-term recovery. Since the 1990s, however, there has been a tremendous ideological shift toward the assumption that people can and should thrive in the community.[1] Here in part 2 of this book, we will see how seemingly self-evident concepts like treatment and recovery take on vastly different meanings in public safety net clinics versus elite private facilities. To make sense of this, I ask, Who do mental health-care providers imagine their clients to be? And to what can patients in the contrasting worlds reasonably aspire?

This chapter introduces two women in their fifties whose divergent lives reveal the wildly different meanings of *recovery* in contemporary psychiatry. Although they share an experience of major depression with psychosis, the contours of illness and intervention are profoundly different in their lives. Their trajectories show how visions of clinical progress emerge against a backdrop of unequal material resources, divergent social networks, and constructions of human value shaped by race and class.

Delilah Jackson is an African American woman who entered Department of Mental Health treatment after losing her job, losing custody of her children, and becoming homeless. We meet Delilah at a moment of tension when her providers are questioning whether independent living is appropriate for her. Noting her self-isolation, case managers conduct home visits to ensure she's safe but are unable to address her psychological needs. Gwen Sennett, on the other hand, is a wealthy white woman from a beach city whose family brought her to the Actualization Clinic after a series of hospitalizations and a stint in residential treatment. We meet Gwen as her providers plot how to get her "voice" back. Beyond symptom abatement and role resumption, they offer a psychotherapeutic plan to empower Gwen and transform her family system.

Unlike inequality in the case of some physical illnesses, where the rich receive far more attention but a similar treatment,[2] psychiatric interventions may diverge in form—that is, patients from different socioeconomic backgrounds may receive strikingly different treatment approaches. This means we can't compare treatment outcomes in a straightforward way. A robust literature in psychiatric epidemiology shows that poverty is linked to worse illness, but here I investigate something else.

Rather than ask who is sicker or whether the public or the private approach is more effective, I show how each type of clinic is relatively "successful" with both mild and severe disability. This is because their respective definitions of success stem from highly stratified understandings of recovery and personhood. Thus, I argue that alongside the psychiatric prognosis of symptoms and projected course of illness, an unspoken *social prognosis* predicts the kind of life a person can expect to live—and it shapes what counts as reasonable treatment.

STABILIZING DELILAH JACKSON

The DMH case management team worked out of Fifth Street and San Pedro, a corner office with a floor-to-ceiling glass window and a waiting area furnished with plastic chairs. Sharing a hallway with a development called the Little Tokyo Lofts, the clinic occupied one of the many unofficial boundaries between Skid Row and up-and-coming

Downtown. Upon entering, clients were greeted by a private security guard's metal-detecting wand, a receptionist in a locked station behind an enclosed plastic window, and a sheriff's deputy. No one would mistake it for a spa or a Malibu doctors' office, but the clinic at least offered respite from the streets.

Behind yet another set of locked doors, I sat with the treatment team in the clinic's cold concrete conference room. They quickly discussed each person on the client roster, noting who had appointments or routine visits coming up, but they stopped and lingered at Delilah Jackson. She hadn't been going out to buy food and had missed some expected meetings at the clinic. They'd found her an independent apartment, but things were going wrong. "She can't live on her own," said Beth, the social worker. "We might have to go over and put her in [the hospital]."

These comments were more questions than assertions, as Delilah had transitioned from the streets to a Board and Care home and now on to her new subsidized apartment unit. She *was* living on her own and wasn't technically gravely disabled, a danger to self or others, or requiring an emergency hospitalization, at least not yet. In trying to account for her missing appointments at the office, a worker said Delilah once reported that a man had sexually assaulted her near the clinic, and perhaps she now feared the area. Everyone acknowledged this was sadly common in Skid Row, but no one knew what was going on. The conversation quickly moved to the practicalities of monitoring her for signs of a crisis.

Laura, the team leader, assigned Carlos, the housing specialist, to check up on Delilah and see whether she'd come to the day's activity—a Panda Express Chinese food party. Carlos didn't drive, so that day I would take him on his rounds in the county car, my small contribution.

As we saw earlier at the Spring Street outreach, Carlos was a master at connecting with vulnerable people. Clients at the clinic loved him, and some praised him as "the people's case manager." He was, in that sense, the perfect person to check on Delilah. Still, his own political analysis had already led him to question what he could do. He'd rail against the system, saying things like "Austerity kills, man!" Why, he asked, was Skid Row disproportionately Black? Why was he, someone who hadn't finished college and had no clinical training, working with "the sickest of the sick"?

We climbed the front walkway of a reconstructed apartment building with freshly painted doors that opened onto an inner courtyard surrounded by pleasant stucco walls. Once dubbed a "Hotel from Hell," the units had been repurposed as permanent supportive housing, with special allocations for formerly homeless DMH clients. As we walked through, we saw little trace of the building's former open-air drug market and reputation for violence.

Then Carlos and I were waved over by the building manager. Along with two women, he was making pancakes in a shared cooking area. He told us that Delilah had been active in the building community, even running Bible study, until recent weeks. The building's job preparation and counseling activities were all voluntary, so her absence from these was unremarkable. Still, like the DMH team, he was at a loss when it came to understanding what—if anything—had happened to her.

With that, we headed to Delilah's room. When we knocked, it took a few moments, but she soon emerged. She looked different from when I'd last seen her at the clinic, shrunken somehow. Her straightened hair was matted against her head, and her shoulders slumped forward. I said hello and she nodded at me, but she kept her eyes toward the ground. Her small, round glasses slid down her nose. Carlos told her about the Panda Express party with Chinese food and games if she wanted to come to the clinic. She didn't say anything but followed us as we left, and I drove us all back to the DMH.

Later, when she was better, she'd tell me her story. Delilah was from a poor neighborhood and had lived in Los Angeles her whole life. After finishing high school, she'd worked various retail jobs and supported herself and her kids. When she was psychiatrically hospitalized while pregnant with her third, she was shocked to be diagnosed with schizophrenia. The diagnosis was later changed to major depression with psychosis, but whatever it was, Delilah couldn't hold a job. She bounced between relatives, eventually ending up on the streets and losing custody of her kids to her ex-partner.

The children's father allowed her visits, sometimes meeting her at church on Sundays. Ever vigilant and streetwise, Delilah proudly noted she'd been robbed only once. She took up residence in front of a grocery store, where she became a fixture. Although other homeless outreach teams had come through and chatted with her, Delilah explained that it was the DMH team that developed a real relationship with her.

"Laura and them came and visited me when I was at King and Crenshaw in front of Albertson's [supermarket] and sat and talk with me and ask me what *I* wanted to do," she said firmly. "They wanted my opinion on what I wanted them to do for me, and I gave them the opinion of what I wanted." What she wanted was housing. After her stint in a motel and then a Board and Care home, the team found out that the former "Hotel from Hell" was developing units for DMH clients, which came at just the right time. Carlos helped Delilah apply, processing the paperwork and taking her to appointments. Soon she had her own apartment.

The DMH case management team's vision for Delilah helps illustrate social prognosis in this context. Workers aimed for her to live on her own, and she managed well enough. After routine visits like the one I went on, however, they eventually hospitalized her. She was, in her retrospective words, "not eating, not cleaning up, not doing what I was supposed to do." After the hospitalization, she resumed living in her unit. The team members visited her once or twice a month, and with their encouragement, she began to come to the clinic for Friday social outings.

I caught up with her during one of those Friday day trips, a picnic in a park outside Downtown. With her housing situation stable now, the team investigated new possibilities for her to move into a mixed-income building or eventually age into qualification for senior housing. A mental health worker described her as being ready for "that next step" away from a building filled with other mental health clients. This possible future trajectory implied a better but still small life. After assistance with housing, a hospitalization, and the recalibration of her medication, Delilah seemed to have stabilized. She was largely symptom free and, in psychiatric terms, recovering.

Missing from her treatment, however, was any focus on the deepening of human relationships, returning to a more active lifestyle, or making meaning of her journey to improved mental health. Delilah had never truly lost touch with her children, but after so much time apart, I wondered whether there would be a concerted effort to repair the connection with family therapy. There wasn't. Nor did the team attempt to get her back to work—possibly this was because of her age or the complications employment presents to people who rely on disability benefits for survival. And I saw little emphasis on exploring her psyche or addressing her traumas of street life and sexual assault.

What Delilah had to look forward to, from the team's perspective, was moving from specialty DMH housing to a non-mental-illness-designated building. So for all the "recovery" that had occurred, I could easily see the possibilities left on the table. For instance, when I asked about her routine, Delilah described a largely isolated life. "I sit at home and I watch TV or listen to some music," she said. "I listen to a lot of gospel. I stay in my room singing and . . . reading the Bible. Or getting rested. And then I get out. I go Downtown sometimes and walk around. Or I eat at Kentucky Fried Chicken. I relax. And there's not too much where to go, 'cause everybody in my family works . . . I don't get to see no one during the weeks, months, years. It's like on holidays or the weekends, stuff like that." This point that "there's not too much where to go" spoke to her relative isolation but also what parts of the city were available to her.

Living adjacent to the thriving parts of Downtown that cater to the well-off, Delilah was within walking distance of many cultural and consumptive opportunities. For her, however, the usable parts consisted of her building and apartment, those fast-food restaurants she could afford, and the DMH clinic. Her social world included family that she rarely saw, clients at the clinic outings, and the DMH staff. These workers offered kindness, safety checks, and entertainment but little in the way of how to process her trauma, what it meant to now be housed and a mental patient, or what she might make herself into next.

When Delilah relates her life story of hardship—surviving disability, losing her kids, experiencing homelessness—we can sense the enormity of her resilience. The treatment team, too, has done something incredible in transitioning her to psychiatric stability and permanent housing. Perhaps Delilah could live a fuller life and recover beyond symptom abatement, but other possibilities and relevant treatments are simply outside the frame of reference for many public safety net clients. The DMH team is constrained by both the limited care resources at its disposal and the limited vision of Delilah's future—that is, by the social prognosis. It stands in clear contrast to the expectations for clients at the Actualization Clinic.

RECLAIMING GWEN SENNETT'S VOICE

Gwen Sennett is a white woman in her early fifties, with blonde bangs and a youthful bounce. She worked as a journalist before becoming a full-time wife and mother. Her husband was in "the industry," as Hollywood types say, and they lived in an exclusive area near the beach. Gwen described herself as a "formerly" busy, social, and energetic woman. She'd first encountered the Actualization Clinic when her teenage son struggled with bipolar disorder, and she'd hired their case managers to help him in the early years.

Thus, when she was in crisis, she already knew of and trusted the Actualization team. Although she'd long been in therapy and medicated for anxiety, it wasn't until later life that she had experienced significant distress, withdrawal, and ideation of both self-harm and harm to others. Now she was being treated for major depression with psychosis.

Unlike those people who struggle to access mental health treatment, Gwen had been through an extensive round of elite facilities. "I've had a *lot* of treatment, and I'm still battling stuff," she told me. This care ranged from multiple hospitalizations at private facilities, a month at a psychodynamic residential program, and now outpatient care with the Actualization team. After her insurance stopped covering visits, she and her husband simply paid for expenses out of pocket.

In a therapy group at Actualization's Intensive Outpatient Program, Gwen related what she had learned through her time at Resolve, the psychoanalytic residential treatment center. "I had a lot of trauma these last few years; that's what we established at Resolve." This trauma included her father's death and becoming an empty nester with her kids heading off to college. Now she was reflecting on the loss of her career. She noted how she'd spent much of her life as a mom.

"Three kids," sighed the therapist. "That's a big job."

Gwen agreed. "I did so much for them, now they're all busy. You give up a lot of yourself for other people. I kinda got lost in all of that—lost myself."

But this moment had potential in it as well, the therapist suggested. "It's a difficult time but also a very exciting time." Indeed, Gwen was starting to consider what she might do now that her kids were grown. "No workplace for twenty-four years. It's hard," she acknowledged. As she expanded in a later interview, "I want to put myself back together. I'm glad I've found some volunteer opportunities, because that's giving me something to do. Because I think, for me, I took care of family for so many years, and now I'm in transition and my friends are in transition too. It's a big life change to have your kids grow up and leave the nest, and then I gave to them for so long and I'm still giving to them."

Gwen's calm narrative masked what clinicians said was a crisis. According to her case manager Norah, Gwen was so psychotic and erratic on their first day together that Actualization told her husband to immediately drive her back to the hospital. After various medications and bouts of electroconvulsive therapy, Gwen was no longer experiencing thoughts of self-harm or aggression. She was, however, struggling with basic cognition and memory, which could be attributed to either the depression or the treatment. Norah told me frankly that she thought it was bizarre that Gwen had been undergoing psychoanalytic treatment, since she believed that the woman's thoughts remained too scattered for in-depth therapy.[3]

At a subsequent treatment meeting, the Actualization clinicians debated the next steps for Gwen's development. Building on the psychodynamic work of Resolve, the case management team saw Gwen's current predicament as entangled with her past, including her career loss, her father's death, and her identity crisis once her kids left for college. Helping Gwen recover her "voice" became a key goal: the team wanted her to become an active and productive person again. More specifically, they wanted her to take a more assertive role in her family.

"She was one of those parents who did everything," said Deirdre, the supervisor. "Her daughter wants her to wake her up and make breakfast. She [Gwen] doesn't want to go back to being a mother-maid. It's a family issue." Nate, the Intensive Outpatient Program director, suggested that the family required intervention as well. Norah said that the family needed psychoeducation to better understand the nature of Gwen's illness. In turn, she needed to learn to stand up to her family.

"I tell her she has to say no to me at least once a session."

Nate agreed. "That was a goal in IOP: Say no to her family once a week." To the clinic team, her beginning to "say no" could indicate empowerment to rediscover herself outside her role as a mother. Norah explained that the family still got mad at Gwen when she was symptomatic rather than understanding what was happening to her. But she couldn't stick up for herself. "We had her write a letter to her daughter and her husband. Two weeks ago. But she can't send it. [She said,] 'I'm too scared to bring any of this back up.'"

The team continued to debate whether the problem lay with Gwen or with her broader family system. One therapist who was pursuing her PhD in depth psychology brought these strands together with a psychodynamic interpretation.

"I had a similar patient who had become psychotic after being a super mom and member of the community. Not consciously, but the psychotic issue was an exit strategy from that life. If it's 'you become this person you used to be or you're disowned,' then she can't progress. She has a sense of what to do, but if the risk is too great, then she's stuck."

The team members pondered whether this was Gwen's predicament. "She has no voice," Joseph, the family psychologist, said finally.

"She has voice here," Deirdre responded. She felt that Gwen was doing well in session but couldn't transport it to the real world. Norah said that it again came down to Gwen's husband and children's understanding of her illness and the slow pace of her growth. "She could have voice if the family expectations were different."

With the Actualization team's help, Gwen would try to establish a new routine and dynamic with her family. In addition, she slowly reduced treatment days, and the team helped her find a series of volunteer activities. Following its recommended protocol, Gwen was poised to move from three days of IOP groups each week down to only two, provided she filled that extra time with volunteering, work, or other productive activity.

•   •   •

Why does the county's most intensive outpatient treatment program mean housing assistance and check-ins for Delilah, rather than trauma therapy for the devastation of sexual assault, family systems therapy and reunification for the loss of her children, or resumption of work? Why, on the other hand, does Gwen receive treatment focused on understanding her internal world, remaking healthy family dynamics, and finding her appropriate activity to empower her? Where, in other words, do these radically different care regimes, definitions of treatment, and possible futures come from?

From a medical perspective, the disease of major depression with psychotic features should look similar and be treated similarly across contexts. The diagnosis describes a person with a combination of severely depressed mood and occasional psychosis, often manifesting in a belief that something terrible is about to happen. The baseline medical intervention is a combined use of antidepressants and antipsychotics, with electroconvulsive treatment increasingly recommended during acute periods.[4] To some degree, both women were biomedically stabilized. But the overall treatment protocols and ways that clinicians discussed their mental illness were radically different.

It's hardly surprising, given the enormity of American social inequality along racial and class lines, that there is inequality in care too. Excellent research has shown how physical health treatment for the poor and the rich diverges in terms of *quality* of or *access* to similar types of care (for instance, with diabetes or geriatric care).[5] But comparing the treatment of Gwen's and Delilah's psychiatric illnesses feels more like comparing apples and oranges. If treatment were simply a medical question of symptom abatement, the solution might be shared. Yet treatment necessarily diverges because it is tied to unequal material resources and visions of possibility—not merely the individual's brain or psyche.

Delilah Jackson and Gwen Sennett inhabit different social worlds. They are separated by a chasm of race and class. And their respective treatment plans illuminate vast disparities in our cultural visions of serious mental illness across the socioeconomic spectrum. Delilah is the marginal person who has fallen through the cracks. She made her way in our urban landscape, stripped of her social roles and left to survive on her own. Gwen is the privileged wife and mother whose performance of socially valued roles might have contributed to her breakdown. Like Charlotte Perkins Gilman's 1892 "The Yellow Wallpaper," where the restrictions of upper-class motherhood and married life drive a woman insane, the Actualization Clinic interpreted Gwen as having lost her "voice" because of family demands.

This differential understanding (and valuing) of human life is shaped by social forces larger than any individual, family, or clinician, and it shapes what constitutes a reasonable treatment practice.

PRACTICAL PROBLEMS AND POSSIBLE FUTURES

In a 2018 conversation, the novelist Esme Wang and the law professor Elyn Saks discussed the need for clinicians to "carry hopes and dreams" when patients cannot.[6] Both women had managed psychosis and ascended to the top of their respective fields. Both were aided, at least in part, by family, money, and access to private care. Saks, for instance, had engaged in years of psychoanalytic talk therapy. Critiquing pessimistic social service providers and drawing on their own lives as examples, these women spoke to the real possibilities of recovery. Yet what kinds of "hopes and dreams" can most people aspire to? These vary tremendously relative to whether they call Skid Row or a wealthy beach town home.

My comparative ethnographic approach here takes a different tack from much research on social inequality and mental illness. There has been a long debate in sociology and psychiatric epidemiology over what is known as social causation versus social drift. Each side seeks to explain a well-established but not fully understood fact: marginalized people are more likely to experience serious mental illness. According to one perspective, the stressors of poverty can cause the onset of illness and worsen it (social causation), while the other says that people who become mentally ill are more likely to lose their jobs and become poor (social drift). The best contemporary evidence suggests that these are not competing explanations at all but interacting ones that compound and keep people trapped in poverty and ill health.[7]

Building on this perspective, I will further show that inequality doesn't just impact the severity of illness—it shapes the very meaning of treatment provision and recovery. To do this, I first examine the everyday practical problems that the clinics must deal with. Whatever kinds of treatment goals they have, clinicians must engage with the demands of the everyday, and thus "treatment" *is* whatever they *do*—whether it's completing a housing voucher or offering psychotherapy. Second, I look at how the clinicians, families, and patients imagine possible futures, not only in terms of symptoms, but in terms of what kind of person the client can be. These practical problems and possible futures are what make up a *social prognosis.*

All this helps us approach debates about the relationship between social class and mental illness with a fresh perspective. Rather than ask, Is this person poor because they got sick, or sick because of poverty? and Will this treatment change the course of illness? my framework investigates something else. I show how social inequality can shape how symptoms are interpreted, what problems become visible, what form stigma takes, and what hope means.

In the context of urban poverty governance and the public safety net ecology, there is a general possibility of *a life off the "institutional circuit."* The DMH case management team members share an imagined future of a person who can perhaps avoid rearrest, eviction, and hospitalization. In the context of family systems governance in the elite private ecology, however, there is a social prognosis of *a viable identity*. These clinicians imagine a human with robust possibilities. If mental illness stigma is defined by what Erving Goffman called "spoiled identity," this form of psychiatric rehabilitation promises to help build someone a life beyond illness.

.   .   .

In the following chapters, we will encounter many puzzles related to these social prognoses. You will come to understand why a DMH nurse thinks he can best perform his job by *not* listening to people; why staff can describe a client who considers his life totally stagnant as "what hope looks like"; and why an excellent public mental health worker is defined not by therapeutic abilities but by knowledge of bureaucratic systems. In the elite private milieu, in contrast, we will see why people think the rich can, in some ways, suffer more than the poor; why clinicians spend so much time arguing with parents over whether a patient is ready to return to healthy activities like school and work; and why therapists do things like build a website to house a client's community college term papers, even though no one reads them.

CHAPTER 5

A LIFE OFF THE "INSTITUTIONAL CIRCUIT"

In the previous chapter, we met Delilah. She had experienced home-lessness, brief hospitalization, and precarity before the Los Angeles County Department of Mental Health (DMH) helped her stabilize in independent housing. Los Angeles's Skid Row presents an extreme case, of course, but the public mental patient's cycling in and out of a variety of inadequate care and control institutions is an unfortunately common experience across the United States.

Rather than the long-term hospitalization of the asylum era or the robust community services promised by the deinstitutionalization movement, low-income psychiatric patients of today often encounter brief ER stays, shelter stays, jail time, and/or abandonment. Social scientists have dubbed this hellish nonsystem the "institutional circuit."[1] The DMH case management team's goal for most of its clients—in effect, the only one that seems possible—is to create *a life off the institutional circuit*. This is already such a daunting aim, and there are so many people in need, that other possibilities recede into the background. As the team leader Laura once noted, "We're not so good at the rehabilitative side. It's no one's fault. It's just once we've covered the basics with one person, we have to move on to the next person to get them housed."

But where does this *social prognosis* come from? For DMH clinicians, practical tasks linked to homelessness, criminal justice involvement, and survival crowd out the ability to envision robust futures. A patient's achieving day-to-day stability is hard enough. Note, for instance, how omnipresent these concerns are in the metrics the DMH uses to measure its success: one county-level outcome report boasts a "67 percent decrease in homelessness, a 35 percent decrease in jail days, and a 15 percent decrease in hospital days" in its opening description of the agency's intensive adult programs.[2] All reasonable priorities, such demands mean that the DMH programs are in the business of saving and sustaining lives rather than rebuilding them.

The practical tasks and limited resources, too, have a history. To understand how the DMH and other mental health-care providers came to this more limited vision of a patient's possible future, we must return to the early years after deinstitutionalization and how successive waves of budget cuts circumscribed the development of public safety net services.

COMMUNITY CARE AND THE GREAT TAX REVOLT

With hindsight, the 1960s vision of community care seems naïvely optimistic. Proponents promised that people could have robust lives and develop their potential—things they arguably couldn't achieve if they were locked away in asylums. In theory, community care would include high-quality, early psychiatric interventions with a variety of treatment modalities as well as all the services people would need to live successfully in their homes, families, and communities. Social scientists of the 1970s and 1980s held out hope that the federal government would help build robust mental health treatment programs offering greater autonomy and real care. Although President Jimmy Carter aimed to deliver sustained federal funding with the Mental Health Systems Act of 1980, it was repealed within a year under the Reagan administration.[3] In the end, far fewer community centers were built than were needed. Many therapists preferred to work with milder cases like sad teenagers than ex-asylum patients with severe needs. And even the gold-standard models of care faltered almost immediately under the weight of social need.

The anthropologist Sue Estroff's classic 1981 study of a pioneering case management team detailed the struggles of ex-patients to live independently and avoid returning to the hospital.[4] Developed during the haphazard early days of deinstitutionalization, the Assertive Community Treatment model aimed to create a "hospital without walls" that could deliver wraparound care throughout the community. The case management teams had their successes, but the researcher nonetheless saw the rise of a new kind of illness "career" funded by Supplemental Security Income and disability benefits. Estroff worried that for the patient, getting *better* could mean the loss of subsidies and the health insurance needed for survival. What if the system was incentivizing the adoption of a perpetually disabled role rather than an independent, flourishing future?

The coming crises of homelessness and mass incarceration (which affected the precarious poor more generally) meant that many patients could not expect even this meager life. By the 1990s, the anthropologist Kim Hopper and colleagues would write of patients rotating through jail stints, emergency psychiatric hospitalization, and time in homeless shelters—of people trapped in the institutional circuit.[5] Rarely receiving real care, they would be triaged rather than treated, sent to the streets rather than housed, or arrested for minor offenses. They might be "free," but was this better than the asylum model?

California again presents a case study of the problems at hand. Recall the DMH leader Harry Brickman's complaint that Ronald Reagan emptied the state hospitals earlier than promised, overwhelming unprepared municipal systems with a flood of severely disabled patients. It got worse, and quickly.

Much as California served as a national model for deinstitutionalization, it was also a model for what would later be called the Great Tax Revolt. In 1978, a powerful movement against taxes swept the state and later the country. Californians voted to alter their tax structure with Proposition 13, slashing property taxes to 1 percent of assessed 1972 value, and then severely limiting the extent to which property taxes could be raised in the future. Ostensibly, the overhaul would help retirees at risk of displacement, but in practice the tax cuts broadly aided privileged landowners who had formerly constituted much of California's tax base.[6]

Shifting to budgets based on income taxes rather than property taxes also meant that state and municipal coffers would now boom and bust along with the economy. In other words, budgets were slashed, and what remained became highly unstable, making it difficult to plan things like mental health provision. The fallout was immediate and profound.

As the *Washington Post* reported, the then California governor Jerry Brown had promised that 1978 would be "the year of mental health" and that he would allocate $82.6 million for community care "as a humane alternative to the beleaguered state hospitals." But in the new fiscal context, he simply couldn't deliver, and "within 48 hours of the passage of Proposition 13, Brown, suddenly committed to strict budget austerity, removed virtually the entire $82.6 million promised appropriation from the state budget."[7]

This belt-tightening had profound ramifications at the local level. *Los Angeles Times* headlines, gathered by the sociologist Alex Barnard, paint an ugly picture:[8]

- 1981 "Budget Ax Hits Mental Health Basics"
- 1986 "Only Most Severe Cases to Receive Care: County Cuts Treatment"
- 1988 "Funding Cuts May End Programs to Aid Mentally Ill"
- 1991 "Board Votes to Shut 7 Mental Health Centers"
- 1992 "Service Cutbacks Squeeze 30,000 out of Clinics and into 'Revolving Door' Facilities"

Now only the "most severe cases" could warrant attention. People had to be especially visible "problems" to gain access to services. Practically speaking, preventive clinical care was over, and the best hope for many indigent psychiatric patients became the "revolving door" of emergency stabilization.

What was happening in these safety net settings? Rather than a place of confinement and refuge for months or years, hospitals focused on brief emergency holds. After all, they were not planning to re-create the asylum era (few had the will or the means to do so). The anthropologist Lorna Rhodes's work on emergency hospital settings has shown how a lack of resources pushed staff to simply "empty beds," rapidly discharging patients with little in the way of concrete care, because the facility needed to make way for yet more people in crisis.[9] The status quo was brief, highly inconsistent treatment provided only in acute phases, rinse, and repeat.

For people trapped in the urban American institutional circuit, the idea of a future had essentially disappeared. In a study of a homeless shelter geared toward mental illness, the anthropologist Robert Desjarlais quotes one woman who described days spent "struggling along." This kind of surviving in the moment broke with how most people experience life. The makings of a future with self-development and a narrative plotline were simply unavailable. Desjarlais came to see that a good day in the shelter—all that could be hoped for—was one where "nothing much happens, where a few bucks are earned, where the voices are not too bad, where pressure is relieved through pacing, and where there are enough cigarettes to last the day."[10] This was a vision of surviving mental illness and poverty as a life unto itself; mental health was too distant a concept to even register.

THE MEANING OF RECOVERY

At the same time that the material base of treatment and social support was being stripped away, an ideal of client independence and choice was taking root. The recovery movement of the early 2000s, built by radical ex-patient activists, brought renewed commitment to the possibility of full recovery from mental illness.[11] Negative prognoses, they argued, could become self-fulfilling prophecies, keeping people from realizing their potential. Clinicians, families, and patients had to believe in the possibility of a robust future. In the psychologist Larry Davidson and colleagues' terms, recovery "identifies and builds upon each individual's assets, strengths, and areas of health and competence to support the person in managing his or her condition while regaining a meaningful, constructive, sense of membership in the broader community."[12] Activists argued that hope was a key to ending stigma and helping people move forward.

Some scholars, however, debated what this recovery meant in a context of budget austerity. As the psychiatrist and historian Joel Braslow has argued, celebrating patient *in*dependence rather than *inter*dependence echoed the earlier wave of deinstitutionalization. He worried that this rhetoric of autonomy might be inappropriately used to demonize "dependency" and justify further cuts to services.[13] In 2015, the anthropologist Neely Myers found ideals of empowerment elusive amid material deprivation, writing that client goals of employment or connecting with people outside the service center rarely came to fruition.[14] Recent journalistic exposés of programs to move institutional patients into independent apartments have found further evidence of gross neglect continuing into the present day.[15]

Updates to Estroff's work on community treatment teams have shown that helping clients survive poverty has become the predominant concern. The sociologist Kerry Dobransky, for example, writes that community mental health workers spend much of their time delivering basic social services but recode these as *medical* services, so that their agencies can bill Medicaid.[16] The anthropologist Paul Brodwin, shadowing a contemporary Assertive Community Treatment team in Wisconsin, notes that the early optimism of community care is nowhere to be found. "Controlling people's symptoms and avoiding evictions dominate the agenda of ordinary clinicians," he points out. "The imperatives are so pressing that clinicians rarely imagine alternative goals of treatment. Given what the system expects of [the local team], how could case managers ever refigure their task as fulfilling human needs . . . [beyond shelter and stability]?"[17] Thus, in some publicly funded services, the lofty goal of addressing human development rather than day-to-day survival has become nearly unthinkable.

In 2004, California initiated one of the country's most robust attempts at systems change with the Mental Health Services Act. The plan was to serve not just the poor but also the middle class with "recovery-oriented" services. Using a 1 percent tax on individual income over $1 million, the state would develop a steady stream of mental health funding targeted at underserved populations. Voters were swayed with a campaign highlighting the large population of unhoused Californians with mental illness—a visible problem many found disturbing—and family advocates' stories of grossly inadequate services.[18]

The flagship program of the Mental Health Services Act was Full Service Partnership (FSP), a variation on the Assertive Community Treatment team model extended throughout the state. FSP teams would prioritize serving patients with histories of homelessness, incarceration, and hospitalization. Under the slogan Whatever It Takes, these programs would have the flexibility to perform case management tasks that did not necessarily fit into conventional ideas of psychiatric care. By the 2010s, the case management teams were up and running across the state—some directly operated by counties, some by contracted nonprofits. That's the setting into which I stepped as I undertook my ethnographic fieldwork, and that was the backdrop to my question: What can the public provision of "recovery-oriented" services really amount to?

THE BANALITY OF CRISIS: MORNING MEETING AT THE DMH

From my field notes:

....

April 2013. 8:30 a.m.
Workers discuss how to schedule and stagger home visits, since there aren't enough county cars to go around. Laura, the team leader, then turns to the important cases.

—A man is moving into a new apartment, but the ride situation is difficult, since the county cars are already spoken for. How will they get him his things? The team decides that they will bring the man's furniture tomorrow.
—An older white man who uses a wheelchair is being evicted. Knowing that this client will likely put up a fight and the landlord will call law

enforcement, social worker Beth begins to sing the Bob Marley song "I Shot the Sheriff," and other team members laugh as she dances in her chair. They then brainstorm places to put him temporarily. Since the sheriffs have a reputation for kicking people out rapidly and forcing them to leave property behind, the team decides to focus on keeping the wheelchair and the walker.

—A young woman in the Snow Lodge Board and Care says she is pregnant again. This has reportedly been a persistent delusion, but someone says it could be true now if she's been trying to get pregnant by sleeping with other residents. Laura says that they should offer to take her to prenatal care, so if she's pregnant, they haven't simply ignored it.

—An African American man who had prostate cancer and went through chemo now has a lump in his breast after a mammogram. There's no diagnosis yet, but he's afraid.

—A Latino man has moved into a new facility where his roommate keeps disrobing, making him very uncomfortable.

—A middle-aged African American man has been going to court and telling officials very different things, including that he wants to go back to jail. Laura says she is okay with this if it is what he really wants.

—A client has now had three separate diagnoses of Axis 2 personality disorders, specifically antisocial personality disorder. Someone jokes that the two recently graduated social workers will ace their licensure exams, because they know so much about difficult, antisocial clients in this clinic.

—Joanne, a thirty-something white recent outreach, will be kicked out of her hotel room. She has neither a full name nor a Social Security number, so the team can't place her somewhere permanent. She has a vaguely European accent. The hotel manager says Joanne has been panhandling and bumming cigarettes, and seems high functioning. As it stands, the DMH is drawing on $1,300 of special county funds a month for the hotel. The nurse Vic says that on her last day at the motel, he can put her on a 5150 emergency hold, because she will either make a scene or wander off, indicating she can't care for herself. Laura says that Joanne is reacting reasonably, though, since they gave her a nice, safe place, but now the team was going to take it away. They offered

a shelter bed near the clinic, but Joanne refused, because she'd been
sexually assaulted Downtown.

—Paperwork, again. Laura says that it is unacceptable that progress notes
do not get done on time and that the note and service are two sides of
the same coin. They can't bill and keep the program funded without it,
so helping a client is not an excuse for failing to get paperwork done.

....

At this case conference meeting, we see the practical problems the
DMH case management team is being asked to manage at the intersection of mental illness and urban poverty. Note how things that might
be addressed in psychological terms are primarily relevant for their
significance to issues like housing. For instance, the violation of sexual
assault is meaningful, not because it harms the self and will need to be
processed with a therapist, but because it prevents Joanne from coming near the clinic (as was the case for Delilah in the previous chapter.)

On this day, alongside the routines of med drops, there were people
moving into new apartments and others getting evicted from apartments; a phantom pregnancy that required a liability cover-your-ass
investigation on the off-chance it's real; cancer and fear of death;
naked roommates; criminal justice entanglements; and a nameless
woman who was about to become homeless again. In some sense, no
two days were the same. But that's because every day was chaos. Like
Laura, who suggested it's hard to work on the "rehabilitative side"
because of problem solving in the present, the DMH team psychologist simply said, "It's just always putting out fires."

There are patterns within the chaos, though. Tasks and clients
cohere into work routines, and case managers develop specific expertise for getting people off the street, accessing housing, dealing with
probation, and achieving basic forms of stability. Clients, in turn, see
their own lives through the realities of their social opportunities. We'll
consider homelessness, criminal justice diversion, and everyday life
revolving around the mental health world.

Sometimes clients had fallen so far through the cracks that enormous effort was spent simply getting them into the system. Consider

the effort (and specific kinds of work) involved in the task of housing "Joanne" when no one knows her legal name. We'll follow Vic the nurse as he goes to see her alongside other recently outreached people temporarily placed in a budget motel. Of the belief that people with "legitimate schizophrenia" won't get much better, Vic focuses on safety and basic stability for the clients—and on getting himself through the shift.

"NO ONE RECOVERS"

Vic's life revolved around food. He'd break up the day's drudgery by selecting a special stop for lunch and then take me on tours of his Los Angeles highlights. "That's where Bruce Springsteen went for pizza," he'd say, or he'd tell me which Zankou's Chicken had the best garlic sauce. He needed to work a few more years for the county so that he could collect a pension.

Having worked jails, hospitals, and emergency services before coming to community care, Vic was used to seeing people at their worst. He rejected the idea that community mental health workers should listen to people with serious mental illness, focusing instead on administering medication, keeping people indoors, and hospitalizing them when needed. For Vic, psychotic clients' thoughts or desires were usually meaningless. Still, he interpreted their behavior with his own variant of psychodynamics—not for a psychological intervention but for the practical work of getting them to stay in place.

At the clinic, Vic received the following assignments: first, check on Valerie, a woman who had left the budget motel to return to the flagpole, her longtime sleeping place in a public park. Second, deliver meds to Alan, a man who'd been outreached beside a river. Third, see whether the mysterious woman, Joanne, who had once lived under a bridge, required hospitalization, as she was "increasingly disorganized." The DMH team couldn't find records of her, and she variously described herself as being from Canada and Europe, a corporate communications expert, and connected to the Vatican. Laura told Vic to take me around that day, and he motioned for me to follow him into the medication room.

Chuckling, Vic stitched the three clients together into a comical story. "Oh, maybe Valerie and Alan were on their way to the Vatican when they stopped at the hospital." As he packed medications into a pillbox, I asked whether he thought Alan would understand which ones to take and when. Shrugging his shoulders, he sighed, "No, the thing with these people is I don't even know if he's gonna take all three of these at once, instead of spreading them out." We then drove out to look for Valerie at the flagpole.

Valerie's former home was an island park containing a monument to Vietnam vets in the middle of a busy intersection. A round lady with big eyes, white hair, and rouged cheeks, she sat on a bench with a young man passed out next to her. "So you want to stay out here on the bench?" Vic asked. Valerie replied she was thankful for his help, but happy where she was. Vic tilted his head. "You don't want our services anymore?" She said she'd think about going back to the motel. We said goodbye and told her the team would check on her again.

Back in the car, Vic began to tell me how he saw the situation, invoking a psychoanalytic interpretation centered on unconscious fear. "Yeah, she looked great, smelled great, was on medication, everything going good. You can go forward or backward or stay the same. She's going backwards." He paused thoughtfully. "And I can relate. People get scared when things are going good. It's all unconscious."

Given his focus on medication as the primary treatment, I was surprised to find that Vic was well versed in psychoanalytic, specifically Freudian, explanations of human behavior. I mentioned that I'd read some interpretive, humanistic approaches to psychosis that saw meaning in even seemingly delusional speech. Vic agreed that unconscious forces were at play but said he didn't think such approaches could be used therapeutically with these clients.

We arrived at the Super 8 Motel and went to Alan's room. His door was open, and he was smoking. Vic noted that Alan had lost some weight after coming out of the hospital, and Alan happily agreed. Vic showed him the pillbox, taking out one day's worth of pills and explaining when to take which ones. "This one is slightly smaller than

this thin one and is more like a tab." The routine was quite complicated, and I thought to myself that I wouldn't have remembered it.
Alan nodded his head, though, and smiled.

Soon Joanne strolled into the motel parking lot. She'd come from
the library, where she went to get a phone number for the president
of a company she claimed to work for. Vic asked what she could tell us
about herself, as the team remained unable to figure out her identity.
She said she had lived in Canada and various other places, including Switzerland. For now, though, she was going to keep her identity secret. She said something about Nortel Communications and
the Vatican and that she needed to protect herself and her identity
because she was an important person in danger.

Vic interrupted, glancing at me as he said, "Oh, so you're a very
important person?" Joanne blushed and averted her eyes. "Yes." Vic
asked whether she needed anything, and she replied that she doesn't
like being indebted to anyone. He suggested that if she continued
panhandling, it was better that she not sit on the busy street, since
he didn't want her to get hit by a car. She agreed and said she would
see us later. He determined that she was far from "holdable" for a
hospitalization.

Back in the car, Vic told me he had been making a point by interrupting her, because "if you just let these people talk, they'll go on
forever." After all, he said, they were delusional, and there were important tasks he needed to accomplish in limited time. Still, he wanted to
return to the idea that psychotic talk might contain important meaning. "You said something pretty profound before, but I don't know
if you know how it was." There is truth in what such people say, he
agreed, but nothing for therapists to make any use of. Even medication would only help so much.

I asked Vic whether he thought people could recover. "No, not if
you're a legitimate schizophrenic. No, no one recovers. Their mind is
gone. Their soul is gone. Really, I mean, brain tumor, cancer. None of
these is as horrifying as being that gone psychologically."

So that was why Vic saw no reason to try and interpret what
patients were saying.

This illustrates a classic point from the sociological literature on labeling and stigma. Once a person is deemed crazy, everything he or she says is suspect.[19] Furthermore, even though Vic cares about the clients' well-being, he has come to view them as essentially nonpersons. He *did* want to help people—he just believed that the best way to do this was to rebuild the state hospitals and lock them away, as he explained in this book's preface.

Other DMH staff members criticized his pessimism. One told me that Vic was the kind of burned-out nurse who gave county workers a bad name. Yet for the tasks at hand, it made little difference—what "legitimate" schizophrenics required was a check-in, a med drop, an evaluation for the hospital. Far from knowing a person's past to interpret the symbolism of current symptoms, the program might not even know someone's name. Vic couldn't be sure that people would take their medication regularly or understand their regimen. The available intervention was to start the housing process, and that was exactly what the DMH case managers did.

Valerie would soon be placed through a specialized "Good Samaritan" Housing Program, which connected clients to fully furnished apartments. She still talked about going back to the flagpole but later learned to stay in her unit. Alan moved temporarily to a Board and Care home, where staff monitored his oral medication. The team then got in touch with Alan's children, who lived in Northern California, and sent him there when they agreed to assume responsibility for his care.

Joanne presented a more serious difficulty, because there was simply no information on her. Laura struggled with ways to figure out who Joanne was, in the official sense. There was no way to force her to reveal her secret identity, presuming she even knew. Hospitalization was difficult, as she didn't present as "dangerous" or "gravely disabled." The team considered fingerprinting her at the police station, but a police representative said they would have to arrest her if there turned out to be any outstanding warrants when they ran her fingerprints. Eventually I went with a team member to an embassy to try and discover whether Joanne was who she claimed to be, but officials there couldn't help either.

"They need to have a loophole in the HIPAA [patient privacy] law for clients like ours," said a case manager. "You don't know who these clients belong to, or what they've done." The health-care regulations prevented the DMH from accessing Joanne's official identity, which in turn might prevent it from accessing benefits or housing subsidies for her.

Beyond the practical complications, the mental health worker's language about clients is deeply revealing. Rather than conceive of them as people having psychologically deep pasts and futures, such a framing of whom they "belong to" indicates a concern with their keepers—perhaps some absent family or custodial institution. "What they've done," on the other hand, usually means the issue of criminal records and whether clients might be dangerous to staff.

Understanding people in these terms easily aligns with a dismal view of future potentialities. Note the circular logic in Vic's claim that certain people could never recover. If a person diagnosed as having schizophrenia did in fact make substantial psychiatric and social gains, it would necessarily mean that he or she was never a "legitimate schizophrenic" in the first place. But in fact, many people did quite well and appeared positioned for a fuller recovery than simple symptom reduction.

Next, we move to a street-outreach-to-stabilization trajectory that the case management team declared a success. In it, I find that Vic is wrong about some people diagnosed with schizophrenia, at least in terms of recovering from *psychiatric symptoms*. Yet I also see how, in terms of *social recovery*, he may well be right.

"WHAT HOPE LOOKS LIKE"

Jeremiah was a Jamaican man in his early thirties who was psychotic and on the street after a long journey to the dumping ground of Downtown Los Angeles. As he eventually became stable, housed, and interested in returning to work, a DMH case manager said, "That's what hope looks like." Examining his trajectory will help us understand precisely what a good future means in a setting like this.

Unlike Delilah, whom the case management team simply planned to wait on until she could transfer to subsidized senior housing, Jeremiah was young enough that there could be possibilities for him to lead a robust life. Yet those possibilities shrink when we consider them up close. The team addressed Jeremiah's life situation as a series of practical problems to solve, shaping, in turn, what kind of possible futures might be had.

A SUCCESSFUL STREET OUTREACH STORY

I first met Jeremiah when the case management team responded to a call about a strange homeless man who might be part of its target population. Shadowing two workers, I went to a little park near a courthouse and watched as they engaged a skinny fellow with a sheet wrapped around his head. He had drawn messages in the dirt and now looked up at us, shielding his eyes from the sun. Sweat dripped from his body as he began gesticulating. I had difficulty following what he was saying, and as we walked away the workers said that they believed him appropriate for the treatment program. Later, Jeremiah recalled the initial outreach interactions: "[The worker said,] 'We may find you a place at the Russ Hotel to stay.' I remember those words. I was, like, 'Oh, that would be nice to find somewhere to live.' When he was saying that, I was, like, 'For real? Yeah? Is that for real or is that some gimmick?' I was thinking of that. But that sounded good to me, and I was, like, 'Yeah, it would be nice to get off the street.'" Jeremiah had been getting his food at a church and didn't like the big missions in Skid Row. He'd figured out how to survive, gathering resources while avoiding the areas that scared him. The treatment team moved him into the Russ Hotel and a month later hospitalized him.

The doctors prescribed Jeremiah the antipsychotic medication Risperdal, which he found made his thinking clearer. He began to think of what he had been experiencing as schizophrenia and decided to continue taking the prescription. While some people experience marked discomfort on Risperdal, Jeremiah reported only weight gain as a side effect. It was substantial, though, so once when he waved to me at the clinic, I didn't recognize his newly chubby face. He struggled to control his eating, but believed it was worth it. "I've been taking the medication, I started doing better, I didn't feel confused anymore, I didn't feel afraid, I didn't feel like anybody was threatening me."

The case management team offered to help him get his own apartment, but he decided to stay in a Board and Care home. I asked why, given that many people prefer to have their own place. He replied that fewer things could go wrong at the Board and Care, and he felt that pretty much anything was better than the street. He would wait until he felt ready to manage an apartment. In the meantime, he participated in activities at the clinic and hoped to find a job.

Learning about Jeremiah's past shows us all the other systems that failed him and how much work it takes to build him a life from scratch. For the DMH team, transforming Jeremiah from a psychotic street denizen to a stable indoor person was a substantial victory. I'd come to see his simultaneous gratitude to the team and despair at his lack of a future. From the perspective of urban poverty governance, however, he was an unqualified success—he was now living indoors and not acting bizarrely in public space.

A SERIES OF SYSTEM FAILURES

How had Jeremiah ended up psychotic and homeless in Downtown LA? Much of what the DMH team members did day to day would be very different if they weren't starting from square one. Thus, when we learn about Jeremiah's trajectory, we can think through a series of possible intervention points that would have kept him off the streets.

As he explained it, Jeremiah had left Jamaica and followed his wife, an American, to Northern California, where she worked as a nurse and he got a job as a school crossing guard. His psychosis seemed to have started at the end of his twenties, a bit later than typical onset. Although he has a fuzzy memory of the time, he presumes that his wife kicked him out of the house because of his "episodes." From there, he lived in a tent and moved through various locales, attempting to keep his job while homeless. Then he began acting in ways that, looking back, he couldn't account for.

For instance, he made friends while camping but soon turned on them. According to Jeremiah, a woman who identified herself as a Christian reached out when she saw him near a creek bed, and they'd begun speaking about God. One day, however, he told her he was going to punch her in the face. He's not sure why he said that—nor why he followed through—but he got arrested then, and again several more times for setting fires while camping. A jail doctor once asked him whether he was taking medications, but Jeremiah says he was never offered any mental health care or diagnosis. The jail simply processed him for minor offenses and released him. Then he began his tour of bus rides through various towns, short arrests, and, eventually, refuge in Downtown Los Angeles.

When I attempted to corroborate these stories, I found news reports describing the attack on the woman at the creek bed. One newspaper noted that law enforcement had to fight Jeremiah to get him into handcuffs and that the responding officers were at a loss to explain the violence. The next article, which came out three months later, described him as a "transient" arrested for making a series of fire pits in a hiking area where he had been camping. The fire department put out the blazes and the police again arrested Jeremiah on a previous assault warrant. This time he was taken to the hospital for dehydration and smoke inhalation but seemingly not psychiatric care. None of the media coverage indicated that authorities saw the incidents in terms of possible mental illness, only criminality.

But let's imagine the contact points at which Jeremiah might have been identified as a potential psychiatric patient. Since his family was overseas, his wife had less access to his social support network and may have found his behavior overwhelming. Perhaps with other material and social resources at her disposal, she might have gotten him care. His employers might have noted the psychosis and sought an alternative to simply firing him. The arresting officers "at a loss" to explain Jeremiah's behavior might have seen him as someone to be taken for a psychiatric evaluation. When he was hospitalized for smoke inhalation, a nurse or doctor, clued in to its source, might have noticed signs of psychosis.

Whether it was a failure of interpretation, insufficient resources, or simple indifference, none of those interventions happened. After his conflicts with his wife, after losing his job, Jeremiah had become homeless and was behaving in ways unfamiliar to even himself. Despite being identified as a problem by authorities, he'd apparently not been treated as a person with a psychiatric disability. Instead, he was processed through the criminal justice system, tossed into and out of jails and shelters, and eventually boarded a bus bound for Los Angeles.

When I went with the DMH homeless outreach team to see him on the street corner, Jeremiah had become a street person disconnected from family and work, behind on his immigration case, and with a criminal record. In effect, given how far he had fallen through the cracks, employees of California's most intensive public outpatient psychiatric treatment model had their hands full with the tasks needed to simply stabilize him. That meant medication and housing as well as straightening out his immigration status.

"IT SHOULD BE MORE TOO, RIGHT?"

The DMH team believed that Jeremiah was "what hope looks like." In his eyes, however, he was stuck. It's not that the DMH refused to believe in his ability to work or resume a productive life. Its program was simply not set up to facilitate these achievements, and the tools at hand had largely been exhausted. Jeremiah had attended DMH-facilitated groups, but these often related to topics like financial literacy or activities of daily living. There was little in the way of therapy. More concerning for Jeremiah, the DMH could not provide job training or a computer class. From this researcher's perspective, what was most striking was what the groups consisted of: not psychoeducation, psychosocial rehabilitation, job training, or psychotherapy but information for surviving as a poor mental patient. If Jeremiah exited treatment or was moved to a lower level of care—that is, if he succeeded in moving forward—he risked losing the DMH's housing support and basic services.

What were the case management team's tasks for helping Jeremiah progress, beyond its work of street outreach, hospitalization, and Board and Care placement? With the state Mental Health Services Act funds, Los Angeles County had been able to help pay for DMH services when he didn't qualify for certain benefits. For a client disconnected from family and with a murky immigration status, the team had moved mountains.

And Jeremiah was deeply grateful. Still, he hoped for something beyond housing and immigration assistance: "It should be more too, right?" He'd told me he wanted a future. In lieu of official work, he'd been doing odd jobs around the Board and Care home to have a little pocket money and stay busy. He felt he still had something to offer. He explained, "I think a big part of it is, like, when you've gotten the person on the meds and they're doing fine, you want to get them to the point where they're working, and it makes more sense instead of just not having anything to do or feeling that you can't do anything, you know? Because there's a lot you could do. Like me, I know there's a lot I can do, you know what I'm saying? I'm still young." He seemed hesitant to criticize the DMH program, given how much the team had helped him. Yet in contrast to the case manager's description of Jeremiah as "what hope looks like," Jeremiah worried that he'd never be able to fulfill his potential.

A LIFE DIVERTED

Criminal justice system involvement was a major determinant of clients' possible futures. Many DMH clients had committed minor offenses when they were in altered states or just trying to survive. Thus, another task for mental health-care providers was to facilitate a person's release from jail, sometimes as a diversion from potential longer-term incarceration. The case management team's work would then be to keep the person on track with probation, prevent reoffending, and carry them through the assigned period without violating terms of release. In this section, I introduce one such person; she didn't know whether she'd return to a productive career, but she held out hope for rebuilding the most meaningful part of her life: her relationship with her children.

Gillian was an African American woman in her late thirties who had been diagnosed alternately as having postpartum depression and bipolar disorder. While in a manic state, she had taken her children from her mother's house and driven off. Since she had previously lost custody, this was considered a kidnapping. Eventually arrested, she cut a deal to avoid prison time by taking a year with the DMH case management team and five years on probation.

COORDINATING THE NONSYSTEM

Gillian's case began with a series of false starts. I accompanied Kevin, the psychiatric technician, to the women's jail to transfer her to a Board and Care home. It was the DMH team's second attempt to get her out since her being set up for transfer to its care, and Kevin had been telling me about how much effort went into coordinating with different social service agencies and housing providers, what a hassle it was simply to get someone out and into a place to stay, when he received a call. We were nearly at the jail, and now Kevin was learning that the Board and Care home would not accept Gillian without the latest paperwork concerning her diagnosis, evaluation, and criminal record. Kevin called the jail psychiatric staff, but he was told that he wouldn't be able to access the records that day. He turned the car around.

Already, the DMH staff had spent hours on the phone and behind the wheel, with one bureaucratic hiccup after another. Kevin, who had worked in prison mental health for years, was furious. A person might have enemies inside the jail, he said, so an extra week before release could mean life or death. Nothing so dramatic happened to Gillian, but the delay was another frustration for the team. In all, it took three separate visits to get her out of the women's jail. What was the team's plan? Its task was to house her and keep her on track for a year, coordinating her probation.

Gillian was short and round, with light-brown skin and straightened hair that she pulled back. She wore a kind smile and a general air of fatigue. When I met up with her at the Board and Care home, she was groggy—a side effect of the antipsychotic medication Seroquel. Soon she was animated, though. She laughed easily in spite of, or perhaps because of, her situation. It was hard to reconcile this portrait with the one painted of her in the news reports. This was the unstable woman who had kidnapped her children and gone on the lam? One website's comments cruelly referred to Gillian and her children in racist terms that likened her to an animal. (Luckily, a friend told her to never Google-search her name.)

Sitting with me outside the facility, Gillian was eager to share her life story. She had pursued a master's degree and worked as a teacher's aide before her first mental health crisis, and she said she was happy to help me out on anything related to education and academic research. Her life was hardly characterized by street smarts and trouble with the law, so she had felt herself to be wholly unprepared for her time being homeless and incarcerated.

FROM FAMILY COURT TO CRIMINAL COURT

How had Gillian ended up here, seeking to avoid a prison sentence for taking her own kids? She had grown up with a social worker mother and a father who received workers' compensation after being injured on a job. Her sisters became a nurse and a social worker, respectively, and she aspired to be a teacher. From such a background, Gillian wasn't used to serious material hardship. In her recounting, her mental health struggles seemed to come at the intersection of two stressful events: a difficult pregnancy and an eviction.

NEIL: When did you first encounter the mental health system?
GILLIAN: About nine years ago. I had my first daughter, and I was pregnant with my second daughter. [In between] was my son. And then I got gestational diabetes at that time. And then it was a lot going on as far as my husband and I were concerned, but I was

teaching and I didn't have any money at that point to pay the bills, because my husband wasn't doing well with making sure that the money was being designated to everything that we were supposed to be doing. . . . We ended up getting evicted. I was very devastated by that, because I had never had a bounced check in my life. I had no problems with money.

After giving birth in this context of financial stress, Gillian became profoundly sad. While taking an antidepressant, however, she experienced episodes of mania in which she lost track of reality. When hospitalized, she also received the diagnosis of bipolar disorder. "I've read research that has said sometimes if you have postpartum depression, it can lead into bipolar disorder," she told me. "My therapist has told me that. I've seen the articles about it."

It's hard to know precisely, and there's considerable debate in the psychiatric community.[20] Had the person always been bipolar, with their mania triggered by an inappropriate administration of an antidepressant? Or was the mania fully medication induced? If the latter, should it be treated with mood stabilizers or antipsychotics, or should it be left alone, in hopes it will resolve naturally? There's no totally agreed-on protocol.

Patient activists have criticized "prescription cascades," where side effects become diagnosed as new symptoms of a different illness, leading to yet more medications and more side effects.[21] These activists argue that when doctors don't recognize that treatment itself may cause harm, or when they refuse to help patients come off psychiatric medications, it can become impossible to sort out what's happening. Whatever it was, Gillian was now dealing with episodes where she had no memory of what she had done.

She said that her husband had taken the kids while she was hospitalized, but he behaved recklessly and was arrested. The couple then lost custody, with their kids briefly in the foster care system before eventually landing with her mother. At the family court, the judge told Gillian and her husband that they had to be evaluated for mental disabilities, but her husband refused to do so and walked out of the courtroom. Her sister offered a place to stay, but then decided that Gillian was too unstable to have around children. Alongside the psychiatric evaluation, Gillian understood that housing was the key to regaining custody. "The judge told me that pretty much, in order to get our kids back, we had to be evaluated [psychiatrically], which I was evaluated. But also my husband had to be evaluated, but also we had to have some kind of housing for them. So that's why I kept thinking to myself, '*If we can get the housing, if we can get the housing, if we can get the housing,* we can finally, you know, be able to get our kids back.'" Her husband agreed to look for a new job and get the mental health evaluation for the court, but when he did neither, Gillian left him.

After a hospitalization, she moved into a Board and Care home. Soon she got in a conflict with the owner, who then kicked her out. Since her medication was stored at the Board and Care, she didn't have access and began withdrawing. Now homeless and entering a hazy period that she can't quite remember, she visited her kids, who were in her mother's custody.

"So, I was with my kids and my kids were hungry. . . . And my mom wasn't there, so I just took my kids to get something to eat. And then I didn't bring them back."

Gillian had been gone for two days before the police found her. Her mother subsequently lost custody of her children, but her sister took over, which kept the kids from entering foster care.

While putting together her deal to get out of jail, Gillian had hoped to go to a women's program that had its residents working at a daycare center. The program almost accepted her, but then her medication side effects disqualified her from participating. She had begun to suffer tardive dyskinesia, a neurological condition characterized by involuntary repetitive motions, which is often associated with antipsychotics. Gillian told me, "They didn't want me to come, because I might drop a child or I'd be a risk to the others that are inside there. . . . When they said no, I was devastated."

Unable to access that work program, she began scaling back her goals for the moment. She had left her husband behind and come to terms with this heartbreak. Her biggest goal was to live with her children, but that, too, was no longer an option. Luckily, the fact that her sister now had custody of them made consistent visitation possible.

Unlike many of the cases I've described at the DMH, Gillian's family was heavily involved with her care. Her mother and sisters visited her when she was confined to the hospital or jail, and they had taken in her children. Unfortunately, even middle-class families—let alone working-class or poor ones—typically lack the resources to fill in all the gaps. For instance, Gillian's family couldn't just pay for an apartment for her when she and her husband had initially gotten evicted. Family might be involved, but they are not a focal point of treatment. Here, with Gillian a prisoner returning to patient status, the goal was not rehabilitating her family system but managing urban poverty and social disorder.

Soon, the DMH case management team came to jail to meet with her. She had once received case management services from a Compton-based FSP program and found it immensely helpful. She recalled, "[DMH staff] were, like, 'Have you heard of a FSP program?' I was, like, 'Yeah. I never even thought that that was even an option again.'" They had told her she'd need to be on top of things and put in as much work as they did. Thus, the team would take her on and assist her with keeping appointments and doing what the judge required for her to get through her probation.

MANAGING BUREAUCRACIES

Much as the team coordinated Gillian's movement between court, jail, and Board and Care, they were essentially her representatives at probation-related hearings and appointments and helped her work through the attendant bureaucracy. Throughout my time with the DMH, I accompanied workers and clients to appointments at the probation office, the Social Security office, and the Housing Authority of the City of Los Angeles, and I came to see this as one of the program's primary functions.

I was able to join Gillian and the DMH case manager Marla to meet with the new probation officer assigned to her case. We arrived and waited briefly before being called back. Gillian stood shoulder to shoulder with Marla, and they addressed the officer in tandem. A white-haired African American man with kind eyes and a relaxed manner, the officer said he'd worked there for years and was nearing retirement. Upon learning that he had attended the University of Southern California, Gillian joked that she, too, came from a "USC family," and she glanced at me to see whether I'd take the bait. She knew I was working toward my PhD at UCLA and teased me about the city's college sports rivalry. They both smiled when I feigned angry school pride.

Marla assured the probation officer that she would help Gillian check in and make all her visits, and he gently replied that he never tried to "trip people up" and send them back to jail for minor violations. In his words, Gillian was "doing what she was supposed to" by seeing the DMH team and jumping through all the bureaucratic hoops. She and Gillian thanked him, and we drove back to the clinic.

The team members had their hands full helping Gillian exit the institutional circuit. So, rather than involving themselves in relational work with her family, their time was dominated by securing housing, adhering to the probation order, and ensuring that she didn't go to state prison.

Not all DMH workers are like Vic. Some members of Gillian's care team listened to her when she spoke of her children or former career dreams. Marla, for instance, was empathetic, encouraging her to hold on to hope—but she wasn't a therapist, and this wasn't a therapeutic intervention. What Gillian experienced as the deeply personal disappointments of her lost career and role as mother were, for her treatment team, indicative of relevant practical tasks to be completed: coordinate the release from jail, house, medicate, and prevent a return to incarceration.

•   •   •

What are the possible futures for patients as the DMH clinic sees them? Workers may have a sense of deep fatalism, as in Vic's lament that "no one recovers." This is because they're starting at square one with their clients: these people are not only in altered states—they are also sleeping on the streets, incarcerated, or unwilling or unable to recall their names. Some people can be easily moved indoors and pawned off on relatives, as when the team finds Alan's children in Northern California. But sometimes people have become acculturated to street life, as with Valerie, who felt safer returning to the flagpole than staying in the motel. Workers can spend an enormous amount of time just getting someone to live inside again, and this stands in place of other, perhaps more transformative interventions.

At the same time, a person like Jeremiah challenges Vic's perception that no one recovers. Stabilized on an antipsychotic, housed, and ready to work, Jeremiah was "what hope looks like." His journey brings him to barriers that are not so much psychiatric as social in origin— immigration difficulties, benefits traps, and the general dilemma of exiting a life as a professional mental patient. Whether Jeremiah will return to gainful employment, reconnect with his wife, or otherwise thrive is not really in the DMH team's purview. Similarly, someone like Gillian may recover and stabilize her psychiatric symptoms, but her felony record for kidnapping will limit her options in terms of work and regaining custody of her kids.

The DMH case management team has an impossible task: managing not only serious mental illness but also the problems of urban poverty. Although the FSP programs were created with new funding from the state, the workers and their clients find themselves at the historical culmination of brutal cuts to housing, welfare, and mental health services. The DMH can offer a life off the institutional circuit but rarely a robust life.

Like clinicians, I sometimes asked myself what treatment would look like if more resources were available. What if the clients had not been through such terrible situations, their family members had the time and money to help them, and mental health workers had all the tools they needed? One research strategy I used was asking mental health-care providers what *they'd* do with more funding. For instance, when an FSP psychiatrist began to describe how material realities prevented proper care, I asked her how she would transform the clinic.

DOCTOR: The ideal would be being able to improve their [patient] social situation, whatever the stressor is, or engage and give this well-rounded mental health treatment approach. But the reality is that that's not—

NEIL: really possible in the Skid Row setting?

DOCTOR: Yeah, understaffed clinic, all that stuff . . .

NEIL: If there was a sudden infusion of cash or staff, what would you see as the first thing to address?

DOCTOR: Here? I think a lot of case managers. And housing specialists so the LCSWs [licensed clinical social workers] could do therapy. Maybe another rehab specialist, skills training. That sort of thing. Definitely, yeah, in a heartbeat. It would take my position down to half time. That's where the need is, really. It's ridiculous, 'cause having therapists who are really skilled having to—

NEIL: fill out paperwork all day.

DOCTOR: And move someone from a house to another house. [Which takes] four hours.

To some operating within this system, the unrelenting *social* need prevented clinicians from doing *therapeutic* work. To explore this insight, I needed to observe how well-resourced settings operated. In the next chapter, we visit the Actualization Clinic and its collaborators, catching a glimpse of care, struggles, and futures from inside the world of elite private mental health services.

CHAPTER 6

A VIABLE IDENTITY

In the elite care sector, the treatment of serious mental illness is tied to expectations about upper-middle-class life milestones. Psychiatric providers aim to restore hope, cultivate clients' talents into respectable activities, and manage paying family members who have unrealistic or inappropriate expectations. Framing these tasks is a vision of the future: college, work, healthy social relationships—or, at the very least, an identity beyond that of "mental patient."

The Actualization Clinic's treatment director, Deirdre, summarized this optimistic philosophy of psychosocial rehabilitation: "We're not interested in how many hospitalizations have you had and what are your umpteen diagnoses. It's basically where do you want to go from here and how can we help you make a better life? . . . What do you want to do? Do you wanna make friends? Do you want to recreate? Do you want to go to school? Let's do it!" Such tasks—socializing, finding hobbies, and returning to productive activity—are the bread and butter of psychiatric rehabilitation in a resource-rich context. On this side of the American mental health system, the social prognosis is entirely different from that envisioned for the public safety net client.

At the end of the previous chapter, a Los Angeles County Department of Mental Health (DMH) psychiatrist suggested that her medical workload would be reduced, and the program's clinical workers could focus on psychotherapy, were there more funding to address the patient's social needs. Without it, the staff managed continual crises—often related to housing instability—that were as much about poverty as psychiatric illness. At places like the Actualization Clinic, where baseline needs are met and resources are abundant, other concerns can dominate. When clients are materially comfortable, other forms of suffering may become existentially salient, clinically visible, and situationally actionable.

William, the director of one of Actualization's sister programs in another city, told me that the privileged patient presented unique challenges. Given his dual doctorates in sociology and social work, William could expound eloquently on issues of social inequality. A key problem for the well-off, he said, was not material survival but "spoiled identity" and stigma in relation to family expectations. These, he thought, could *increase* with privilege. "[A client might say,] 'My brother's some corporate executive, my sister's a lawyer over here, I'm at [treatment center],'" he explained. "So, the level of a sense of failure in relationship to your family—I feel like what we work in is the field of . . . 'spoiled identity,' as Goffman would call it . . . and so it's pretty extreme for somebody from a successful family." This reference to the foundational sociologist Erving Goffman points to the author's famous 1963 book *Stigma*,[1] published two years after his critique of mental hospitals, *Asylums*. In *Stigma*, Goffman examines how people navigate their lives marked by "discrediting" attributes like disability or minority status, which bring negative stereotypes and rejection.

Many of us can imagine the cruel stigmatization of impoverished mental patients, as when people mock, ignore, or fear them on the street. Yet William pointed to another form of suffering: a state in which a privileged person's once-promising identity has gone rotten, so to speak. Wealthy clients struggled with a disconnect between dreams and reality, particularly when compared with highly successful family members. Richard, owner of the Actualization Clinic, similarly told me that some therapists struggled to empathize with privileged clients who seemingly had the world at their fingertips. A good mental health worker would need to see how suffering was, in fact, relative and tied to expectation.

In a context of family privilege, where "spoiled identity" is the key problem, elite mental health-care providers attempt to build something experientially meaningful and socially respectable—*a viable identity*—out of a stalled life. It is the social prognosis appropriate to this environment. The relevant tasks are time consuming and difficult, and they unfold in ways that contrast markedly with the work undertaken at the DMH. As we did in the previous chapter, we can look inside a case management meeting to get a better sense of the day-to-day tragedies, triumphs, and tedium of the governance project—this time aimed not at baseline stability but at class-appropriate functioning.

ROUTINES OF RECOVERY: MORNING MEETING AT THE ACTUALIZATION CLINIC

From my field notes:

....

May 2016. 9:00 a.m.
Deirdre points to a quote she's written on the whiteboard. "If you judge a fish by its ability to climb a tree, it will live its whole life thinking it's stupid." She looks around the conference table. "What's this mean?"

Nate, the group therapy director, says with a snort, "Don't expect too much."

Deirdre rolled her eyes. "Not quite."

"I got the Cliff-Notes version," Nate quips.

Deirdre asks me what I think, and I say I think it means that a person in the wrong environment might look incapable, but in the right environment they can flourish. She nods her head.

Our kids are in the wrong learning environment and think they are stupid, but it's really the teaching style. . . . It's helping our kids develop what they're good at, which many of them have lost since becoming ill. They need to find an environment where they can succeed.

Deirdre asks her case managers to keep this in mind as they consider what clients are capable of.

The conference begins with brief updates before transitioning to situations that require more in-depth attention.

—Jobs: A man will begin selling cars at Ford, and another got a Prius and will start driving for Uber.

—Hospitalization: A woman is inpatient again, and her mother will come to visit.

—Hobbies: A woman played tennis for the first time in a year.

—Legal/emotional dynamics: A family is finally open to someone else serving as their loved one's conservator [legal guardian].

—Healthy changes: A woman in her fifties with diabetes, bipolar disorder, and developmental disabilities bought healthy food when the case manager took her grocery shopping. Usually, she wants tasty junk food.

—A young man struggling with psychosis was supposed to start a job teaching art to seniors, but "got emotional and lashed out" at his case manager. She helped him process the event, and he apologized to her. She's happy he feels safe enough to discuss it.

—A man wants to leave treatment in CA to be closer to his family in another state. The case manager thinks this is a bad idea. Deirdre says, "It's 'cause [his mother] thinks he'll be better closer to the family. But it's actually the opposite." She thinks he wants to be "coddled," which will be unhealthy. He only wants to take Gabapentin [an anxiety and nerve pain medication] now, and not prescriptions for his bipolar disorder diagnosis. The case managers think this is a terrible plan and that he'll end up back in a residential program.

—A man in his 20s won his disability case and will receive [Supplemental Security Income] back pay. Since his family supports him, he will suddenly have $11,000 with no expenses. Deirdre says he should pay back his uncle, who is funding his treatment. "He cannot have that money under any circumstance," she said. "He'll go to Vegas."

—A 50-year-old man diagnosed with Asperger's is trying to create a tutoring business. He has a juris doctorate, and although he hasn't been able to work as a lawyer, wants to tutor advanced placement government for high schoolers. His rigid protocol (students must pass his test before he'll take them on) and odd demeanor are hampering his business. Nate says, "He's in fantasy land." Deirdre reframes, "He needs more treatment, needs to work on things first before he goes back to work."

Notice two striking points of contrast with my notes from the DMH meeting in the previous chapter. First is the level of family involvement and the paternalistic mind-set: Deirdre calls adult clients kids and frequently references family in relation to clients' situations. Second is how the work is oriented toward building lives and schedules. The opening quotation about fish and trees speaks to the belief that within the right environment, people can be successful. Some of the Actualization Clinic's clients are employed—driving Uber, starting a tutoring business, and working at an auto dealership. Even the man who won Supplemental Security Income back pay had until recently been working at the family business, which allows for employment and role development.

Some victories, such as a person playing tennis, have a particularly classed tone, but the breakthrough need not be tennis. What's important is resuming activities, having hobbies that involve other people, leaving the house, and finding greater personal autonomy.

Helping a man run his own tutoring business is potentially very time consuming—he presents problems by being too rigid—but it's hard in a different way from the DMH trying to get "Joanne," the woman with no name or government benefits, into stable housing. Note that Deirdre counters Nate's dismissive statement about this client ("he's in fantasy land") by suggesting that the man *could* run the business *if* he undergoes more treatment. Getting a woman to *choose* healthy food on her own is also an accomplishment, though again, it's a different kind from negotiating a jail release when limited community resources are available.

Notice as well that some of the elements here are shared across the two psychiatric settings: people going into the hospital, people wanting to stop medication, or the complications of legal conservatorship that take a person's rights away. Yet the social dimensions shaping problems and linked futures look immensely different.

"WE DREAM KINDA BIG"

William, the sociologist social worker, explained the importance of seeing recovery not just in psychiatric terms but in social terms.

> [A client], when they're ostracized, has a profound psychological event going on. Negative signs of schizophrenia look like despair to me, they don't look connected to schizophrenia. They look like a person who's slowly becoming isolated from the world and becoming lethargic because of that, not something that's created by the schizophrenia.
>
> It's impossible to treat with medication, and it's the bigger predictor for dysfunction than psychosis. To me, that social event that slows a person down when they're having psychotic symptoms is the thing we should be working on with schizophrenia, right?

Here William asks me to see what he sees: the many multidirectional causal connections between the psychosocial and the medical dimensions of illness. Not only do symptoms lead to social difficulties; social difficulties can lead to things that resemble psychopathology.

"Negative signs" of withdrawal and isolation represent a relational rather than a purely medical crisis. William is not a radical social constructionist—he believes in mental illness, speaking of "the schizophrenia." But, as he points out, the larger question of functioning is about not just psychosis but the kind of social environment a client is in.

Since William once ran a public program, he had insight into the comparison.[2] His public case management team had been able to move people forward, he said, but once the county forced them to take on larger caseloads, they could only work on "maintenance." His goal for all clients, across settings, was to get "acuity so low that all they need to do is go to a clinic, they don't need this [intensive program]." After that, the difference was one of potential futures: "So, somebody in our program [current private case management] going back to college with our supports possibly for a while and that kind of thing, because they're on their way to becoming an MBA [master's in business administration]. For the other group [his previous public clients], someone getting a job at a restaurant where that's going to support them and they're going to maybe get off of SSDI [public benefits], have their own apartment, and build a social life independent of a social life with other psychiatric patients." To William, "They're kind of similar goals," but the public program, once overloaded, was forced to make its goal "more about maintenance," or keeping people stable, rather than moving them forward with new or expanded social roles.

William's experience in the changing public sector of mental health care is instructive in another way. Recall that we encountered extreme budget cuts, high client-to-staff ratios, and programs taking on more than initially intended at the Los Angeles County DMH. William's solution to avoiding the burnout that threatened workers in the public sector was to instead serve the wealthy, moving to a context in which he could practice his craft at the highest level and feel the professional satisfaction of transforming lives.

Most clinicians were too pessimistic about serious mental illness, he believed, so they failed to understand clients' true potential. But he also knew that this potential was dependent on social dynamics. For people who were young and well resourced, a schizophrenia or bipolar diagnosis was hardly a life sentence of disability. William's program could exert concerted efforts to make dreams come true. Drawing on the language of radical patient advocacy groups, he said his clients might even learn to reframe "symptoms" as "gifts."[3] "I feel completely unlimited in what they can achieve. I really do," he declared. "So, you know, [having] a family, kids, job. Their symptoms are integrated into their lives where they don't bother them, or maybe they even begin to see them as gifts. If they have extreme issues with reality, those issues with reality become something metaphorical and supportive rather than something that hurts them. So yeah. We dream kinda big about what we can do. 'Cause you're not worried about the socioeconomic stuff."

This stands in stark contrast to the jaded DMH nurse Vic, who suggested that "no one recovers" and that "legitimate schizophrenics" had essentially lost their souls. Although other workers at the DMH frowned on Vic's negativity, their practical tasks ultimately oriented them similarly. They were trying to keep people housed and out of jail, maybe get them consistent with medication. For practitioners like William, who hoped to help clients lead rewarding lives, such settings were demoralizing. Crucially, he wanted me to understand that after he left public services, he was *only* able to treat the very privileged— there was, to him, no way to provide intensive, wraparound case management for the middle class. It was simply not reimbursed by most private insurance, so he could only serve those who paid directly.

Let's dig into this idea of the unservable middle-class patient for a moment. In the previous chapter, I described how community care was affected by the Great Tax Revolt, state budget austerity, and the shrinking of municipal services. But in many private insurance–based settings, treatment opportunities were being slashed too. Beginning in the 1980s, managed care profoundly altered what services were available to the insured.[4] The new system was a reaction to spiraling health costs and concerns that unnecessary treatment was taking place, and it limited which medical providers a patient could see, used external reviewers to monitor doctor's decisions, and pushed clinicians to justify their billing.

Managed care affected all forms of health care but hit psychiatric services—sometimes treated as luxuries rather than legitimate health care—especially hard. In part, this is because many forms of mental health treatment are arguably not medical at all in that they are social and community integration activities, and psychotherapies often have ambiguous outcomes. Driven also by pharmaceutical company influence and the perceived (if overhyped) effectiveness of new medications, private insurance companies began cutting back on reimbursements for long-term psychotherapy and hospital stays. Health maintenance organizations (HMOs), in attempting to limit costs, increasingly prioritized medication-based treatment over psychosocial care.

The reduction of long-term psychotherapies in inpatient psychiatric units made practical sense. If the average hospitalization had dwindled from months on the ward to less than a week, little progress could be made with in-depth therapies. Still, the use of such treatments for people in severe crisis did not disappear entirely. Instead, they became the province of elite residential settings, perhaps bundled with wraparound case management, like the Actualization Clinic or William's program. Such narrowing of the possibilities for the middle-class patient underscores the kind of profound bifurcation that was occurring in treatment as well as its multiple sources: public austerity in the wake of tax cuts, changes in welfare policy, provider burnout, and managed care after deinstitutionalization and the floundering attempt to build community psychiatry. In the end, we have come to a mental health system that is meager but open to the very poor (if they've become a social problem), tight-fisted with the middle class, but full of options and possibilities for the rich.

THE COLLEGE TRANSITION

Helping people become self-efficacious and achieve vibrant futures presents practical problems different from those seen in housing the homeless mental patient. Surprisingly, assets like highly involved parents and high hopes for the future come with difficulties of their own. For a clear instance of how these expectations and resources shape treatment and recovery, we start with the college transition.

Let's consider two men in their twenties, each of whom left school because of psychosis (recall that serious mental illness commonly emerges in the late teens and early twenties).

RJ

Coming from a wealthy white family, RJ illustrates the difficult task of working with parents who haven't adjusted to the idea of having a disabled adult child. The Actualization Clinic held out hope for RJ's future, but it also believed that his family was pressing for too much of the right activities—namely, school and work—at the wrong time.

Diagnosed alternately as schizophrenic or suffering from drug-induced psychosis, RJ had been doing well in elite treatment. As Ian, the Buddhist therapist case manager, explained, "He'd been in a wilderness program, then had been at Menninger's [an elite private hospital] for a few weeks, then at a sober living, where he was stabilized on Invega [an antipsychotic]. He was doing much better, and then his parents let him go to school in [another area], where he fell apart in the dorms. He freaked people out by staring, and one of his symptoms was hysterical laughter without knowing what it was from." Although Actualization recommended that RJ live at Namaste Gardens, its favored dual-diagnosis sober living facility for young men, his parents brought him back home. At a team meeting afterward, Actualization staff discussed what it called family noncompliance: RJ's mother was monitoring his every move, and his father assigned him to work in various family businesses.

"His mom called and asked, 'What am I supposed to do for him?'" Deirdre said in frustration. "[She should] be his mom, back the fuck off, and let us do our job!"

Ian sighed. "She's his crutch since letting him home. Now she wakes him up, makes sure he takes his medication, et cetera."

Deirdre complained about RJ's father, who was "in denial" about RJ's psychotic disorder and found part-time work for his son. Mimicking a deep, manly voice, she said, "All he needs is work. And now he's got three jobs!"

. . .

"I'm kind of serving the whole family," Ian said.

Deirdre noted the family's high expectations. "They will not tolerate his failure."

From Actualization's perspective, RJ's latest mental break in college had led to his family enveloping him in an enormous amount of surveillance and time management. Here, what seems to be a clear good—a dedicated family that can provide opportunities—becomes a problem. The father has connected his son with multiple jobs, an eventual treatment goal, yet the team doesn't believe that RJ is ready for these. In "serving the whole family," the team decides that Ian can only help RJ through influencing the young man's family system.

Actualization reported that such dynamics were common. Where some rich families didn't demand enough from the loved one, others had unrealistic expectations for their child's achievement, and they alternately paid for stretches of treatment in private facilities or brought the adult child home and micromanaged them. There were examples in which families' expectations relative to social class even led to clients dropping seemingly positive activities. For instance, the Actualization Clinic once helped a young man diagnosed with schizophrenia secure a job at a P.F. Chang's restaurant. It believed his employment to be a great psychosocial rehabilitation achievement. The young man's wealthy family made him quit, however, because it believed he could "do much better."

Often there is uncertainty about whether and when work, school, or other psychosocial activities are appropriate. In RJ's case, this was partly because no one knew whether he had a drug-induced psychosis or schizophrenia. In theory, the former might clear up on its own. Yet, as the anthropologist-psychiatrist Helena Hansen notes, this diagnosis is often applied to upper-class young white people for social rather than medical reasons: it helps avoid the stigma of a *schizophrenia* label.[5] Perhaps the alternate diagnosis could prevent a negative self-fulfilling prophecy, but it might ultimately prove harmful. Someone like RJ may indeed have a persistent disability, and the family's attributing it all to drugs might mean an unproductive denial of his actual needs. This push and pull between hope and realism continues, however, because clinicians struggle to make clear diagnoses and can never make a fully confident prognosis. At least for now, they'd struggle over the right form of pushing him toward a better future.[6]

BRANDON

An intensely intellectual African American man named Brandon, on the other hand, illustrates the difficult process of reshaping dreams. He had taken a leave of absence from an Ivy League school after a roommate accused him of stalking. Although Brandon acknowledged experiencing delusions that he was Albert Einstein, he insisted that the "stalking" was a misunderstanding. Whatever the situation, he was hospitalized on the East Coast and eventually diagnosed as having schizophrenia. His family wasn't wealthy, but his mother's insurance was one of the few that covered Actualization's Intensive Outpatient Program (IOP) and some additional services. Relatives still had high hopes for his future career.

Since returning to Los Angeles, Brandon had also attended UCLA's IOP and the Aftercare program, which enrolled people in research and services for early psychosis intervention. In the four years since, he had been hospitalized nine times and was now taking Clozaril, the most powerful of the antipsychotics.

In Brandon's case, the family management task was expectation adjustment. When I first met him, he talked about returning to the northeastern college to resume work toward his applied physics degree. He was excited about Actualization's IOP curriculum, comparing the dialectical behavioral therapy and life skills therapy favorably to what he'd witnessed at a local nonprofit. But despite the intensive services and the powerful medications, he was soon hospitalized again. Hallucinations related to his favorite comic books continued to break through, and he became terrified that he had the power to destroy the world with his mind. He also struggled with the Clozaril regimen, becoming so constipated that he needed medical attention. By the last time we played cards together at the Actualization social group, Brandon had scaled back his academic goal to attending community college. The dream of a return to the Ivy League was, at least for now, over.

No one believed that Brandon had lost his soul, as Vic said of clients at the DMH, but clinicians thought that elite education might be unrealistic or overwhelming for him.

A LIFE TO COME BACK TO

For people who experienced later-stage psychotic breaks, there might be a substantial level of achievement to return to. Success in school and at work before the onset of psychosis is often associated with better psychiatric outcomes.[7] Whether this is because such people have a different underlying manifestation of illness, or simply have better resources correlative with their social class, is unclear. As I've suggested throughout this book, such factors interact in complex ways.

Recall Jeremiah from the previous chapter, who had married, immigrated to the United States, and worked as a crossing guard with hopes of upward career mobility. Experiencing a psychotic break at the end of his twenties and falling into homelessness, his situation and the DMH's resource realities made it unlikely that he would recover either his marriage or his career goals. Now consider Franklin, a white man in his thirties who had a law degree and an established career as a certified public accountant before his first crisis. Diagnosed with schizophrenia, he believed that he was in purgatory and that his wife and children weren't his actual family. When he started a two-week fast that he said would help him escape back to reality, he was involuntarily hospitalized.

Early on, Franklin had met with the Actualization case management team, but he ultimately connected the most with Dev, the peer worker who sometimes collaborated on cases. Franklin's wife didn't want him back home, and so he was living with an aunt. Though eventually stabilized, he remained unsure of which reality he was living in. Still, he moved back in with his wife and kids, and the family hoped for a partial return to his old life.

In the following excerpt from my field notes, I joined Dev and Franklin for a session at a Yard House chain restaurant:

> As we walked through the parking lot, Dev asked Franklin what percentage he was sure that he was in purgatory. He was 90 percent sure, an increase over last time. Dev asked whether the doctor had lowered the Clozaril dose, and Franklin said he had. He believed

that the Clozaril was acting not medically but through Dev and his powers.

Franklin believed Dev to be a supernatural being, maybe Jesus, "placed here to help me through this process." When he'd first met Richard at the Actualization Clinic, he'd wondered whether the man was God. "He's a pretty charismatic dude," I agreed. Now Franklin said he felt more and more like his everyday experience was real, but he couldn't account for the last five years of his life.

While we waited for dinner to arrive, Dev pulled out his *Cognitive Behavioral Therapy for Severe Mental Illness* illustrated guide and flipped to a scale on delusions. He then measured Franklin on such issues as how preoccupied he is, conviction about his unusual beliefs, distress, and disruption to life. Franklin stated that on distress and disruption, his numbers had gone down considerably over time, and he was now trying to work again. Still, he believed he was likely in purgatory.

Now the big struggle was going for job interviews and worrying that the boss was reading his mind. Dev flipped to a chapter of his book that discussed research debunking extrasensory perception. "What do you think of this book saying there is no telepathy?"

Franklin smirked and said this didn't prove anything. "I agree. That means I'm not on earth."

It took me a second to register his argument—namely, that his mysterious experiences were real rather than delusions, so he must truly be in another dimension—and I burst out laughing. He grinned at me, and we turned to nonpurgatory matters.

Note how Franklin's respectable identity is sustained and possibly even resurrected here. Although he waffled on his belief that he is living in an alternate reality, 90 percent certain he's in purgatory, his goals remain the same: he will resume family relations and working as a professional.

All this is quite bizarre, for by Franklin's own logic his children are not his children but purgatory doubles. It also makes little sense for him to go to work if he's still trying to get home to Earth. Still, through his trust in Dev, whom he thinks is a supernatural being, he's giving it a chance.

Productivity and family life are more attainable in such a situation, because employment won't threaten government medical, housing, and cash survival benefits as it would for a poor patient like Jeremiah. With the ability to stay with his aunt and a family who could pay for private mental health treatment, Franklin neither became homeless nor soured the marital relationship with his wife to the point that he lost custody of his children. Thus, he had a shorter road to bare stability, leaving him more room to be in an altered state while regaining status and possibility.

TREATED AND TRANSFORMED

In chapter 3, I discussed how the diagnostic specificity and strong referral network available to privileged people mean that they can receive specialized care. Cassie's case illustrates the possibilities when a person's rediagnosis and enrollment in the right therapy can remake a life.

Thirty-something and recently married, Cassie was a former Actualization client who had become a social worker. Her story offers a particularly vivid example of what kinds of goals elite clinics could aim for, as she eventually worked at Actualization and then a hospital. She told me that she had been in various forms of therapy throughout her childhood and "was the identified patient of the family." After several suicide attempts and a series of hospitalizations, she felt hopeless. Diagnosed with bipolar II disorder and a profound body dysmorphia, she had tried nearly twenty medications and was unable to hold down a job. At the age of twenty-four, she was living on disability benefits and her family had locked her out of the home. They didn't have the money to pay for out-of-pocket care, but when Cassie began to live in her car, a wealthy aunt stepped in and paid for private psychiatric services from a famous university doctor.

Cassie came to believe, however, that this prominent psychiatrist had misdiagnosed and overmedicated her. The Actualization Clinic placed a premium on diagnostic specificity, as it could lead to

specialized interventions. Yet given the messiness of psychiatric diagnosis, there was no guarantee that even famous doctors would get
things right. Since bipolar II can function as a catchall category for
many disturbances of mood and behavior, there was an open question
as to whether it accurately characterized her suffering. Then, during another hospitalization, Cassie was diagnosed as having borderline personality disorder. She resisted the pronouncement, she said,
because of the stigma associated with that mental illness category.
Some argue that borderline, characterized by unstable relationships, a
distorted sense of self, and emotionality, is the modern-day equivalent
of *hysteria*—a term often applied in sexist ways to "difficult" women
rather than serving as a genuinely useful diagnostic category.[8] Cassie
had also come to identify heavily with being bipolar, so the new diagnosis felt disorienting. Her family brought on Actualization for clinical community care and Dev to offer peer services. It was Dev who
persuaded her to attend a clinic that specialized in "mentalization-
based therapy," a cutting-edge approach to borderline.

But an issue arose—not resources or access, for the rich aunt could
cover the case management and any private therapies. It was that
Cassie would not, or could not, get out of the house. She related that
her body dysmorphia was so severe that she couldn't stop staring at
herself in the mirror. Having the "right" diagnosis and access to specialized treatment might not matter if she couldn't participate.

Deirdre, then a frontline case manager at Actualization, worked to
get Cassie out into the world. Together they completed such tasks as
picking up the mail and going outside to places Cassie was initially
uncomfortable with. Soon the case management team got her a plant
to take care of, and then a dog, which required that she go outside
twice a day to walk it. Cassie described Deirdre's involvement in her
treatment as like a friend gently coaxing her: "Let's not wear sweats
today. Let's do your hair." Through months of slowly building her
capacity to leave home, the Actualization team helped her get to the
specialized therapy center.

The theoretical base of mentalization-based treatment is that those
with borderline personality disorder struggle to understand how other

peoples' behavior is related to their thoughts. Mentalization is "the process by which we implicitly and explicitly interpret the actions of oneself and others as meaningful on the basis of intentional mental states."[9] Cassie explained that the staff of the therapy center worked to help her properly attribute motivations to others in situations that had previously led her to massive emotional outbursts. In a major turning point, for instance, she'd been out to a dinner party at a restaurant when she was served a slice of cake that was smaller than those received by others at the table. Cassie believed that it had been a deliberate slight and began to get upset, but when a woman suggested that they must have run out of cake, she sensed her mentalization-based therapy kicking in.

According to Cassie, without the Actualization and mentalization clinics, "I'd be dead or on the streets." This might sound hyperbolic coming from a person with wealthy relatives, but she had indeed tried to kill herself and lived in her car. But receiving the proper diagnosis and then having access to specialized care were only the first steps in her recovery. Her success also required the Actualization team, especially her close relationship with Deirdre, to help her move from simply living in an apartment to doing the psychotherapeutic work that changed her life. Cassie then completed her advanced education, got married, and became a mental health-care provider herself.

Note that Cassie did not suffer from a psychotic disorder, and her bipolar diagnosis was eventually rejected. Perhaps all the intensive treatment in the world wouldn't have made such a transformative difference for someone experiencing a more profound disability, like RJ and Brandon, the young men with psychosis who tried to return to college. This is hard to say for certain, however. The point is that in this treatment world, the trajectory of a person like Cassie can be held up as a possible future outcome for others.

"NOBODY KNOWS THE FUTURE"

For some patients, such dreams seemed unlikely. The Actualization Clinic served some older clients who were motivated to improve their lives, but they remained profoundly disabled—despite all the treatment money could buy. Anthony, an international client who came to Actualization on a medical visa, illustrates the other side of hope: dreaming of a life in line with classed expectations, all while the clinical staff secretly doubts that it is possible.

After we became friendly at the clinic's group therapy sessions, Anthony agreed to tell me his story. Fifty years old and of European descent, he had grown up in a former colony where his family once ruled. After decolonization, the family transitioned from possessing government power to controlling business interests throughout the country.

Diagnosed in his twenties as having schizophrenia and alcoholism, Anthony was placed on what he called a "vintage 1950s medication." His father hired a nurse to monitor him, which he found humiliating. After having been through "like ten thousand hospitals in my country," Anthony's family sent him to California, then a treatment destination for the global elite. He got sober in a matter of months.

Rid of the destructive side of his alcoholism, Anthony returned home and made various attempts to work in the family business, though he still struggled with voices. In his telling, he had his biggest mental breakdown at age thirty-three. Wanting to demonstrate his independence from his family, he saved up his allowance and brokered a large raw materials deal. But when the buyer and seller cut him out as middleman, he lost his money. Then Anthony's girlfriend left him, and his life was in shambles.

Since then, he had struggled with intrusive thoughts about a historic battle between good and evil. His family checked him into a place he likened to a "primitive, third-world rehab" that "broke me, traumatized me. . . . And so I thought, I need to go back to America. I keep thinking that. I need to go back to America and fix whatever problem I have."

In this most recent round of medical tourism, he stayed at a hotel near the Actualization Clinic, where he would come in for the IOP group therapy. Case managers took him to do skills training and socializing in public, and nonclinical helpers assisted him with daily living activities. He saw a specialist, a holistic psychiatrist who prescribed both medication and customized vitamins, as well as a private therapist who helped him process childhood trauma.

Anthony's access to unending resources played out in complicated ways. Ironically, his wealth and upper-class cultural dispositions isolated him. A talented visual artist, he took me to his hotel room to see his paintings—a giant syringe symbolizing the terror of emergency hospitalization, a haunting self-portrait of morbid obesity stemming from his medication side effects. I was excited when Actualization brought him to the Painted Brain, a nonprofit that runs art classes for people with psychiatric disabilities. I had visited the center earlier and hoped he could find a sense of community with other artists. Unfortunately, Anthony was uncomfortable with the place and declined to return. He thought the hallway smelled bad, and the center seemed too "low class." After passing by an art gallery in Hollywood, he told me he'd like to rent the space and display his work there. Having money could facilitate such a highly individualized intervention, but it also meant that he avoided important *social* connections.

The promises of elite treatment also created a trap of optimism. For all Anthony's motivation and the attention afforded by his wealth, the Actualization case management team secretly believed that he wouldn't get better. I watched in the IOP group as he grew frustrated by his intrusive thoughts yet held onto his high hopes for the future.

"[My childhood trauma] has been pushed down all these years, and now I'm going to therapy and it's bubbling up." He was holding on to his notepad, and when another client asked what he was writing, Anthony responded, "I'm doodling garbage." The therapist exclaimed, "That's a judgment!" She wanted him to observe his mind's workings without evaluation, but Anthony simply wanted to be rid of his strange thoughts.

Someone asked him to read it, and Anthony said, "The asshole wants the whore, who is stronger than Super Girl, she wants me to never marry."

"It's like a movie script," someone said with a smile.

Anthony continued, "He wants Super Girl to beat me up so I can never marry a woman. They'll make me into a priest." He explained that these characters were interrupting his goals. "My biggest dream is to be cured and married."

For Nate, the director of the IOP, Anthony presented a difficult case. It was unusual to find a person who had been debilitated for so long yet wanted to continue working hard with intensive treatment. Yet Nate was skeptical that Anthony was ever going to achieve these dreams, and he echoed William's point that the wealthy suffer "spoiled identity" from sibling comparison.

> His brother is married and has a couple of kids, and runs a success-
> ful business, and Anthony wants all that for himself, in his life. But
> he's fifty, and he's still struggling with his hallucinations and some
> of his plans to try to lead that normal life the way he sees it. Getting
> married to someone rich and successful, and having children, and
> living that happily ever after. . . . His expectation might be a little
> ambitious for where he's at with his mental health status.
>
> The challenge there is, you want clients to have hope. You want
> them to have something to shoot for and stay motivated to remain
> in treatment, keep taking their meds, keep moving forward in posi-
> tive ways. But the treatment providers may have a different view of
> the likelihood of his ultimate plan succeeding, unfortunately. It's a
> tricky thing, because you don't want to communicate that to a client.
> You don't want to discourage them from their dreams in any way.
> Nobody knows the future.

Thus, to keep Anthony engaged—and his family paying—the Actu-alization Clinic would stoke the embers of hope. Maybe his ambitions were out of reach, but striving toward them was a class-appropriate task that made some sense in this milieu.

THE ACTRESS AND THE PROFESSOR

Finally, I consider two clients who were relatively stable in terms of symptoms and had achieved the appearance of viable identities, but they were nonetheless isolated and unhappy. Their stories reveal the limits of highly resourced and highly individualized care if providers can't figure out how to *socially integrate* clientele. Here again we see how money may become part of the problem.

Shelly was a forty-eight-year-old white woman who had been engaged in some form of mental health treatment for most of her life. Diagnosed with bipolar and borderline personality disorders, she'd undergone eight psychiatric hospitalizations when suicidal. She consumed an enormous amount of health and other services but still felt stuck. The Actualization Clinic, in turn, worked to help cultivate her career as an actress, encouraging her auditions and artistic identity.

On a sunny afternoon, Shelly and I sat by the pool in her apartment complex, watching her video reel of dramatic and comedic clips. She recounted some of the painful traumas of her youth, from an older man preying on her when she was thirteen to a physically abusive boyfriend. She longed for success in the film industry—it would show up her brother and his wife, who didn't believe in her and controlled her disbursements from the family trust. Aside from her father, she complained, the family had never taken her seriously. She was eternally grateful to Actualization's founder, Richard, for telling her siblings that they didn't understand her talent.

The treatment team members debated why Shelly was stuck. Some believed her still to be profoundly ill, while others thought she could have held a job if she hadn't been so indulged by family wealth. Therapists joke about the term *affluenza*, but there can be a real problem when people have never had to develop grit. A clinical psychologist explained to me that extremely privileged clients often lacked coping skills. Shelly was one of these cases where mental illness and problems of affluence seemed bound together.

To be clear, sometimes her money seemed great for her situation. When her beloved father died, for instance, Shelly was in crisis but did not want to go to the mental hospital: "I told Actualization, take me to Forward Steps"—one of the premier dual-diagnosis rehab and mental health centers in Malibu, costing around $50,000 a month. Although Shelly had no drug or alcohol problem, she found the rehab's mountain air, daily therapy groups, individual sessions, farm-to-table organic food, and kindhearted staff better than what she'd experience at a psychiatric institution. "I'm never going back to a mental place," she told me. "I'll get ten massages a week if I have to." Other times, the Actualization team thought that her money was bad, since she simply hired companions like psychics and crystal healers rather than make friends.

Whatever the precise cause—serious mental illness, family dynamics, affluenza—Shelly wasn't well. At one team meeting, the Actualization Clinic staff tried to parse out what was going on and what to do. The family psychologist Joseph explained, "She was paranoid and fearful, and now nonstop talking. She said to me three times, 'I'm not manic.'" For Joseph, this only proved that in fact she *was*. Yet Richard argued that her current predicament wasn't about the bipolar or borderline personality disorders per se. At the root of her problems was that she was only "taking" from the world, not giving of herself, and therefore leading a miserable existence. A meaningful role and social connections, perhaps some volunteer work, would make her better. But "she doesn't want to change her attitude," Richard said in frustration. "All I can tell her is, 'You're getting what you're putting out.'" For Joseph, this attitude was a product of the family systems dynamic: "She's been enabled and accommodated by family her whole life." The intervention became to focus again on Shelly's identity. "Let's get her back to auditions," he concluded.

This clinical approach, which considers a variety of biopsychosocial factors in mental illness and health, is sophisticated. Resuming acting seems like a wholesome and holistic intervention. But, as I came to see it, the focus on auditions ignored Richard's key insight about taking versus giving: in Shelly's pursuit of fame, and her consumption of acting lessons and psychic readings, she was entirely focused on herself. The viable identity of actress gave her activity, purpose, and a cover for her unusual life as a wealthy person (most actors in LA are underemployed and auditioning rather than consistently working). But with her paid friends and self-obsession, she—and the Actualization Clinic—failed to create the social integration that the program proclaimed to be its mission.

I learned that such a dynamic could be sustained across a lifetime. The clearest illustration of this is the client that Actualization clinicians affectionately dubbed "The Professor." Now in his sixties, Sherman had his first psychotic break while attending a prestigious liberal arts college. Diagnosed with schizophrenia, he had by this point been an Actualization client for decades. "I got sick, I fell behind in my studies, and I became a mental patient," he summarized. Although he lived alongside some public clients in a Board and Care home, Sherman's deceased family had left a trust that provided for private case management and living expenses as well as a little spending money. His story illustrates the possibilities and limitations of care when even well-resourced, kind mental health-care providers can't change the broader social context in which disabled people live.

Sherman was an intellectual, and the case managers supported this identity by driving him to all the community colleges around Los Angeles. He claimed to have taken nearly every possible course and recounted the trajectory of his broad liberal arts education. "When I'm old, I studied literature. When I'm young, I studied philosophy, politics, and history and psychology. Middle, I studied economics, anthropology, and art history." I once accompanied Sherman and a case manager to a museum, which I learned was one of his favorite activities. He occasionally went on longer trips, as when he was driven to attend Shakespeare plays for several days in another city.

Moreover, Actualization designed a website to house Sherman's collected papers. As Deirdre explained to a case manager, "He has no immediate family and wanted his legacy to live on. He wanted the knowledge passed down." I learned that he would occasionally ask his case managers to scan and upload the papers he'd written. This all presented an opportunity to help Sherman maintain an identity and honor his contribution to the world.

I was moved by the website, but as we sat chatting in the Board and Care home, Sherman was ambivalent. "I don't know who reads it, or anything about it. Maybe people read it; it'd be nice if they did." When we talked about classes, he said dejectedly that they were only for his own edification: "Just no purpose but self-improvement."

His love of knowledge and wisdom was evident, but he was not an actual professor.

Furthermore, Sherman's life was *socially* empty. "I have no family," he said, adding, "No, I have no friends, I didn't have [them] for years. One of them showed up at my parent's funeral, but besides that I haven't had anyone." A case manager said that Sherman still talked about his college days, when he had girlfriends and drove around in his own car. His social network now consisted of his treatment team and the people he paid to bring him coffee or hot dogs.

Sherman's money ensured security and access to reputable providers. There were the accoutrements of culture as well. But despite his activities and classes, he lacked an intellectual community and lived an isolated life in a Board and Care home. His world revolved around paid pseudofriends who were enthusiastic because it was their job, and Sherman knew it. As I wrote in a memo later that day,

> Sherman [shows] both the greatness and the sadness of what money can buy you in advanced capitalist America. He has hired help to take him to cultural events and museums, and he has taken nearly every class around at community colleges. Always had housing, no long-term hospitalizations in years. Doesn't have to work. But he doesn't have a social network—friends who aren't paid for. No people like himself at the Board and Care, with similar interests or educational background. It is a sad existence but much better than what a lot of people have.

The website and highly personalized case management were more than most could ask for. But for Sherman, it wasn't a meaningful life.

•   •   •

In elite care settings, family wealth facilitates impressive interventions that nonetheless butt up against the realities of mental illness and a world not designed for people with psychiatric disabilities. The fact that elite care workers "dream big" in a context of material comfort means they must resolve a variety of issues quite different from those that present at the DMH. Helping people like RJ and Brandon return to college after a psychotic break, for instance, may mean negotiating with overbearing families, planning out self-management strategies, and re-envisioning dreams.

Perhaps these promising clients will end up like Cassie, finding a truly transformative therapy and pursuing an advanced degree, or like Franklin, who believes he is in purgatory yet will resume engagement with work and family anyway. Others may burn out and live at home, doing nothing. Or they may end up like Anthony, still pushing for an unlikely career and family at fifty. Here, holding on to a vision of a robust future—but one that's always just out of reach— may mean tremendous effort and disappointment. Treatment providers sometimes craft an alternative identity for those who won't hold a job and start families, such as helping Shelly become an actress or designing Sherman's "professor" website. Notably, these people may have the trappings of a viable identity, but their lives remain socially thin. Identity in isolation can be profoundly alienating, as Sherman's case shows.

Significant resources and effort may be devoted to getting people what they want—recreation, activities, and the like—but not necessarily the *social* integration that these programs putatively aim for. Put differently, highly individualized treatments may risk becoming too *individualistic*. And sometimes money and upper-class values become a problem. If money means that Shelly and Sherman hire company rather than make friends, Anthony rents gallery space instead of returning to the art workshop he deems "low class," or a young man must quit his job because his family feels it's beneath him, huge social recovery opportunities are lost.

In the next section, we'll encounter a different irony regarding money and family involvement: DMH clients receive far less attention, and no one is trying to "fix" them, but this can become its own kind of benefit. Where the rich may feel overwhelmed, disciplined, or controlled by extensive therapeutics, the poor are largely left alone. In some sense, their self-determination might be a greater freedom than that afforded the rich.

PART III

THE PARADOX OF CLIENT CHOICE

CHAPTER 7

OF LOVE AND LIABILITY

Before the civil liberties revolution in mental health law, patient autonomy was largely subordinate to the psychiatric institution's presumed need for protection and control. But deinstitutionalization and the legal changes of the 1960s fundamentally shifted the locus of psychiatric power from coercion in confined settings to choice in the community. Outside emergency situations, below the legal thresholds of "danger" and "grave disability," patients gained a set of rights to self-determination. In the third section of this book, I investigate the management of everyday choice and behavior when patients are formally free. What does it take for people with significant psychiatric disabilities to become autonomous, to freely function in their respective environments?

For both the public safety net and elite private settings, choice has been defined in ways corresponding to the very different social worlds and visions of the future addressed earlier. In what follows, we will encounter two young men whose partial compliance and ambiguously problematic behavior reveal the still-unresolved dilemmas of post-deinstitutionalization psychiatry. The men's freedoms, while rarely leading to danger, nonetheless complicate the maintenance of social order—and their own well-being.

Hugo Castile is a light-skinned Hispanic man who was referred to the adult DMH program after aging out of Hollywood's youth homeless services. His treatment team, believing he might get evicted or start fights based on apparent delusions, looks for ways to mitigate potential legal liability. As agents of the local state, the DMH tries to tolerate and contain Hugo's choices and behavior. Tom Burton, by contrast, is a white man who came to the Actualization Clinic after his psychosis interrupted his plans as a tech entrepreneur. We'll get to know Tom as he's questioning his intensive care regimen, the contradictory expectations of his parents, and whether he'll continue in treatment. As agents of his loving family, Tom's mental health-care providers try to constrain his choices, cultivate his self-control, and secure his future.

In the United States, it makes sense to us—in a perverse sort of way—when impoverished "problem people" are micromanaged and punished by the local state while the privileged live in an alternate world of indulgence and choice. We tend to associate freedom with class advantage in many domains. Challenging both common sense and sociological theory, however, impoverished Hugo is given latitude, while privileged Tom is constrained. This forces us to question the meaning of "client choice" in the case of serious mental illness. In our consumer society, economists speak of "superior goods" purchased as incomes rise, and "inferior goods" mostly consumed by the poor. Freedom, at least in blunt economic terms, appears to be the inferior good.

TOLERATING HUGO CASTILE

It was time, Vic said to his DMH colleagues around the conference table, for someone to check on Hugo. The young man had been claiming that he was hearing rapists' whispers and thoughts and intimating that he would fight them to protect his female friends. To Vic's mind, Hugo was experiencing auditory hallucinations that might lead to public conflict. The veteran nurse reminded those at the morning meeting that he was requesting not therapeutic dialogue—"Trying to understand what schizophrenics are thinking is impossible," he had said—but danger evaluation.

Laura, the leader of the intensive treatment team, agreed about not trying to "understand deeply" as she assigned nurse Leticia and social worker Beth to visit Hugo in his new, subsidized Hollywood apartment. Noting that eviction was a concern (he'd taken in several homeless youth and angered his neighbors by throwing loud parties), Laura asked the team to listen practically—if they failed to anticipate a client's violence, well, "this is how we get sued." Then she looked at me. Since I was "chill," around the same age as Hugo, and had hung out with the man at the clinic, Laura suggested that I could go along to be a calming presence.

That's how I ended up in the county car, listening to Leticia and Beth discuss the possibility of hospitalization. Beth was not yet certified to initiate emergency holds, but Leticia had the credentials and considerable experience from her years on the DMH Psychiatric Emergency Team. If a "5150" became necessary, she'd show Beth the ropes.

Hugo's building was a classic Southern California remodel, with newly painted stucco and a surprisingly attractive open-air corridor. Leticia identified his unit and rapped her knuckles on the apartment door. Hugo soon appeared, clad in a punk rock T-shirt and pants with one leg rolled up, with his messy dreadlocks draped to one side of his face. He stood awkwardly, clutching his shoulder, and said he'd hurt his arm skateboarding. As we entered, we were smacked by the pungent odor of cat urine. Dishes overflowed from the sink, and an adolescent boy stood by the couch. When a teenage girl of about fifteen came out of the bathroom, Leticia and Beth exchanged a look of worry and asked these guests to step outside.

Beth explained to Hugo that she was concerned about his "protecting" these kids. He might be trying to do the right thing, but it looked bad to have an underage girl in the house. Plus, Hugo had a way of thinking he needed to protect all women. He'd said that all those he knew during his years on the street had been either rape survivors or sex workers. There was a risk, Beth said, that Hugo might encounter any man—"even Neil," she said, gesturing to me—and think he was planning on hurting a woman. What would happen then?

Leticia leaned in toward the conversation, listening for any indication that she and Beth needed to initiate a psychiatric hold, but Hugo gave the "right" response, avoiding coercive hospitalization. "Men can talk all the shit they want," he said. But until they "lay hands" on a woman, he claimed that he wouldn't "do anything." Leticia smiled and shifted her tactics. Now she would have to work with his choices.

"Hugo, would you like a medication appointment?"

"I'd rather have my friends than be zonked out on meds," he replied, and we all cracked up as he made a zombie face and stiffened his arms.

Hugo did say a few odd things during our visit, though none that would invite coercion. He told us that birds spoke to him, and at one point, when Beth moved some trash, he said, "Don't do that, Mom." Still, as we left, Leticia called the office and reported, "He said the right thing about not reacting until men 'laid hands' on a girl." She was an experienced emergency evaluator, and Hugo was an experienced refuser. Since the DMH couldn't put him in the hospital or force medication, it would concentrate on keeping him housed.

Beth suggested that Hugo might move—find a building where the neighbors wouldn't complain. Then he could have friends over and party late, "because it will be in a shitty building." For now, she hoped he'd just kick his friends out.

Later I learned that Hugo's family had come from a Spanish-speaking Caribbean nation, and he grew up in Los Angeles, later making trips in friends' crummy cars to Kentucky and experiencing adventures all along the East Coast. He was proud that, unlike many traveling-punk kids, he'd finished high school. After his girlfriend became pregnant, he tried to work to support them, but she soon moved away with their son. These days, she had a restraining order against him, although Hugo did not explain the grounds.

Other parts of his background were mysterious too. The DMH team knew little about his earliest experiences with altered states and treatment, in part because he didn't say much about them. It suspected he might be an unreliable narrator, complicating things further. For instance, he once claimed that his mother was dead—which she most certainly was not.

When Beth tracked down Hugo's mom, she found a parent who was afraid. The woman said Hugo was too erratic to live with, and that multiple family members had received schizophrenia diagnoses. To Beth, that meant Hugo was "screwed from birth." With neither his mother nor his ex in the picture, he now had little contact with anyone beyond his street friends. Beth told him that the only way for him to get better was to stay on medication, but he continued to refuse. Chagrined, she pointed out to me that during his most recent hospitalization, he'd been put on nothing more than the antidepressant Celexa. "That's what *I'm* on!" she exclaimed. "He needs an antipsychotic, not an antidepressant."

Ultimately, Hugo's building's management company got fed up. It threatened to kick him out after he hesitated to pay even his small portion of the subsidized rent. So, to avoid getting an official eviction on his record (which would disrupt his ability to secure other housing), the team persuaded him to move to a new place Downtown. The DMH housing specialist Carlos, Beth, and I helped him pack. As if following Beth's advice, Hugo was off to live in a "shitty building," where his behavior might be better tolerated.

TRANSFORMING TOM BURTON

Upstairs from the Actualization Clinic's main conference room, I inhaled deeply, scanned my body for tension, and filled in a work sheet about my SUDS, or Subjective Units of Distress Scale. Scribbling away on his sheet with great zeal was Tom Burton, a curly haired man in his midtwenties dressed in a blue-checked shirt. We were participating in the dialectical behavioral therapy (DBT) group, me as researcher and him as reluctant but motivated patient. Tom hoped that attending DBT would provide an exit from his current situation. He was living with his father, who required that he attend an Intensive Outpatient Program (IOP) three days a week and regularly meet with the Actualization case management team. His dad doubted his business ideas and hoped he'd rethink his life's direction.

Meanwhile, Tom said he would soon return to his plans to become a Silicon Valley entrepreneur, which had ground to a halt when he experienced mania, then psychosis, then a monthlong hospitalization. He had become convinced that he was seeing humans and artificially intelligent machines melding together—that he was witnessing the "singularity," in tech-speak. More than a few of his futurist friends believed him—before deciding he had lost his mind.

Speaking in the language of DBT, Tom described how the therapy was helping him live harmoniously with his father and make better choices. By "naming and taming" feeling states, he said, he now understood that he could turn immediate *reaction* into purposeful, reflective *action*. Tom's DBT therapist commended his newly "wise" choices as he described the most recent argument at home.

TOM: [In the past] he'd say I was full of shit. I'd say eff you, Dad. But I stayed mindful during the trigger, and he gave me the best advice—I don't have to be an entrepreneur to be happy. I could do other things and be just as happy.

THERAPIST: You're so much more open.

TOM: Yes, more growthful. DBT gave me the skills to *choose.*

ANOTHER GROUP MEMBER: Choose what?

THERAPIST: The choice to remain calm and present. What did "emotional mind" say?

TOM: He's going to judge the last two years of my life.

THERAPIST: You're making assumptions.

TOM: Yes. I felt afraid. Fear and hurt.

THERAPIST: "Rational mind" said what?

TOM: Maybe I should listen to my dad, he pays my bills.

THERAPIST: "Wise mind" is a melding of the emotional and rational.

At least in theory, DBT presented Tom with a new way of conducting himself in relation to his father. Now he had the ability to choose his actions instead of simply reacting emotionally, along with the wisdom of understanding his financial situation with his family. Learning to stay "mindful" through fear and anger could generate new forms of choice.

In a later group, drama therapy, Tom was just as engaged, conceding that he needed to control his grandiosity. The facilitator, a short, energetic Asian American woman with a bright smile, brought out a deck of cards inscribed with archetypes. Our task was to choose cards fitting different aspects of our personality and act out any archetypes that we had been suppressing. Tom chose the warrior and the she-hero. He said that he had traveled India pondering what it meant to be a leader and that he wanted to inspire people. The therapist said that she would role-play his heroic personality and that he should practice speaking to himself from a more practical perspective. She flounced around the room, waving her arms and saying, "I love this energy! I want to help you, you, and you" as she tapped group members on the shoulder.

Then Tom took center stage, waited for the therapist to fall silent, and knowingly told her that she had to become more emotionally grounded. "Why?" she asked. "I love the feeling of all this energy!" He spoke to her, and through her, to himself: "But remember the last time—remember what happened with your girlfriend and job, and relationships with your family?" He told her that only by being more stable could she help people. The drama therapist smiled at this response, and we moved on to the next patient.

Away from the Actualization Clinic, however, Tom stopped using its lingo. He told me he was skeptical of the therapy groups. In his words, he was only there "to appease my investors," by which he meant his parents. They were well off but not wealthy; Tom was one of the rare people whose private insurance was covering both case management and IOP, and he was annoyed by the time suck of it all. As he noted in DBT group, Tom knew he was supposed to listen to his father, who paid the bills. Yet this "leverage" dynamic also grated on him. Like other patients, he chafed at this push and pull, in which family offered or retracted funds or emotional support, contingent on participation in psychiatric treatment.

Adding to his annoyance, Tom didn't believe that his extreme states were pathological. "Steve Jobs was probably bipolar," he told me. He'd begun watching *Bipolar Advantage*, an online guide to thriving with the condition rather than trying to eliminate it. It wasn't that he dismissed the ideas from drama therapy—Tom agreed that he had grown out of control—but he felt that he was being held back. His full potential, it seemed, lay in his extreme states. The only time he really enjoyed the Actualization program was during community-based sessions with the case managers Ian and Zach. They mostly went on hikes and talked about spirituality (not far off from clichés about Silicon Valley whizzes, in fact).

I could understand why Tom didn't see himself as sick. With his intensity and ability to think outside of the box, he had made good use of his privileges in life. He had elite university credentials, a web of high-placed business connections, and plans to develop a technology to deepen meditation practice. He'd been to Hong Kong to learn about manufacturing and to India for spiritual exploration. The world was at his fingertips. As the clinicians took in his story as well as his present state, they had conflicting views on how to help him. Ian, the Buddhist psychologist, drew on tropes from 1970s antipsychiatry to claim it was wrong to pathologize Tom's experiences. Out of earshot of his colleagues, he told me that people like Tom revealed how the larger society is sick. On the other end, Nate, the director of the IOP, was worried when Tom said that he was fed up with "Western medicine." Nate took this as a sign he was about to go off his medications again.

Soon Tom began to consume marijuana, a previous trigger, and indeed stopped his antipsychotic and mood-stabilizing meds while attending an eclipse festival. The Actualization case management team reported that he became psychotic, and although he initially agreed to enter the hospital, he was not allowed to leave. The psychiatrists there initiated a 5250 to keep him for fourteen days, then a *Riese* hearing, the procedure to authorize forced medication (more on these in a bit).

Ian visited the hospital, and then the Actualization team met to discuss whether to seek further legal control. Where the clinical supervisor Deirdre saw the need to clamp down, Ian and Zach drew on a humanistic philosophy about break*down* leading to break*through*.

DDEIRDRE: His mom and I talked about possible conservatorship. We gave the number of our mental health attorney.

IAN: You think a conservatorship is necessary?

DEIRDRE: Yes, for now . . . until he understands that the antipsychotic will be part of his life, he needs to be on an injectable.

IAN: I've never seen anything like [Tom in the hospital]. It was beautiful to behold, actually. I could see it [psychosis] peaking. All the same stuff [from before], with AI [artificial intelligence], the world ending. . . .

ZACH: And he'll learn from it.

DEIRDRE: I wouldn't go there.

ZACH [*pointing to an inspirational quote on the whiteboard*]: "A man's errors are his portal to discovery."

In holistic mental health care, there is a tension between Zach and Ian's psycho-social-spiritual model of psychosis and Deirdre's insistence on the need for antipsychotic medication. For Ian, Tom's psychosis was profound and powerful, and for Zach, the crisis presented an opportunity for learning. Deirdre, however, thought that they must take advantage of this opportunity, with Tom under coercive control, to further revoke his rights and keep him medicated.

After stabilizing on an injection of the antipsychotic Invega, Tom was discharged to Resolve, a private residential psychoanalytic treatment center. Here the staff would try a different form of therapy, working to get to the childhood roots of his experience. Tom had been at Resolve for a few weeks when Nate, the Actualization IOP director, and I toured its facility. One of the therapists noted that Tom was coming to see how his sense of insignificance as a child fed his adult desire for grandiosity. As with Gwen (see chapter 4), who also attended Resolve, the staff was developing a psychodynamic narrative alongside the more practical therapeutic interventions like DBT and cognitive behavioral therapy offered through the Actualization Clinic.

Upon his discharge from Resolve, Tom decided to live in Northern California with his mother. The Actualization team would continue with phone contact but were unsure about how much they could do from afar. Tom planned to go off the injection. Though Deirdre thought that "his mom should have conserved his butt," Ian explained that the hospital staff said the legal order wouldn't have gone through. "He seemed on board and was doing really good [psycho]analytic work on the source of the psychosis," Ian said. "They've got a cool program [at Resolve]." Deirdre remained unconvinced. "How many times does it take?" she asked of obtaining a conservatorship. "It's not enough to be at [elite hospital] for five weeks?" Soon Tom would return to the community, once again able to choose or refuse care.

•   •   •

Despite the significant differences between the Hollywood street youth scene and Silicon Valley, Hugo's and Tom's experiences converge on dilemmas of freedom and choice in mental illness—what clinicians would call noncompliance with treatment. This is clearest regarding medication, which each man intermittently refuses. In Hugo's terms, it's to avoid being "zonked" like a zombie, while Tom hopes to harness the creativity and energy he feels during manic phases. They both also use marijuana, which, legal and common enough in California, can exacerbate psychosis.

The men are periodically coerced in the form of hospitalization, but this is not a long-term "solution." At the DMH, Beth expresses frustration that Hugo was hospitalized briefly and discharged on an antidepressant, and at the Actualization Clinic, Deirdre is upset that they can't secure a conservatorship to keep Tom on the injectable antipsychotic. Both care and control will take place in outpatient rather than hospital settings and will involve choice rather than coercion.

In some sense, the tension between individual choice and group needs, or a person's desires and their supposed best interests, is a story as old as time. The legal empowerment of people with serious psychiatric disabilities, however, is historically novel. Enshrining a *right* to refuse treatment in law and celebrating an ideal of client choice are recent and culturally specific, and we must not take them for granted. Understanding the clinics' actions will require grappling with a final dimension of the history of deinstitutionalization—the changing form of psychiatric power—and the development of highly unequal forms of community care and control.

PSYCHIATRIC POWER AFTER THE CIVIL LIBERTARIAN TURN

During the asylum era, it was within a doctor's professional prerogative to commit a person to a psychiatric hospital or mandate them into treatment, with minimal judicial oversight. Yet after documenting abuses in state hospitals, a coalition of ex-patient activists, advocates, and civil libertarian groups like the ACLU began to agitate for new patients' rights. Beyond the reduction in hospital beds and the question of where treatment would take place, deinstitutionalization fundamentally transformed the question of psychiatric power. The democratic ideals mobilized in the 1960s social movements for racial and gender equality, however, fit more awkwardly with mental health. By shifting the treatment model from coercion under confinement to one of choice in the community, deinstitutionalization initiated a series of new dilemmas surrounding power and freedom that continue to this day.

In 1967, California governor Ronald Reagan signed the Lanterman-Petris-Short Act, which introduced new legal protections for patients into psychiatric commitment procedures. Doctors now had to work more closely with lawyers and judges. The legislation created the famous criteria for emergency holds, namely "danger to self or others" and "grave disability," and it limited those "5150s" to seventy-two hours before a secondary process to apply for extended fourteen-day "5250" holds. Combined with the cuts to hospital infrastructure, the Lanterman-Petris-Short Act drastically reduced long-term hospitalization outside criminal justice cases. It would become model legislation for other states.

The dilemmas of psychiatric power would soon be addressed in the nation's highest court. In the 1975 case *O'Connor v. Donaldson*, the

Supreme Court ruled that a person could no longer be held simply by a "need for treatment" standard, whereby a psychiatrist determined they required care.[1] As the court concluded, "a State cannot constitutionally confine without more [additional justification] a non-dangerous individual who is capable of surviving safely in freedom by himself or with the help of willing and responsible family members or friends." Of course, the precise definition of "non-dangerous" and "surviving safely in freedom" was subject to debate, but it generally became far more difficult to lock people away for more than a few days at a time.

In California, the ability to coerce people to take medication was further transformed by the 1987 case *Riese v. St. Mary's Hospital*, which found that even those who had been temporarily confined under Lanterman-Petris-Short Act 5150 or 5250 holds retained the right to refuse medication.[2] Until then, it had been assumed that a person confined under "danger to self or others" or "gravely disabled" status could be forcibly medicated. Henceforth a "*Riese* hearing" would be required. In practice, and given that many emergency holds lasted only three days, patients were often released without having been forced to take psychiatric medications.

The legal empowerment of patients and the turn to community care profoundly disrupted the form and content of psychiatric authority. Previously, many social theorists had claimed that psychiatry was like an iron fist in a velvet glove, with the gentler side of care inextricably bound to the power to confine. For the philosopher Michel Foucault, asylum psychiatry was in fact a paradigmatic instance of "disciplinary power."[3] This power organized a person's time, movement, and comportment, and it sought to make people into "docile bodies" who would behave appropriately. Foucault traced this marriage of physical segregation and normalization to pioneering seventeenth-century protopsychiatrists like Philippe Pinel, who argued that humanistic engagement with mental illness must be backed up by the threat of more direct repression.[4]

Physical intervention with the confined could take brutal forms. Care and control during the nineteenth and twentieth centuries might include pulling teeth, spinning patients in chairs, extended baths, insulin shock therapy, lobotomy, electroshock therapy, and eventually heavy doses of antipsychotic medications.[5] Each could be imposed for the patient's "own good"—or held out as a potential punishment for those who hesitated to behave.

For those who acted "properly," asylum wardens provided privileges and the possibility of freedom. The English Quakers of the eighteenth century famously induced patients to work in the asylum gardens, socialize with staff, engage in mock dinner parties, and look inward to seek out their own hidden faults. This was no doubt kinder than beatings or pulling someone's teeth out, but for critics like Foucault, this "moral treatment" was itself an insidious exercise of power. Such treatment techniques, once stripped of Quaker dogma, still had an almost religious quality. Foucault wrote, "The asylum is a religious domain without religion, a domain of pure morality, of ethical uniformity."[6] For Foucault and other social critics of the 1960s, the union of physical confinement and psychological and religious normalization—again, all for the patient's "own good"—represented the ultimate form of social control.

This was a plausible if contrarian and countercultural theory of psychiatric control *before* the Lanterman-Petris-Short Act and *before* *O'Connor v. Donaldson* and *Riese v. St. Mary's Hospital.* Yet deinstitutionalization would radically and rapidly transform psychiatric power into something no one had predicted. Within just a few decades, hospitalizations would become brief, emergency affairs and community living de rigeur. Moreover, patients were imbued with the right to refuse any of these treatments. If mental health-care providers could only rarely confine people, force them to take medications, or demand engagement in psychosocial activities, how would psychiatric power operate?

To better understand the consequences of the civil libertarian turn, I must take a bit of a detour to the new institutional spaces into which people were inserted. Since the responsibility for psychiatric patients was transferred from the state to local governments and families, we need to understand trends in the governance of urban poverty and family systems.

GOVERNING BEHAVIOR FOR THE CITY AND THE FAMILY

Punishment and abandonment, not therapeutic management, was the fate of many patients in the community. It was much the same for other marginalized people in the United States, given the country's overarching punitive turn and welfare retrenchment. During the late twentieth century, the nation rolled out hyperpolicing and mass incarceration while policies like welfare reform reduced cash benefits for the poor.[7] These actions were partly due to real rises in crime and perceived problems of benefit dependency, but they also stemmed from politicians who feared looking soft and an ideological turn toward privatization and a more extreme free-market capitalism. The management of urban poverty, social scientists have documented, became a hybrid project, characterized by work requirements (rather than cash disbursement), punitive sanctioning, and "therapeutic policing" to push wayward people toward (scant) social services under threat of arrest. Overwhelmingly harsh jails and welfare cuts were authorized to discipline poor people not through micromanagement but through fear, forcing them into taking up undesirable, low-wage labor.[8]

This new approach to control stripped away any pretenses of rehabilitation and behavioral change for those who would step out of line or threatened to upset the social order of the day. The legal scholars Malcolm Feeley and Jonathan Simon suggest that during this period, the criminal justice system refocused toward affecting overall *rates* of crime by incapacitating people or putting them under supervision via probation.[9] Others noted that prison warehousing served to merely "neutralize" social problems through "punitive containment" rather than any attempt at correction.[10] On the streets, cities policed the homeless, not to reform them, but to disperse them to less visible, more undesirable areas.[11] Emergency services, in some situations, began to merely "burden shuffle" people between different state social service and law enforcement agencies,[12] with some relegated to "zones of social abandonment"—essentially, left to die, out of sight and out of mind.[13]

Of course, there are always dedicated reformers trying to change the status quo, and certain concurrent developments ran counter to such discipline, punitiveness, and abandonment. For instance, in the 2000s federal and municipal governments came to embrace the ideal of the Housing First approach to homelessness, or the provision of subsidized housing without preconditions such as medication compliance or sobriety. The clinical rationale of Housing First is that mental health and addiction needs cannot be addressed without establishing safe, stable housing.[14] In this, the policy echoed the logic of "harm reduction," as seen in needle exchanges and safer-sex initiatives; these assume that people will engage in risky behaviors and need assistance to do so as safely as possible. There was also an economic basis for this shift: homeless people with disabilities, researchers found, were consuming substantial emergency resources, which might be offset by getting them into subsidized apartments.[15] Housing First has served as a counterweight to the harsh bent of urban governance, and such "permanent supportive housing" has become an integral part of new psychiatric policies like California's 2004 Mental Health Services Act. Today, harm reduction is, if only rhetorically in some places, part of the public mental health provider's tool kit.

Like municipal governments, families suddenly tasked with managing disabled relatives after deinstitutionalization had to cope with a new landscape. They had little financial help and could no longer put a family member away or force them to behave. As I've noted, aside from works addressing the family member social movement, there is a paucity of empirical research on patient families as well as on elite private care in the United States. But recall that classical liberals like John Locke argued that "lunaticks" were to forever remain "under the governance of their parents." Following Locke, my solution to approaching this lacuna is to turn to a body of literature that seems quite distant from the asylum, the prison, and the dispersal of the homeless encampment. I look to the literature on child rearing.

The sociologist Annette Lareau's celebrated comparative ethnography of family life offers the clearest account of differential classed logics of parenting in the United States. Working-class and poor families, Lareau finds, engage in an "accomplishment of natural growth" model of parenting, believing that "as long as they provide love, food, and safety, their children will grow and thrive."[16] In these families, children have few structured activities and there is little emphasis on talk. Lareau's middle- and upper-middle-class families, in contrast, engage in a "concerted cultivation," a style of parenting that aims to develop talents and capacity in individual children. This "deliberate and sustained effort to stimulate children's development" requires "organized activities that dominate family life and create enormous labor."[17] The socioeconomically privileged parents use talk as a preferred method of discipline as they attempt to reason with rather than isolate or otherwise punish their children.

Certainly, these parenting styles are partially rooted in the material factors of class; some families can afford to pay for things like violin and karate lessons, while others cannot. Some families have the time to go to and from activities and to talk through disciplinary problems, while others do not. But these styles are also linked to different parenting ideals. Lareau writes that middle-class parents see their children as "projects," while working-class parents think that children should be allowed to pursue their own ends. Lareau argues that the resulting divergent forms of socialization reproduce class advantage through differentially rewarded dispositions—poorer children are endowed with less social capital and lack the cultural tools to navigate middle-class institutions like school, while more privileged children with more parent-driven social capital begin to feel entitled to resources and learn cultural skills for interacting with authority figures, such as doctors and teachers.

The writer Andrew Solomon, exploring the experience of parents with disabled children in his best seller *Far from the Tree*, notes a class-based distinction in the acceptability of difference that can be read as resonant with Lareau. He writes, "People of higher socioeconomic status tend toward perfectionism, and have a harder time living with perceived defects." Similarly, he cites a French study that found "the lower classes show a higher tolerance for severely handicapped children." Indeed, in his interviews with parents, Solomon saw significant differences in how a wealthy white mother and a poor Black mother, both with autistic sons, viewed their situations.

The more privileged woman had spent years futilely trying to make her son better. The less advantaged woman never thought she could make her son better because she'd never been able to make her own life better, and she was not afflicted with feelings of failure. The first woman found it extremely difficult to deal with her son. "He breaks everything," she said unhappily. The other woman had a relatively happy life with her son. "Whatever could be broken got broken a long time ago," she said.[18]

Such findings regarding class and disability fit well with other social scientists' takes on resource opportunities and parenting approaches.

For our purposes, the fact that parenting styles diverge along class lines is relevant for understanding how differently situated clinics might manage disabled adults. The natural-growth approach, pursued by parents who lack the time and resources to invest heavily in child rearing beyond safety and bare needs, may mirror public safety net settings, in which mental health-care providers can offer survival resources but minimal oversight. Concerted cultivation, with its emphasis on scheduling, achievement, highly verbal interactions, and the development of individual talents and interests, might illuminate the logic of clinical care purchased by the affluent family.

Putting this insight into dialogue with the urban social control literature, I began to recognize intriguing parallels unexplored by Lareau and other family scholars. Most important, I noticed the intersection between concerted cultivation, typically viewed as a form of privilege, and the techniques of Foucauldian disciplinary power, often seen as an illegitimate form of social control. Each aims to develop self-efficacious people who can appropriately participate in modern social institutions, and they share such tools as surveillance, the time schedule, and controlled activity. The tools are, however, wielded differently.

Whether as soon-to-be adults or workers in a free market, these systems need people to make free choices—a departure from the idea that power is always oriented toward stunting individuals' freedoms. This is what the sociologist Nikolas Rose calls "governing *through* freedom" rather than governing *over* freedom. These attempts to make people choose correctly are supposed to be subtle, for force may be neither legally feasible nor culturally appropriate. What unites the developments in the governance of urban poverty and family systems is the goal of shaping free and responsible actors who can function autonomously. After deinstitutionalization, psychiatric patients became the responsibility of municipal governments and the family. Understanding those two contexts helps us make sense of the contrasting and sometimes surprising approaches to managing patient freedom in community care today.

OF LOVE AND LIABILITY

Now we can return to Hugo and Tom and the actions taken by their respective psychiatric care teams. The history of patients' rights mobilization and the civil liberties revolution in mental health law explain why neither the DMH nor the Actualization clinics can simply hospitalize a client long term or enforce treatment compliance. Thus, the clinics may try to bargain, leverage behavior, generate habits, or alter the environment such that they can induce the proper choices from people who are legally endowed with freedom. But the choices available to each man are bound to a different and unequal context—what I've earlier called governance projects, ecologies, and a social prognosis with its linked possible future.

Hugo's mental illness is a problem of *urban poverty governance.* He is considered an "issue" in public space because he panhandles and says bizarre things that frighten people, and in housing because he is loud and associates with the "wrong" friends. His best possible future in the care ecology, seen from the perspective of the DMH, is *a life off the institutional circuit.* The challenge is to channel his free behavior in ways that keep him out of jail and off the streets. Contrary to literature that might suggest a punitive or disciplinary approach to managing indigent people with psychiatric disabilities, the public safety net programs engage in what I call *tolerant containment.* It is a spatially specific acceptance of disruptive behaviors, with the goal of preventing eviction, arrest, or troubling of the social order. With few resources for cultivation or constraint, public providers do their best to keep their patients safe, contained, and out of the way while limiting their own legal liability.

Tom's mental illness, on the other hand, is a problem of *family systems governance*. He's been derailed from his successful upper-middle-class life, and now he argues with his father about not just medication but his career. His possible future is *a viable identity* as some sort of respectable person by the standards of his class. The challenge is to guide Tom to harness his drive and talents, to help him see that his interests dovetail with his family's interest in medicating and therapeutically reshaping him. Although a simplistic approach to privilege might assume that the better-off are free to do whatever they like, the whole point of expensive treatment is to shape Tom's available choices and steer him toward making the "right" ones. Akin to Lareau's concerted cultivation of the privileged child, this approach exemplifies *concerted constraint*.

•   •   •

Reorienting analysis from the politics of coercion to the politics of unequal choices helps us avoid overly reductive discussions of psychiatric power. Instead of asking whether a specific intervention represents care versus control, or whether an individual's decision is freely made versus coerced, we can investigate subtler questions. What kind of choices do the authorities hope to elicit—and to what end? How do unequal circumstances impact the range of choices they can offer to clients? Are mental health-care providers trying to pattern everyday life or manage periodic emergencies—and do their interventions target thoughts, physical actions, feelings, habits, or something else entirely?

In the following chapters, we will see these unequal forms of client choice at work across a range of puzzling situations. You will learn why workers at the DMH clinic instruct a person to choose crack cocaine instead of methamphetamine; why undocumented immigrant neighbors who are scared to call the police may become an unanticipated asset; and why Board and Care operators liken the drudgery of flop-house life to a vacation in the Catskills. You will also learn why elite providers think rich people with trust funds are especially hard to control; why some private residential programs insist on work and pastoral activities; and why a success story at the DMH could be one of failure for the Actualization Clinic.

These findings bring a provocative new perspective to older theo-ries of psychiatric power. For instance, recall Michel Foucault's claim that an intensive care regime like the Quakers' "moral treatment" was a form of domination. Perhaps, in a resource-poor context, the county DMH's tolerant containment and minimal intervention represent a kind of liberation. And perhaps, disciplinary power, manifested as concerted constraint, is now a privilege available only to the rich.

CHAPTER 8

TOLERANT CONTAINMENT

Officials in places like Downtown Los Angeles have long managed "problem people" by incarcerating them in jails, sticking them in bare-bones shelters, or simply banishing them from the area. More tolerant approaches have recently emerged, however, as last-ditch attempts at pragmatic problem solving. Since formerly homeless psychiatric clients' needs and accumulated traumas drastically outpace the public safety net's capacity for care, and because harsh treatment or policing often exacerbates problems, clinicians learn to focus on generalized harm reduction. Their primary goal is spatial containment in tolerant settings to help prevent arrest, avoid eviction, and appease the genteel public. This approach means radically lowering behavioral expectations and accepting problematic choices—so long as patients remain out of the way.

Recall that the Los Angeles County Department of Mental Health works in a project of *urban poverty governance* to create a client's possible future of *a life off the institutional circuit*. Operating within the civil libertarian legacy of deinstitutionalization and laws that limit the use of force, the trick is to somehow manage clients' strange or even chaotic behavior without hospitalization or incarceration, and all with minimal resources. The result, which sees mental health-care providers bringing people into independent apartments and low-demand flophouses, is what I call *tolerant containment*.

Ironically, the outcome is that disadvantaged clients, imbued as they are with legal rights, are now allowed to express their civil liberties and act in ways that violate mainstream cultural standards. Laura, the DMH team leader, once described an alcoholic patient who had moved into an independent apartment with a smile, a shrug, and the assurance that "he's still housed, still drinking, and still defying gravity!"

Tolerant containment can facilitate trust and provide the dignity of self-determination. It can also become neglect veiled in the language of freedom.

HOUSING AS A PSYCHIATRIC INTERVENTION

My fieldwork with the DMH case management team came during a large-scale shift in the ethos of housing, medication, and harm reduction in Los Angeles County (and nationwide). Both local policy rhetoric and research reports on Full Service Partnership intensive outpatient treatment teams describe their practices as an adaptation of the Housing First model to address homelessness.[1] As explained earlier, this philosophy does not require that people be "housing ready" in terms of sobriety and psychiatric compliance, but it does suggest that housing is itself a precondition for addressing mental health and addiction needs. People who in the past would never have had such a chance may now be provided with independent apartments and minimal oversight.

Although ostensibly a homelessness intervention, Housing First began as a psychiatric engagement technique during the post-deinstitutionalization period. This idea was hatched when the community psychologist Sam Tsemberis struggled to engage "treatment-resistant" patients on the streets of New York City.[2] His approach, codified in the 1990s as the Pathways to Housing model, was to get people apartments with Section 8 housing vouchers and *then* deliver wraparound social services to ensure they succeeded in staying housed. Even when the program became a "representative payee" and controlled a person's disability check, it would distribute cash to the patient without treatment demands. It understood that people might purchase drugs, a fact that marked Pathways to Housing as part of the harm-reduction movement.

In Downtown Los Angeles, harm reduction was hardly a foreign concept. As Laura put it, "This is Skid Row—who are you kidding?" If the DMH staff only assisted people who were sober or medication compliant, the way that some shelters and programs required, it would never be able to engage its targeted clientele. The new national focus on Housing First cohered with this existing approach as well as the "whatever it takes" attitude of the state Mental Health Services Act.

In practice, LA County could hardly offer everyone an apartment. The scale of the housing and homelessness crises is simply too broad. Thus, I observed a mix of rapid housing in subsidized apartments, refurbished single-room-occupancy hotels, and older parts of the mental health housing ecology, such as Board and Care homes and specialty shelters. Carlos, the DMH housing specialist, once told me that since there were never enough vouchers, and people sometimes left or got evicted from their apartment, less than half the clients at any given time were situated in permanent supportive housing. When space was available, however, these apartments offered a way for clinicians and street-level homeless outreach workers to connect with people who otherwise refused conventional engagement.

"YOU HAVE TO SIT BACK . . . UNTIL SOMETHING BAD HAPPENS"

It frustrated the DMH psychiatrist Dr. Wong that little was to be done paternalistically until a person crossed that line of "danger to self or others." "Gone are the days where we tie them [mental patients] to a post and beat them. . . . But now we're too far over to the other side, the pendulum swung over," Wong declared. "Now they're saying my job is to educate a person about their mental illness, and their options, and you have to sit back and hope that the person chooses the right choice. . . . Until something bad happens." Even when the team tried to hospitalize people, voluntarily or involuntarily, it was prepared for a rapid release. Holds—if they held—rarely lasted more than seventy-two hours; often the emergency room wouldn't even admit the patient, let alone set up a plan for a longer-term hospital bed.

Ironically, the combined realities of resource constraints and patients' rights laws meant that treatment was all or nothing, leading to eventual coercion that was particularly brutal. Poor people in psychosis were essentially left alone until things got so bad that clinicians saw no option but a chemical straitjacket. Laura once speculated that some clients refused meds because their introductory experience of them was during a chaotic emergency, and a hospital doctor had "punched them in the face" with a heavy dose of injectable antipsychotics (which, of course, come with side effects). We could imagine an alternative world in which clients had access to early, high-quality community care that stabilized with psychosocial interventions and offered lowest-effective medication dosing. Instead, many DMH clients live in a world with a lot of already burned bridges. For them to consider medication treatment, a long trust-building process would be necessary.

Constrained by the system and unable to take his preferred paternalistic route, Dr. Wong saw the appeal of working backward by utilizing Housing First—helping people feel safe and comfortable so that they might try treatment: "As an old-timer, as a meat and potatoes psychiatrist who believes in hospitalization and making sure the clients take their medications, how do we address that issue if they don't want to take that medication? They continue to live on the streets. Perhaps they're happy getting subsidized housing right now, and so, 'Now, I want medications.' You have to slowly talk to them about that." Even within the DMH, tensions arose concerning whether all this was, in fact, "enablement." As a DMH addiction psychiatrist told me, "I've learned the wisdom of harm reduction, because housing gives people a chance. But I don't see the wisdom of enabling people and not kicking them out when they're smoking crack and messing with their neighbors." For this clinician, the most practical issue I could address with my research was to figure out what community treatment teams like DMH's should do when the Housing First approach *didn't* lead to clinical improvement.

In theory, housing could provide a basis for clinical improvement, but in practice its important but limited function was just getting clients off the institutional circuit.[3] Some people do well—what I'll describe as the incidental accomplishment of natural growth—but others only moved their problem behaviors inside, prompting the treatment team to focus on mitigation—the sometimes Sisyphean task of appeasing landlords and neighbors and preventing eviction. There was nothing else to be done, and at least housing provided safety, a locked door.

I saw this practical logic come to the fore in a debate between Laura and a licensed practical nurse. The nurse was complaining about people recently outreached and housed from a targeted encampment. With dismay she asked, "We know they were sick—why did we put them in these apartments?" She described her latest contact with a woman who glared menacingly and intentionally broke the key off in the door lock so that no one could get in. Laura responded, "They were this way on the street. At least [now] they are safe. People like them are not gonna do what we want. But what can we do? These are the behaviors that kept them in the streets."

Notice the disjuncture between the nurse's suggestion that people who are "sick" do not belong in independent living and Laura's high tolerance of the woman's behavior. With the awareness that such clients won't "do what we want," Laura prioritizes the basic *safety* that comes with a locked door. Here the clinician's aim of keeping these people away from the dangers of street life dovetails with the community's need to bring the most disruptive homeless people out of public sight. Once they have been neutralized as a problem of visible disorder, their behaviors could be tolerated unless they reached the point of "danger."

REDIRECTING BEHAVIORS TO PREVENT EVICTION

When a person was symptomatic, seemed to replicate elements of their former street life, or was relatively stable and safe yet disruptive to the broader public, the DMH case management team worked to redirect their problematic behaviors. Frequently, this involved responding to landlords inclined to evict. Sandy is emblematic of those whose apparent symptoms and deviant behavior were not eliminated but creatively redirected. A middle-aged white client, she had been found on the streets and placed in a women's center before coming to the treatment team. DMH staff members secured her an apartment, though she was disturbing her neighbors—diagnosed with schizophrenia and cognitive issues, she refused medication and repetitively banged her head against the wall.

I accompanied Beth, the social worker, to Sandy's new apartment, just outside Downtown. Her building manager had called to say that a neighbor who shared a wall with Sandy was complaining about the head-banging. We also had to check that she was keeping her unit clean. DMH workers believed that landlords sometimes generated or embellished accusations to evict undesirable tenants, but they took this building manager at her word.

"First the positives," Beth said over the sounds of a small TV playing the teen vampire flick *Twilight*. "It's good to see you, and I'm glad you are alive." Bags and trash from takeout food had been piled in the center of the room. Beth took a whiff and told Sandy to open a window. Then she explained how Sandy could stay in the building. She needed to bang her head on the *other* wall, the one facing the street, and clean the apartment more. Doing these things would lessen the noise for the complaining neighbor and, she hoped, satisfy the building manager. Otherwise, Sandy might have to move. "You can choose to live like this, but not in this building," Beth said. "We might need to find you a dirtier building."

Rather than seek the internalization of norms through therapy or attempt to fully eliminate problem behaviors, tolerant containment involves redirecting those behaviors to minimize the harm to clientele, the nuisance to the public, and the chances that the patient would become unhoused again. The team's creative plan honored Sandy's compulsion, and caseworkers came to believe that the building manager was exaggerating her troublemaking. Even so, they worried that an eviction was imminent. As with Hugo in chapter 7, Sandy liked her neighborhood, but an eviction could jeopardize her housing access in the future. So, the team persuaded her to move to a "dirtier building" Downtown. It appeared that tolerant containment was only possible in certain areas—those with the adequately permissive form of social order.

PREPARING FOR "GRACEFUL EXITS"

Samuel, a social worker filling in as team leader while Laura was on maternity leave, was ambivalent about the Housing First approach.

> Some clients are—Housing First model is perfect for you. You stick them in, you get them the rest of the resources and move forward.
>
> [But] a lot of clients are not ready to be in housing. I don't think that's something we like to admit, that "he's really not ready to be in a place." If you've seen some of the units that we've seen, you'll realize [that] "we knew he wasn't ready for this." Or, this person really needed to be in inpatient care. He's got trash stacked up high to the doors. We see a lot of that stuff. The staff, if you talk to us, we go back and forth on the Housing First model. Because we get to see the other side of when you put into housing and they're getting evicted.

But Samuel also took pride in honoring clients' wishes and giving them a chance to try independent living.

> Here's the funny thing. If a client tells us they wanna be in permanent housing, we will do it. At the end of the day, we will do it. Even if we don't think it's—we will do it. Try to give them the support that they need and hope for the best. We still end up doing it, because that's what the client really wants. We try to provide that support and the help to be successful. We're trying to figure out a graceful exit so that they don't get an eviction.

Those "graceful exits," the moves from outlying neighborhoods to chaos-friendly buildings Downtown, kept the possibility of other stable housing alive.

IDLE BODIES IN THE BOARD AND CARE

There are, in essence, two types of order that the DMH case management team can produce, linked to two types of people. Some people will continue to be bizarre, noncompliant (i.e., resisting conventional medication treatment), and drug using, and they can be contained to some degree in permanent housing, should vouchers be available. Another group will be contained in Board and Care homes, if they can get along with other people to a minimal degree.

The pace of the Snow Lodge, a Board and Care facility in Northeast LA, is slower than the city's hustle and bustle. In contrast to some of the dungeon-like institutional homes, this one consists of a series of small bungalows arranged around a grassy area. On this day, four DMH clients ambled into the facility's cafeteria, where Beth asked each of them to describe what had happened to them in the past week.

A young Latino man said that his thirty-first birthday was coming up, and he wanted to spend time with his aunt and relatives. We all wished him a happy birthday. Smiling, he replied, "I just want to thank the staff, because if they hadn't come gotten me, I would still be on the street or the mission, all dirty. So, thanks to you guys." Next, Beth asked a woman about her new earrings. She replied that she got them from a "friend," and someone teased, "Su novio?" Everyone laughed, but she insisted it was not a boyfriend—"No, just a friend."

A middle-aged Black woman reported taking a van to another program but said there was "nothing to do there." Beth, looking concerned, asked, "You mean, like, it's not fun, or really there's nothing?" The woman responded that there's "no production." Rather than receiving any therapeutic day services, the woman said that the clients just went to sit in a nearly empty room. Beth and I speculated that perhaps this program was fraudulently charging Medicaid for services, but the cafeteria was beginning to serve lunch, so Beth wrapped up the weekly check-in.

Only minimal structure is imposed in a Board and Care home. Most people's lives, like these clients', consist of walking or sitting around, chatting, maybe hoping to visit some family. There is very little to the daily routine beyond medication dispensation and meals. With all the time in the world—and none of the money—residents seem to live out their days in boredom and idleness.

THE ONCE-PROFITABLE TRADE IN LUNACY

Funded by residents' Supplemental Security Income (SSI) checks and minor subsidies from the county, Board and Care homes do provide a shared room, food, and basic medication management. I observed facilities that ranged from hideous institutional structures to mom-and-pop household operations, with varying degrees of warmth demonstrated by the staff. Clients shared with me a diversity of opinions on their situations. Some liked the easy pace of life. Others hated the boredom and dismal conditions. From a tolerant containment perspective, the key feature of Board and Care homes is that they are so minimal in staffing and activities as to offer residents a kind of de facto freedom.

This system of private, for-profit housing arose in the wake of deinstitutionalization and represented what the sociologist Andrew Scull called a "new trade in lunacy."[4] Yet unlike the old trade in lunacy catering to the wealthy families of eighteenth-century England, or the elite, private treatment in contemporary West Los Angeles, the Board and Care business model was based on volume. The only way to generate profit with these poor residents was to keep costs as low as possible, eliminating unnecessary services, and that had been the approach from the get-go.

In other words, the residents' "choice" to do nothing was built into the homes. Responding to a critical report entitled "From Asylum to Ghetto,"[5] Christopher Smith, one defender of deinstitutionalization in 1975 equated the nonrehabilitative Board and Care home with freedom: "It is possible that living in the 'ghetto' . . . may not actually be

disastrous. . . . For the mentally ill, living in a place which has no normative community expectations may prove to be satisfactory—it may
allow the individual to live as he or she chooses. It is by no means clear
that we all have similar needs for community, and a 'low-key setting
may prove conducive to recuperation.'"[6]

Note the emphasis on *living as one chooses* and on the idea that
not all people have a need for community. Apparently earnest senti-
ments written against the backdrop of fears of oppressive psychiatric services, these can be read charitably: idle, undirected time, such
accounts claim, is actually a bulwark against "normative community
expectations." Read cynically, these same statements justify neglecting
people en masse.

Ethnographic research during the deinstitutionalization period
showed that even if Board and Care homes aimed to provide real rehabilitative services, their economic model put that goal out of reach. In
a 1981 examination of the business, the sociologist Robert Emerson
and collaborators were matter of fact: "The SSI-derived economic
base of the current board and care system fails to encourage rehabilitation, and in fact offers a number of disincentives to this end. This
funding procedure generates strong pressures toward minimizing
costs; treatment programs and services are expensive, and are only
rarely provided in board and care."[7] In the simple terms of money in
and money out, it made little sense for Board and Care operators to
invest in transforming their residents, only ensuring a kind of basic,
general order. And as the system became decreasingly profitable over
time, the minimal behavioral regulation has thinned. SSI payments
in the past forty years or so have not kept up with increases in cost of
living, especially in Southern California.

Mr. Daniels, the owner of two Board and Care homes and licensing
consultant to the elite ecology, whom we met in chapter 3, explained
that most homes could barely pay their staff. Since the 2010s, these
operations had been at risk of shutting down, he said, and the county
began recognizing even flophouses as a valuable housing resource.
Costs were always rising, but the federal checks that supported residents and housing operators alike never kept pace with inflation.

You have to see it in its historical component. Five years ago, the average resident here who is an SSI client . . . was paying per month $1,003 per month. It works out to about 30 bucks a day. Today, that SSI is paying $1,050 a month. Without doing it cumulatively, a straight-line percentage increase, about 5 percent increase. So we have been receiving 5 percent more per person. Five years ago, just on matter of payroll, minimum wage was $9 an hour. As of July 1, because we have leeway, less than twenty-five employees, it's $13.25. How much is that? How much is $13.25 over $9? 35 percent!

Spitting out that last figure, Mr. Daniels was clearly bitter. He had spiking costs but nearly static revenue. To those who accused him of providing bad services, he challenged, what else could he do?

That discrepancy between a 5 percent increase in income versus a 35 percent increase in staff costs and the remarkably low figure of $1,050 received in SSI funding meant to house and feed one person for one month in Los Angeles should help explain why Board and Cares don't keep their residents busy or monitor them, let alone offer therapies. Ironically, this amplifies the freedom from surveillance experienced by residents in these implicit flophouses compared with the expensive private facilities that oversee their rich clients minute by minute.

DE FACTO HARM REDUCTION

Board and Cares are restrictive settings, with behavioral regulations, requirements to take medication, and bans on drug and alcohol use. Yet rules mean little when there's no one there to enforce them. This became clear to me in conversation with a pair of residents in one of Mr. Daniels's Board and Cares. It was after midnight in the entrance of the building, located near an upscale shopping district, and one man was rolling a joint. I'd heard of places that had nighttime curfews, but this one didn't seem to have any of the staff watching; I'd seen marijuana in my research subject's room, but I was surprised to see someone openly lighting up. When I asked whether anyone felt the need to hide such activity, he stated, "Well, people hide to smoke meth. But not pot." After all, weed was legal in California.

The scene returned to my mind when Mr. Daniels answered my questions about drug and alcohol use. "Now, do we have rules that say you're not supposed to be drinking? Yeah. So? I don't have a guard standing in front of each room twenty-four hours a day, smelling if they smell any alcohol on anybody's breath. Not possible." He tried to screen out heavy drug users at intake, but he was a realist. Drug use was a consistent part of life at his residences, and though he had kicked people out for serious behavioral infractions (attacking another person, major property destruction), he hadn't turned anyone out for drug use or drinking alone. In fact, he said he could understand why people turned to drugs.

Describing a former resident as "a quiet meth user," a "nice guy, a veteran" who managed to use the drug in his room without being destructive, Mr. Daniels explained the leeway he offered. Residents didn't have much to look forward to, he pointed out, trying to get me to appreciate his perspective.

> Imagine in your own life, you're young in your twenties to thirties, and in school, I don't know. And then you have a serious break. Whether it's hormonal, or it's a traumatic family problem, whatever it happens to be. And you find yourself thirty-five, forty, forty-five, asking, "What the hell happened? I'm sort of either couch surfing, or on the street, and my life wasn't supposed to be like this." . . . [The quiet meth user] said, "So this meth gives, I get out of body, out of my mind, out of my life, and it gives me that momentary high, that whatever it is. What do I have in my life? Look! Look!" And I felt so bad. Because . . . it's true.

Sympathetic and understaffed, he tolerated the veteran's drug behavior until the man distributed meth to other residents. Then Mr. Daniels threatened eviction, and the VA relocated the man.

This is a de facto harm-reduction model that is at odds with the formal rules of the residence. It's not the logic of the needle exchange program for disease prevention or Housing First for a safe start to recovery from addiction and/or mental illness. It's tolerance for problematic behaviors—a default, because there's not much else to be done. Mr. Daniels offers empathy, but it's not a therapeutic encounter. Feeling for the man's plight, Mr. Daniels allows him to use meth in the building.

THE FREEDOM OF IDLENESS

The Board and Cares I observed didn't really expect anything from their residents. Echoing that 1975 report by Christopher Smith, Mr. Daniels maintained that people in his facilities truly chose to sit around. He said that his staff would arrange for a walk after lunch and a social hour or arts and crafts program, yet only four or five of their eighty residents would show up for those activities. To him, people just wanted to do nothing. Unlike a facility that required its residents to participate in treatment or meetings, he likened the Board and Care life to retirement. To illustrate, he drew an analogy from his time as a waiter in a resort town.

> You ever hear of the Catskill Mountains? . . . When I was a teen and early college, I use to work there during the summer and make good money. One of the things that you'd notice about people, they would wake up in the morning, go to breakfast, sit on the veranda, take a little rowboat out on the lake, come back lunch, take a nap, take a walk, come back for cocktails, for dinner. They're happy! "Leave me alone, that's what I paid for!" So, you have many of the people [in the Board and Care], [their] affect is flat. I'm not happy, or I'm not aware, I'm not sad.

There are a few ways to interpret Mr. Daniels's comparison. As with Smith's 1975 report, the generous reading is that he respects people's freedom to choose what they do with their days—whether in the Catskills or a Board and Care home, they could choose to wander about aimlessly from morning 'til night.

The less charitable read is to note that people living in a Board and

Care aren't afforded access to rowboats and cocktail hours and bucolic hikes. They get little more than a weekly game of bingo and hours upon hours to wander urban landscapes, penniless. Maybe if the programming was better, maybe if people weren't lethargic from medication, struggling with symptoms, or experiencing the situational depression of a life with no opportunities, maybe then they'd participate. But framing *doing nothing* as a personal choice is stretching the idea of choice.

Despite affable operators like Mr. Daniels, I found Board and Cares almost universally awful. Some DMH clients did everything in their power to get out, as with one woman who moved from a Board and Care into a market-rate Skid Row studio without a Section 8 housing voucher. This meant that she would have to spend all her disability money on rent and go to food banks to try and access enough to eat. That was how much she hated the Board and Care system.

Still, some DMH clients claimed that they were truly happy with their life there. Bernardo, in his late thirties, told me he "loved" the one he'd been living at for nine years. "It's too much hassle cooking and cleaning [in an apartment]." He'd also had to do those chores when living with his family. "I'm very happy [here]," he said. "They do everything for us." Unlike facilities that pushed people to learn new skills, his home had few expectations. The schedule included med dispensing, meals, and a weekly arts and crafts activity. Bernardo used to smoke pot with the small leftover from his SSI check, but he decided he'd rather save his money. Violating curfew, he'd leave the building when he wanted, visiting his aunt for a few days at a time. It was as if Bernardo had already achieved the future that DMH programs envision for the poor: life off the streets, out of jail, and without causing trouble.

Once I asked Mr. Daniels what kind of care services he might provide if he had a larger "patch" of supplemental funding from the county. Here he offered the structural, economic explanation of the Board and Care model as its sole purpose. He implied that I was misunderstanding the model if I thought that the goal was rehabilitation or occupying people's time. The goal was housing people and keeping them out of expensive hospitals, period. "If we got more money in the patch, I believe we could do some more," he acknowledged. "But what is it you want us to do? Do you want us—you know the economics of this thing. One of the reasons why we exist, and I don't mean just us, is so that people are not burdening Medi-Cal [California's Medicaid system] and therefore the state and their budget, by being in the hospital . . . so even that from a fiscal point of view, we're really providing a service!" Mr. Daniels's pivot helps us see Board and Care homes for what they are: a private, for-profit component of an urban poverty governance project to keep mentally ill people off the street and out of expensive institutions that drain county or state coffers. In this view, someone like Bernardo was an unequivocal success story.

Perhaps there was therapeutic normalization of residents' behavior in earlier iterations of Board and Care, but it is minimal today. Low staffing leads to lack of rule enforcement. Residents are neglected until in crisis, even if their behaviors impede fellow residents' recoveries. Where the lack of a schedule might be empowering under some circumstances, for the poor and disabled, for those who aren't oriented to their own life projects, this unstructured time can seem endless. Here there is a freedom to be a particular kind of public mental patient: a medicated lump who sits inside and stares at the wall, a person who wanders the streets during the day and comes back for meals, or a "quiet" drug user who manages to just barely avoid eviction.

.   .   .

So what happens when a person *isn't* able to become a quiet lump? In the rest of the chapter, I'll offer three variations on how tolerant containment works (and doesn't work) through a series of middle-aged clients who have already cycled through the institutional circuit. First is Janey, a formerly incarcerated, crack-addicted sex worker who drastically reduces her drug use once housed. Her case shows how safety and repeated connection with the DMH staff can indeed lead to natural growth, if of a limited kind. Then I introduce Lola, an aggressive, formerly homeless woman who menaces her undocumented neighbors. Here we learn how tolerance may come at the cost of great difficulties for other vulnerable people. And third we meet Bobby, a white man who continues to be hospitalized and arrested repeatedly, as well as Roxanne, an African American woman who drinks herself to death in her apartment—such cases vividly show how people continue to slip through the cracks.

THE INCIDENTAL ACCOMPLISHMENT OF NATURAL GROWTH

Sometimes tolerant containment works: people who finally receive safety and stability begin to improve clinically. Recall that the corollary to Annette Lareau's concept of "concerted cultivation" in the privileged classes is an "accomplishment of natural growth" model of parenting for the poorer child. Low-income families offer safety and love and assume their children will develop, in part because there aren't resources to invest in anything else. Tolerant containment echoes this process, though the expectations of development are far more limited. The DMH is treating adult clients who present with significant mental illness, trauma, and street habits. Although mental health-care providers certainly hope for clinical improvements or drug use reduction, such natural growth is often secondary and incidental to the focus on maintaining safe housing.

Janey Talbot, an African American woman in her early fifties, had begun mental health care during a recent prison stint. She'd spent much of her adult life as a criminalized, intermittently homeless, drug-using sex worker. Though she'd done time in both jail and prison, she wasn't identified, diagnosed as having schizophrenia, and rebranded a *patient* until this late stage of life. In this success story, housing facilitates lessened drug use and reconnection with family.

MISSED OPPORTUNITIES

As we sat in her one-bedroom apartment, Janey reread her childhood through the diagnoses and treatment she *didn't* get. From Mississippi, her family moved to California when she was five and raised her in the LA housing projects. As a child, she recalled, she struggled to look people in the eye or speak. A television commercial later introduced her to the idea of autism. "It's not retarded, but that's what I thought it was," she explained. "That little boy [in the commercial] couldn't talk, didn't want to see no light. . . . Anyway, that's how I was when I was young until I become a prostitute. Couldn't talk to people, just smiled every time. If they asked me a question, I just said, 'Mmm hmm.'" I asked whether Janey meant autism, and she said, "That's it!"

At age fifteen, Janey became pregnant and went to continuation school. Her baby died eight days after birth, and Janey never graduated. At eighteen, she began selling sex and cycling in and out of jail. Later she would have three children, all raised by her mother. Janey briefly worked in the aboveground economy, but by the time she reached her early thirties she had become addicted to crack and was living off her sex work on the streets of Downtown. She described a life of instability, always paying for her hotel room by the day to avoid risking the money she put down. "I couldn't pay by the month, 'cause I didn't know when I'd go to jail."

This went on for nearly twenty years, throughout which Janey often heard a mysterious man's voice. He's "a snake," she told me. "I think he's Satan." She couldn't recall the precise details of her trajectory, but it wasn't jail staff who connected her to psychiatric help. It was a friend on the street who offered Janey money if she would seek services. "A friend of mine, he told me, 'I'll give you $20 if you go down there and sign the paperwork.' I said okay, they took me up to Maple [a DMH walk-in clinic]. There they said, 'I gotta call your parole officer,' and I said, "I ain't goin' to jail for you!" . . . Then I went back, and he gives me a worker, and I tell her, "I need housing, I need housing, I need housing." And she referred me to Full Service [Partnership]." Janey's journey to an independent apartment had finally begun.

"LIKE GETTING ANGRY AT A SCORPION"

Janey still smoked crack multiple times a day, a fact that complicated some housing situations. Carlos at the DMH got her an individual room in the Weingarten, for instance, but she was ejected

when employees discovered her crack pipe. The LAMP Community
(formerly the Los Angeles Men's Place), on the other hand, was a nonprofit homeless center that took a harm-reduction approach to drug
usage, so Janey stayed there for six months until her housing voucher
finally came through.

Janey's lease signing was the stuff of legend among the DMH
workers. Carlos shared that he and Kevin, the psychiatric technician, had taken her to meet with Mr. Jong, a Koreatown landlord who
was accommodating toward DMH clients. When Mr. Jong turned
his back, though, Janey reportedly tried to punch Kevin in the head.
Carlos commented, "We were literally signing the lease. And something agitated her. I can't say what happened, you hear me? She did
a left hook, like. And almost landed. How 'bout that? I don't know.
Would we have continued with the signing of the lease at that point?"

The blow didn't connect, however, and Mr. Jong hadn't witnessed
the attack. So, upon securing the paperwork, the trio rushed out before
the landlord could change his mind. When I asked Kevin about the situation, he just shrugged. "It'd be like getting angry at a scorpion that's
trying to sting you." In other words, he didn't hold Janey accountable
for her actions that day, because she lacked any self-control.

I was struck by both the animalistic metaphor and Kevin's non-
chalant delivery. If I hadn't spent more time with him, I might have
read this comment—in which a white man likened a Black woman to
a nonhuman creature—as racist condescension. But I saw how Kevin's
metaphor was about his ability to tolerate an attack, relieve Janey of
blame, and ensure that she got her housing. He may not ever get to
know or appreciate Janey's full humanity, but there was a kind of care
in his dehumanizing remark.

Further, I understood that like other paraprofessionals at the DMH,
Kevin's task was not deep engagement with a multifaceted human
being. His work disposition was likely shaped by his experiences as
a psychiatric technician in penal settings, where his job consisted of
delivering medication injections to people he thought were beyond
transformation. He was no therapist, and although the scorpion metaphor was unflattering, his mind-set gave him a way to move forward,

justifying the work to secure independent housing for a person with a serious crack addiction and violent outbursts.

HITTING THE PIPE RECREATIONALLY,
NOT PROFESSIONALLY

Illustrative of tolerant containment's success, Janey surprised the DMH staff by reducing her crack intake to once a week. In the past, she'd smoked crack "all day. All night. I'd sit there, get me the money, and spend it." Now, with her own place and things to do, she reduced on her own. Housing and safety seemed to have worked like magic. I asked Janey whether she remembered what had changed for her.

"Well, now I can sit here and watch TV, and in the other one [temporary housing] I didn't even watch TV. When I was in jail, I don't watch TV."

I followed up: "So now you have a place to be and something to do, and you don't feel the need to smoke as much crack?"

"Yeah, that's right, that's it, that's it," she agreed.

Even without an explicit plan to help her decrease drug use, the stability of housing facilitated Janey's natural growth. It even led to her reconnecting with family. The case manager Marla helped track down contact information, and Janey asked Carlos to be by her side and dial the number for her. Carlos imagined what Janey's mother had told the children: "Now, what do you say when you're talking to the kids about her? She was a crack addict? A crack whore? Crazy?" He noted that some families rejected their prodigal relative—it was a risk phoning Janey's out of the blue.

Yet Janey's family was excited to bring her back into the fold. She had an emotionally satisfying reconnection with her mother, who then put her in touch with her kids. Carlos attributed her newfound interest in seeing a primary care physician to this family love. In contrast to her previous self-destructive habits and low regard for the future, he had come to believe that Janey was "trying to stay around awhile."

Though a significant transformation, Janey's journey was still a limited one. As Carlos put it with a grin, "Janey still hits the pipe, but recreationally. Not professionally anymore, twenty times a day!" His tone wasn't mocking but instead suggested a regard for her growth and his expectations for what's possible for her. After all, his and Kevin's intervention had been limited too. They tolerated Janey's crack smoking and punches, managing to get her into safe housing. From then on, Carlos, a college dropout with no therapeutic training, simply checked up on her regularly. This wasn't intensive treatment, but Janey attributed her newfound communication abilities to Carlos's consistent presence in her life.

When I asked her whether there was any way she'd improve the DMH team, Janey had no suggestions. "Nothing. Stay the same. They're great to me. It was hard for me to talk to anybody. But now I can." The only thing she wanted was for Carlos to help her get a new refrigerator. Her freezer didn't stay cold and "wouldn't hold no ice cream."

THE VICTIMS OF TOLERANCE

In some cases of tolerant containment, people are moved around several times before finding a reasonable fit with their housing. Unfortunately, the only neighbors who will put up with an extremely difficult person might be those at the bottom of the social hierarchy, since they believe they have no other recourse. Here the agreement between DMH, client, and landlord creates spillover consequences for others outside the transaction—what economists would call a negative externality. Put less academically, successfully housing some clients in the community can be to the detriment of other vulnerable people.

Lola, a Salvadorean woman in her forties with thick, curly hair that reached her shoulders, bounced between placements before landing in a building that seemed to accept her explosive anger. Diagnosed with schizophrenia but refusing treatment that might subdue her outbursts, she'd lived five years on the street and knew she could survive there if she had to do it again.

As we sat in the clinic accompanied by Lola's young adult daughter,

I listened to a life story marked by instability. Lola's father had sent her at age sixteen to the United States to escape the civil war in El Salvador. An older sister who was already established in Los Angeles agreed to take her in, and Lola worked as a babysitter and elder-care provider through her twenties. She became pregnant, but the baby's father didn't stick around. Without their own place, Lola and her daughter had to stay with various relatives for short stints. Throughout, Lola explained, there were times when she would get very angry and, unable to control her behavior, be hospitalized.

The DMH outreach team visited Lola in Exposition Park, where she'd been living since her brother-in-law kicked her out. By her account, she had befriended workers in an adjacent café, washed herself in the restroom, and surprised other homeless people, who felt she was too clean to actually be living on the streets. In her memory, things had been going alright. But the DMH team members recount a different scene. Carlos said that Lola yelled and threw feces at him when they first met near the Rose Garden. Stationing herself outside a politician's office, she had been causing enough trouble to be singled out for mental health services. And though she wasn't interested in psychiatric care, she told the team she wanted help with getting off the street. They soon secured her a Section 8 voucher and moved her into an apartment.

BENEVOLENT SLUMLORDS

A Korean immigrant, Mr. Kwan (much like Janey's landlord, Mr. Jong) was hoping to ascend the class ladder by renting out apartment units to the county. He liked DMH clients like Lola, because their Section 8 vouchers assured payment via federal subsidies, and the treatment team promised to assist if their renters became too difficult. So no one was surprised when Lola got into conflict with her neighbors over the shared backyard garden space. Supposedly, she had cut down someone else's tree, and so Kevin, the psychiatric technician, and Beth, the social worker, invited me to go along on their visit. They wondered whether they might need to hospitalize Lola.

Standing in her unit, Mr. Kwan said that he didn't want to evict her. He had asked Lola to stay away from the backyard and just garden in the front. Lola, however, retorted that a man had thrown his trash water onto *her* tomato plant. Kevin said calmly that he understood why she would get angry, but Lola seethed, "Not just angry—like, I want to *kill* him." When she began to shake her fist, Kevin said soothingly, "When you shake your fist, I can't hear your words. I just see your fist." Mr. Kwan interjected that she sometimes waved an object in front of people, and even though it wasn't a weapon, it looked threatening. Turning to me as if for confirmation, he emphasized, "She is a strong woman!"

In the future, Kevin asked Lola, could she promise to talk with Mr. Kwan instead of confronting anyone? She refused but said she wouldn't put her hands on people unless they do so first—a clear indication she wasn't "dangerous" (this hews closely with Hugo's assurances in chapter 7 that he wouldn't go after anyone unless they "laid hands" on a woman in front of him—enough to evidence his modicum of self-control). Lola and Mr. Kwan hammered out an agreement and embraced.

This arrangement fell apart, however, when Mr. Kwan sold the building. The new property management company issued Lola a ninety-day notice to leave. Whereas Mr. Kwan used to contact the DMH case managers to come work out conflicts as they arose, this company wasn't so tolerant. What would happen now if Lola (or others placed in Mr. Kwan's facility) ended up back on the street? A social worker sighed, "Everything will destabilize and start over."

Luckily, the DMH was able to move Lola from Mr. Kwan's to Mr. Jong's. In a twist of simultaneous misfortune and luck, she suffered an aneurysm rupture, which meant that her daughter could become her paid live-in health aide. This obviated the bureaucratic difficulty involved in having a tenant's friends or family stay with them in the subsidized units. As Lola regained her strength, however, the team began to hear complaints from Mr. Jong: she had been yelling or banging on doors, but no one had called the police.

THE RIGHT NEIGHBORS

Seemingly, the case management team had found a living situation that could tolerate Lola and her outbursts. But this tolerance wasn't born purely out of goodwill or some utopian acceptance of psychic difference. Soon a neighbor stopped Carlos and said, "Please help us." He responded that the residents could call the authorities—maybe police would arrest her or put her on a 5150 hold. Carlos wondered why her neighbors hesitated to contact law enforcement if she was menacing them.

Later he told me with a mix of excitement and sadness that he'd figured it out. A son of Mexican immigrants himself, he had spoken with the neighbors and concluded that some were undocumented. Calling the police could bring unwanted scrutiny and with it the risk of deportation. Lola's neighbors assessed their own situations and decided they were essentially forced to put up with her behavior. Outside Downtown and in a building with families, the team had unintentionally found a setting where Lola could be tolerated because people *had to* tolerate her.

Regarding another "problem" client who lived at Mr. Jong's, a young DMH worker expressed disbelief at the havoc created for others there. Noting how much money was spent managing the clients, he said, "These people are millionaires and don't know it." It amazed him that society would "babysit people until they're in their sixties." He felt bad to say it, he told me, but he wondered whether it would be better to either execute these patients or keep them in jail for life.

WHAT TOLERANCE CAN'T CONTAIN

The DMH team's best attempts to stabilize someone with housing and wraparound services were often heroic but nonetheless inadequate. In the cases of two people whose overlapping mental illness and addiction problems were unrelenting, the DMH had no solution. One continually cycled through the institutional circuit. The other died in her subsidized apartment.

PRIORITIZING PROBLEM PEOPLE

Bobby, a fifty-year-old white man diagnosed with bipolar disorder, had spent many years in prison. Then he had been homeless Downtown and staying at the LAMP center when a resource prioritization algorithm used by the area's service providers determined he was among the "most vulnerable." Los Angeles, like many cities, had developed a Coordinated Entry System to streamline work between different service agencies and allocate housing based on need, although critics have since argued that the prioritizations often make little sense and may even be racially biased.[8] However it happened, Bobby went to the top of the wait list for the limited stock of permanent supportive housing. As I'd learn, Bobby was repeatedly hospitalized when high on methamphetamine, then rapidly released because he'd calm down once sober. He would eventually go on to gain and lose multiple apartments before being arrested and sent to a locked rehab facility. But in this moment, the DMH was just planning his entry into housing.

Carlos and I sat with Bobby in the LAMP meeting room. When he stood, Bobby's height was remarkable. He was physically imposing, with his white shirt tucked into tan Dickies pants, shaved head, and sinewy, muscled arms waving in the air. He told us he was manic, then quickly picked up the meeting room's phone receiver to say, "Robin, bring around the Batmobile!" He had been refusing psychiatric medications for years. Soon Bobby launched into a story about how his girlfriend had been out on the streets of Downtown, searching for crack. He claimed that Black men had raped her, and he needed to replace their negative energy with his good energy by having sex with her. As if chastising the men, he said angrily, "You think because you give her crack you get to take what's mine?"

Bobby further explained that he couldn't leave the LAMP center, because he owed money to some "gorillas" on the street who might try to kill him. After using the N-word, he looked up at us and insisted that he wasn't racist. Carlos, who I knew was highly attuned to racial discrimination, sat calmly and asked Bobby to think about whether he needed to return to the hospital. They'd missed one Housing Authority of the City of Los Angeles visit, and after three missed visits they could lose his voucher.

Later that day, Carlos was dropping off paperwork at the Housing Authority when he became angry with the Coordinated Entry System's findings. Not only was Bobby getting housing, but he was also being assigned to a nice furnished unit outside Skid Row. Other DMH clients were stuck waiting on worse units in a worse neighborhood, Downtown. He fumed, "Why is Bobby in this unit while [a woman outreached on Spring Street] is in the Cobb [Downtown housing project]? Who is more vulnerable? Who is more crazy?"

I shrugged and responded that they were "different kinds of crazy," but to Carlos, Bobby was getting priority only because he was a costly troublemaker: if not prioritized for housing, he would likely be hospitalized or jailed.

BACK TO THE INSTITUTIONAL CIRCUIT

Bobby moved to one of Mr. Jong's buildings. Soon he was throwing parties and turning his apartment into a drug den. Carlos described "waking up drug addicts at 8 a.m." Fed up, Mr. Jong threatened to kick Bobby out. Then Bobby wound up in a locked rehabilitation facility, and Mr. Jong agreed to avoid an official eviction so long as the DMH paid him for the rest of the month.

Thus began a longer cycle, in which Bobby was hospitalized, arrested, and continually diverted from carceral facilities. In more than one instance, he was able to utilize Proposition 36, a bill permitting drug offenders to take rehab instead of jail time. He briefly ended up in a sober living home in Boyle Heights. When I visited, I saw— and other residents confirmed—that it was a bare-bones program. Few activities or therapeutic exercises were available. In contrast to the "bubble" sober livings for the privileged that we'll encounter in chapter 9, this was what people call a flophouse sober living. It wasn't long before I heard that Bobby had been arrested again.

When I returned to the DMH after my time studying the elite

private sector, not much had changed. A worker described a recent incident in which Bobby had been on meth and PCP, and the police arrived with their shotguns out: "I said, 'Hold on, let me handle him.'" Then she told Bobby, "They're gonna shoot you if you don't go in the car." He got in and promptly urinated. Still, the psychiatric ward only held him from Friday to Monday, for seventy-two hours. She pointed out, "He speaks the language—'I don't want to harm myself, I don't want to harm anyone.'" Bobby would continue to cycle in and out of emergency services.

One day Carlos and I ran into him outside the clinic. Now on his third chance at a subsidized apartment, he continued to use drugs, and the team could only mitigate harm. Beth had told him to smoke crack instead of using crystal methamphetamine. "She was right," he said. He'd ended up with some sort of infection from bad meth Downtown. Bobby was drinking alcohol mixed in with a fountain soda, and he said sadly, "I won't lie about it." Carlos gently told him not to worry. Bobby pointed to a fresh scar on his neck as if to explain his growly voice. He had apparently tried to slit his own throat.

Even Carlos finally seemed to feel sorry for the man.

DELAYING DEATH

In a handful of cases, the DMH case management team believed it was merely postponing the inevitable. Roxanne, a Black woman in her late fifties and a long-term street drinker, provides an illustrative example. Diagnosed with major depressive disorder, she was housed in collaboration with a nonprofit social service agency. Carlos had the best relationship with her. After making sure that she had food, he'd remind her that the doctors said more drinking could kill her, and Roxanne would always acknowledge as much. Still, she refused to slow her drinking. At least Roxanne and Carlos got along—she was open to the visits and even laughed a little here and there. The two of them, similarly aged, made fun of me when I didn't recognize the old TV shows she was watching.

Carlos confided in me that the DMH wanted to schedule Roxanne for more contact, to try for a better connection and to encourage her to drink less. Yet with other "fires" to put out, and with the departure of some staff who had yet to be replaced, its workers were reduced to seeing her every two weeks. Carlos, meanwhile, feared that he would find her dead. Indeed, shortly after my fieldwork ended, he'd be right.

Roxanne had contacted her family after years of separation, but unlike Janey, she got rejected. Carlos felt that to have been the beginning of the end. "She took the leap, and they literally said [*raising his middle finger*], 'Fuck you.' Then she gave up. A year later, she was dead." He speculated, "What would have happened if they had said, 'Roxanne, we love you. Where were you?'"

Even mental health providers who know this possibility struggle to cope with such a death. Although the DMH's program lacks the resources or legal tools to prevent it, its staff members nonetheless worry when they feel they've failed a client. They try their best to make sense of it all by emphasizing two achievements: slowing the death process and giving the patient a modicum of dignity. As a psychiatrist stated regarding another client's passing from alcoholism, "This is a societal group where premature death is enormous. And you're pushing it in the other direction." Keeping people alive for the time being, keeping them housed and away from the most dangerous drugs, presented a large enough task. Staff could then speak of the small acts of kindness and dignity that its services offered. As Kevin once said of another deceased man, "At least he didn't die homeless on the street."

I wish I had more to say about these losses. There is something disturbing about using the virtually anonymous deaths of individuals to make an analytical point. But there was, in fact, little time spent at the DMH discussing who they were as human beings. I've come to believe that this reflects neither the clinicians' callousness nor my own. It is a symptom of treatment provision in this setting.

·   ·   ·

The above findings illustrate the kind of client choice that makes sense for Downtown LA street life. In an *urban poverty governance project* that aims to get people *off the institutional circuit*, the DMH places clients where their bizarre or self-destructive behavior can be accommodated—what I've called *tolerant containment*. Assuming that clients won't learn to make objectively "proper" choices, the strategy is to nudge them toward slightly more adaptive ones. This might mean autonomy from paternalism but also the dubious freedom of drinking excessively but indoors, banging one's head on a wall *other than* the one shared with a neighbor, or using crack cocaine instead of crystal meth.

Note that such an approach may fail in buildings with middle-class expectations. It can "work," however, in a "dirtier building," a Board and Care home with low staffing, or a neighborhood surrounded by vulnerable, undocumented immigrants. A small number of people experience natural growth, moderating their drug use or voluntarily engaging in psychiatric care. Some stabilize in housing, if without substantial clinical improvement. Others will return to the street or jail. And some will die prematurely.

What happens in the other world of mental health care? It's time to return to the elite private mental health settings to observe the type of freedom reserved for patients who might still have a respectable future.

CHAPTER 9

CONCERTED CONSTRAINT

"But what if you want more than that for your loved one?" Dev's words neatly illustrate a stark divide between the meaning of client choice in public safety net versus elite private mental health settings. Providers in each world must navigate the practical dilemmas produced by deinstitutionalization and the patients' rights revolution in mental health law. But where places like the Department of Mental Health have developed the generalized harm-reduction and laissez-faire attitude I call *tolerant containment*, elite providers like the Actualization Clinic assume that real care means constraining choices. They seek to reduce inappropriate behaviors, encourage normative ones, and cultivate self-efficacious people who can perform upper-middle-class adulthood. I term this intensive care and control—which must typically proceed without legal force—*concerted constraint*.

One way to understand what private mental health-care providers and privileged families want is to hear about what they hope to avoid. The above-mentioned Dev, the former Actualization client who became a private case manager, had completed his social work internship at the Village, a famous nonprofit mental health center. Its low-barrier housing approach had served as one of the inspirations for the California Mental Health Service Act's programs—an exemplar for making the Housing First model succeed. Now working in the private care sphere, Dev fondly remembered his internship and how the

Village helped the downtrodden get off the institutional circuit. He also told me why it was, from his current vantage point, undesirable: "I think the Village does it [case management and housing] in a good way. But the Village is also fine if you don't take meds, even if you do drugs to a certain extent, they're more about keeping you out of prison, keeping you out of the revolving door of hospitalizations. That's ultimately their goal. It saves the county a lot of money. But what if you want more than that for your loved one?" With its emphasis on harm reduction and client choice when it came to medication, drug use, and problematic behaviors, the Village was both a model program in the public safety net and deeply problematic from an elite care perspective.

Socioeconomically advantaged parents who remained hopeful for their children's futures expressed related fears about "the system." To them, watching their child be idle in a Board and Care home was also plainly unacceptable. One mother had hired private case management and paid for exclusive sober living homes for her son, who was in his early thirties and diagnosed with schizoaffective disorder. He had been arrested and hospitalized in the past, usually while on meth, and she once had a conservatorship over him. Today, however, he was stable. Without guardianship powers, she couldn't make her son attend intensive outpatient programs, participate in in-depth therapy, or engage with her at all. He had once asked to live in a Board and Care home, but she insisted she would never allow him to give up his potential to lay around all day in a flophouse. "What if we stopped fighting? What if we put him into a Board and Care? I'll tell you what, I can't. I wouldn't put my dog [there]," she declared. "I don't want him in the system like that. I think once you're in like that, you are not out. Once you're in the Board and Care system, you are in it. Because I believe that it's very easy to sink to the lowest common denominator." This mother couldn't bear the thought of her child sitting idly in a "lowest common denominator" setting. That picture looked nothing like the respectable, successful life she believed he could achieve. Ironically, however, he seemed to feel oppressed by her efforts to keep him in the private system that promised to rehabilitate him, to mold him into his mother's ideal.

Unlike in the public safety net, treatment providers in the private world don't tolerate people choosing a life of drug use and treatment noncompliance in ghettoized housing. The legally empowered patient here is free to choose respectability and class-appropriate actions but is not free to be crazy.

MANAGING FAMILY EXPECTATIONS

Recall that tolerant containment in the public safety net emerges as a commonsense release valve in a context of criminalization, homelessness, and hopelessness. For resource-rich families at places like the Actualization Clinic, however, treatment is driven by hope for robust futures. Since it is hard to know whether a troubled young person is a "failure to launch" case who will soon spread their wings rather than a significantly disabled person, and there is money to be spent to help them, hope for transformation can seem sensible—until it doesn't.

In *Far from the Tree*, Andrew Solomon notes that psychiatric disabilities pose a different challenge from early onset or developmental ones, because they frequently emerge as disruptions to what seemed like a successful trajectory. "The shock of schizophrenia is that it manifests in late adolescence or early adulthood, and parents must accept that the child they have known and loved for more than a decade may be irrevocably lost, even as that child looks much the same as ever."[1] This resonates with how Cheryl, the director of the Therapeutic Farm, a pastoral residential treatment center with roots more than a century old, interpreted family demands in the private sphere. "[Parents] are looking to us to 'fix' the person . . . the person you had dreamt your son or daughter would be is *different*," she explained. "And their future is not what you had hoped it would be. So we're walking through a period and a process of grieving and helping them adjust and accept and understand."

This is what is at stake in concerted constraint. Mental healthcare providers are tasked with "fixing" people while also recognizing that for some, the future may need a new definition. Attempting even scaled-back dreams can mean both going against what clients say they desire and tempering family expectations. The art of concerted constraint is to change and narrow what patients want, bringing it into alignment with provider and family goals—all without coercion.

The distinction is not merely that the private providers aim to enforce medication compliance and sobriety, although this is often true. It's that they deploy a whole different set of tools for an entirely different terrain of intervention. These are forms of care and control not offered to a poor person who has spent years in the institutional circuit or abandoned on the street. Even if a privileged client can't fulfill their own or their family's dreams, at the very least they might be kept from becoming like the poor.

LEVERAGING RESOURCES TO MOTIVATE COMPLIANCE

At the Actualization Clinic, as with other elite private mental health providers, one crucial practice for engaging a noncompliant patient was *leveraging* resources to incentivize new behavior. This required working on the family system to generate the right conditions. As Dev explained, "In the private mental health system, you can create situations in which the individual is likely to comply as a result of the work you do with the family." Note that this doesn't have the certainty of force—it's about making things more *likely*. Here money was key.

In contrast to the DMH's immense struggle to secure Section 8 housing vouchers or qualify its clients for benefits, the Actualization Clinic's workers coached well-off families on *restricting* goods. As Richard, the owner, put it, "Would you rather try to deal with someone that's psychotic but homeless and broke and desperate, or someone that's psychotic and got a lot of money in the bank?" In other words, cash was an asset for these families as well as a liability. Some, for instance, had tried a form of tolerant containment by keeping disruptive relatives at home or "throwing money" at the problem. Flush with funds, these clients had little incentive to engage in any treatment that didn't suit them.

Withholding funds, then, seemed like a reasonable way to encourage compliance. Regarding a young man who refused an antipsychotic medication, Richard said, "I don't care how disorganized you are [psychologically]. When you see it [the budget] in black and white, you'll get on board." Here we see a clear formulation of governing through freedom: in the absence of coercion, even psychotic people understood money and would likely comport themselves appropriately. This meant a gradated set of incentives, with cash attached to "healthy" behaviors that might become internalized over time.

Deirdre, the clinical supervisor, explained how leveraging became most necessary when people didn't understand that they were mentally ill. "Most people who have a lack of insight need leverage. It's not like they wake up one day and go, 'Oh, yeah, I *am* psychotic.' It really is through leverage like, 'Do you want to be supported? Well, then you got to see a doctor and follow their recommendations. And if not, you can choose what you want to do.' And there's a risk either way. We tell families there's a risk of them on the street, but there's also a risk being unmedicated where they could die either way."

When clients dug in their heels, providers had to teach families to threaten retraction of money and social support. Richard made the whole team howl with laughter when he quipped, "What is that saying? You can bring a horse to water, but you can't make him drink? Well, you can make him thirsty. It's called the homeless lifestyle." No, homelessness wasn't a joke at the Actualization Clinic, but the metaphor was funny to the team because their prescribed bouts of deprivation were highly controlled. The team worked to ensure that "spoiled" clients wouldn't be vulnerable to actual harm.

In one instance, clinic staff coached a family into kicking their daughter out of their house—an attempt to leverage her into accepting treatment at a residential eating disorder center. "She spent two hours on the street in the middle of the day," Deirdre reported to chuckles. A case manager smiled and said, "I was so impressed with her parents that they kicked her out. And she spent twenty-four hours in the car in her driveway. I told her dad, 'I bet she's in your neighborhood.' And he saw her when he walked the dogs." The family fretted about putting their daughter through "homelessness," but in the safety of her own car in an upscale neighborhood, it turned out that a minimal threat did the job without actual danger. Soon the young woman agreed to enter residential treatment.

Other cases demanded a stronger scare. Steven, an Asian American and Jewish man in his midtwenties, said he had resisted treatment for his psychosis and drug use. He told me that after his release from the hospital, he rejected a residential program, as was his right. He planned to continue using drugs and thought he could make it on the streets, until a case manager helped him see what that would be like. "When I was using, and my mom really wanted me to stop because I found out I had schizophrenia, my case manager took me down to Skid Row and was, like, 'This could easily be you.'" Steven had never seen such poverty, so the trip got him to agree to treatment.

In these examples, where providers could work with families to leverage resources, the same money and support that was once "enabling" could also become a disciplinary tool that helped set their loved one on the "right" path. Still, as Deirdre acknowledged, there were risks. During my fieldwork, one leveraging case made national news: "Princeton Graduate Killed Father over Allowance," announced the *New York Times*.[2] The Ivy Leaguer in question was the thirty-year-old son of a wealthy Manhattan hedge fund manager. As his mother later explained, he had become paranoid while away at college, but he didn't want treatment. The family sought legal counsel but learned that he did not qualify for long-term involuntary care.

When his parents decided to cut his allowance to leverage him into psychiatric services, the young man confronted his parents violently, shooting his father in the head. Despite many private psychiatrists testifying to his psychosis, he was eventually sentenced to life in prison for murder.

This shocking tale has already been optioned for film. Violent acts committed by people with psychiatric disabilities are extremely rare, but they do happen. Alongside fear for a client's well-being, that outside chance explains why families hesitate to do to their loved one what mental health-care providers see as the obvious way to assert control.

My observations at Actualization showed that families' fear was well founded. Sometimes clients retaliated, other times they disappeared. Families worried, in fact, that if a person learned to survive on their own, what little connection remained might be lost. For instance, one young man agreed to live in a treatment center and take antipsychotic medication to gain access to a car. As soon as he received the vehicle, however, he drove away. Although his family cut off his funds, he applied for General Relief (GR) from the city and began to sell his plasma, earning just enough money to continue to live out of his car. "That's why we have no leverage," Deirdre said. "It's freakin' GR!" When noncompliant elite clients transferred into public safety net systems, the Actualization team began to lose control. Eventually, the man drove off to Texas and was arrested for marijuana possession, bringing him into contact with another part of the public sector: jail. Once released, he returned to California, where a homeless outreach program began to visit him on the street.

Teaching privileged adults a lesson was a tightrope walk for the clinic's staff and the families. The point of leverage was not to make these clients suffer but to create enough fear to constrain their behavior and encourage participation in treatment. From that point, medication, specialized therapies, and scheduled activity might generate the internal control needed for self-governance.

•   •   •

So, what does concerted constraint look like? In the following sections, I examine treatment as clients flow through multiple mental health settings. First, I consider hopeful places like "the bubble" of a private sober living home, a pastoral therapeutic farm, and a variety of community-based therapeutic programs. Then, I take readers into one of the few "nice" Board and Care homes for those who are more profoundly disabled. Finally, I show where the treatment model breaks down and how even wealthy clients may experience the same risks on the street as any poor person. From there, families must decide whether to create their own harm-reduction models or give up on their loved ones.

CONTROLLING THE ENVIRONMENT:
THE SOBER LIVING "BUBBLE"

At the Actualization Clinic, it was viewed as a wasted therapeutic opportunity to allow a symptomatic or substance-abusing person to live in an unstructured setting. According to an Actualization therapist who had once worked in nonprofit services for the poor, "Harm reduction is all the county *can* do. They can't control the environment like we can." Concerted constraint meant keeping people in the *right* housing situations and away from the *wrong* people. As a stepdown from hospitals, private residential therapy centers, or rehab, the clinical team sought placements that offered surveillance but also community activity. Actualization worked with dual-diagnosis sober living and transitional homes, preferring residences with a great deal of programming and structure. Its staff introduced me to one it considered exemplary, a Buddhist-themed sober house near the beach.

Namaste Gardens served men in their twenties, thirties, and occasionally forties at a cost of around $4,000 a month. It boasted a highly regimented schedule with daily therapeutics, exercise, a meatless diet, multiple urine tests a week, and Twelve Step meetings. Residents told me that Namaste was a "bubble" sober living home, structured and semiremoved from the real world, in contrast to the "flophouse" sober living facilities that helped poor people. They spent their first six months attending an Intensive Outpatient Program (IOP) at a nearby center—in some cases, this was Actualization's mental health IOP, in others an adjacent addiction facility. Treatment was sometimes covered by insurance, but the sober homes themselves usually required cash up front.

Geoffrey, the owner of Namaste Gardens, contrasted the intensive scheduling of healthy activities at his sober house with what he saw as unhealthy treatment settings that let people choose idleness or tried to use punitive approaches that were inappropriate for mental illness. "[Some residences] allow the person to just take their meds, sleep in . . . kind of shuffle through life," he noted. "That's not going to happen here, I'm not going to want it. . . . We're doing so much together, meditating every day, surfing every day, going to the gym every day. . . . I feel like those bipolar and . . . schizoaffective clients, they can't handle any kind of confrontation or stress. It exacerbates it, but they flourish in a healthy rhythm." Neither allowing people to "shuffle through life" nor relying on the harsh "confrontation" seen in some rehabs,[3] Geoffrey delivered the "healthy rhythm" of scheduled time, therapies, and an active California lifestyle.

This is an idealized representation. The men at Namaste Gardens don't surf every day, but I did join them on trips to the gym and the Self-Realization Fellowship Temple, a famed center for meditation. There was a general level of activity and programming simply absent in settings for poorer people. Geoffrey had aptly distilled the ideal of power in this milieu: keeping people moving forward, within certain behavioral boundaries, until they "flourish."

That doesn't mean that residents always liked the program or saw it as a legitimate form of control. Justin, a white thirty-something, had come to Namaste after 135 days in a dual-diagnosis residential treatment center in San Clemente. Balding prematurely, with glasses that slipped down his nose and a diagnosis of treatment-resistant schizophrenia, Justin exuded a positivity that defied his situation. He'd attended more than twenty different residences already, but he still hoped that this one would "take." He was on a large dose of Clozaril, a powerful antipsychotic that quieted the voices in his head but left him tired.

Sitting on Namaste's roof, Justin told me his story of dreams derailed. He had planned on becoming a filmmaker until college drug experimentation triggered a psychotic episode. Like the young people I described in chapter 6, he struggled after the disruption and hadn't been able to resume his studies. Over the past ten years, he attended a variety of treatment programs. Few could address dual diagnosis— most were primarily for addiction care and others were psychiatric— but he did manage to stop using street drugs. Then, trying to mute the voices in his head, he turned to huffing compressed-air computer dusters. The voices always came back, louder every time. Finally, Justin's family sent him to Southern California for the dual-diagnosis residential program, and now he would soft launch from Namaste Gardens with the help of Actualization's case managers.

When I asked about conflicts with his parents and whether he wanted to live on his own, Justin was adamant that he was invested in his future.

> I need this. The structure and the discipline and the program in general. I'm going to need [stability] for my career [as a film-maker]. If I do make my career, it's going to be a hard one. I'm going to be very busy. I'm going to have a lot of different appointments. I'm going to have to be responsible enough to handle a car out here. Just stuff like that. It's hard at times. Someone waking you up at eight or eight-thirty in the morning just saying, "Chores." It's not the easiest thing in the world, but I know it's good for me.

Six months later, Justin's patience was wearing thin. When I saw him at Actualization's group therapy in the mornings, he would begin to doze off and ask to lie down. He participated in treatment in terms of medication, trying to stay sober, and meeting with his case manager, who was "like family." Still, Justin resisted the intensive schedule and lack of privacy. He had already passed the time frame for gaining new privileges at Namaste and believed he was ready for more autonomy.

This was not to be. A few weeks later, I attended a "sober party" with the Namaste Gardens residents at a women's treatment home. As the men danced, I stood with the Namaste house manager and talked about the facility's dual-diagnosis treatment. Often, he said, Namaste had three or four men with very serious mental illness, and the rest of the residents were addicts who had lesser issues with depression and anxiety. There could be tensions when the latter thought that the former were being given too much slack. "I try to teach them [the residents with minor needs] gratitude," said the house manager. "Like, hey, you have the chance to get married, have a job—these [other] guys are gonna have to live in a sober living the rest of their life, or at least some kind of care." He worried about Justin and thought, if left to his own devices, he might become a psychotic homeless person.

Which is to say, the house manager didn't share Justin's faith in a future career in filmmaking. And that led to a crushing public humiliation.

The next month, I watched as Justin, in front of all Namaste Gardens' residents, approached the house manager and requested to walk around alone and phone his mother without staff listening in. He asked for a "a leap of faith" but was told, "We can't take a leap of faith with people's lives." Justin slumped against a wall, silent as tears flowed down his cheeks.

That night, he ran away. He got high on the beach, where he was later found by police. When he said that he felt suicidal, the officers put him on a psychiatric hold in the hospital. When he eventually returned to Namaste Gardens, he had to begin his climb toward privileges all over again. The program was voluntary, but Justin told me with an air of resignation, "You kinda can't get out of Namaste." He felt trapped.

DIVERTED INTO THE BUBBLE

Other residents were more literally trapped, court-ordered to their time at Namaste. It is instructive to learn what this meant versus jail, a Board and Care home, or a "flophouse" sober living facility. The following case shows how leverage gone wrong can be made right if a family has the money for the right mental health-care providers and legal team.

Channing, twenty-eight when we met, came to Namaste after time in jail and a private psychiatric hospital. Pleasant, wide-eyed, and eager to share his story, he told me he had first experienced paranoia while studying abroad during college. His most persistent delusion was that he was in a *Truman Show* scenario, wherein his family and friends were paid actors, like the characters in the Jim Carrey movie. Still, Channing stabilized at the Actualization Clinic's IOP, finished college, and began working in the mailroom of a film production company.

Things took a turn when the young man went off his antipsychotics and began smoking marijuana. The Actualization Clinic told his parents to leverage him back into treatment by threatening eviction. He was surprised, since his parents had previously said he could take over another family property. "Either get evicted, be homeless, that was literally the implication, get out of the house," he remembered. The rest was a bit fuzzy, though the fact was, he flew into a rage and set his family's guesthouse on fire. Arrested for felony arson, he spent the next six weeks in Los Angeles County's Twin Towers jail. Channing's family covered his bail and hired a private attorney, who helped divert him to a private hospital. From there, he was court-ordered to stay at Namaste Gardens and submit to monitoring with an electronic ankle bracelet.

Channing was in the somewhat unique position of having experienced both county jail and elite private services. His comments about incarceration helped me better understand the form of power he was subjected to in each setting.

Jail, for instance, meant having his freedom of movement revoked, though there were few expectations around how else he filled his time. In fact, there was so little going on that people competed to get into basic activities—they just needed something to do, somewhere to go.

There was "nothing for mental health," he said, but "on Saturdays and Sundays, I believe, they have an AA meeting, which you can go to. But they only take two people out of each pod [division of jail unit]. So, you have to bum-rush the pod door" for the privilege of attending a Twelve Step meeting. Channing, uninterested, simply slept a lot.

When I asked about medications, Channing said he'd been surprised at how many people refused meds, misused them, or sold them in jail. "I'm sure the guards and the nurses know this—a lot of medication was either crushed up or snorted or traded away for a cookie."

The intensity of Namaste Gardens, by contrast, caught him off guard. For one thing, there were the Twelve Step meetings. They were required here, even though Channing didn't consider himself an addict. He wished he could be left alone to sleep. "It's very structured, this place. Sometimes I like to take afternoon naps for a little bit. I get very tired during the day. It's a lot to take in." To be clear, Channing briefly preferred jail, but he didn't *like* it ("It's not a pleasant experience"). Sure, he could nap there, but those naps were interrupted by announcements blaring from loudspeakers. What I found fascinating was the contrast between settings that required activity, like Namaste, and the ones like jail that produced idleness.[4]

As the months passed, Channing came to appreciate Namaste and Actualization. He got into the "healthy rhythm" and believed he was on his way back to work. His family hired a forensic psychiatrist to attest that he was not a pyromaniac, and his private attorney secured a deal to keep him in treatment rather than state prison for the arson. Although his parents had a restraining order against him, they all began meeting at family therapy sessions. He was annoyed that they wanted a conservatorship, but the lawyer said it wouldn't go through, so they dropped it. And, last I heard, Channing was thriving—he read business books, discussed possible careers. Moreover, Actualization reported that he was "becoming a leader," working the program, and helping the new residents get their bearings.

THE LEGACY OF MORAL TREATMENT

The concerted constraint imposed by places like Namaste and the Actualization Clinic is a mishmash of Southern California lifestyle, IOP therapy, sober living home, Alcoholics Anonymous, and case management. It is a product of post-deinstitutionalization community care techniques combined with a fast-growing addiction industry, booming after Obamacare expanded insurance coverage for behavioral health. Yet I also observed programs that built directly on the more than two-hundred-year-old pastoral mental health-care approach of *moral treatment.*

The Therapeutic Farm, an East Coast facility that has been around since the early 1900s, remains a small-scale operation. It's expensive, at roughly $10,000 a month, though less expensive than many Malibu settings. Additionally, the operators believe in making their facility accessible, so well-off families that pay full price subsidize those who pay on a sliding scale, including occasional public mental patients.

Today, as it has since its inception, the farm emphasizes the practices of meaningful work, community, and spiritual discipline. But
recall how the philosopher Michel Foucault viewed the eighteenth-
century Quakers' version of moral treatment: as an "instrument of
moral and religious segregation"[5] that replaced brute force with insidious psychological control. "We see that at the [Quaker] Retreat the
partial suppression of physical constraint [i.e., minimizing the use of
chains] was part of a system whose essential element was the constitution of a 'self-restraint' in which the patient's freedom, engaged by
work and the observation of others, was ceaselessly threatened by the
recognition of guilt."[6] With constant surveillance and work routines,
the Quaker forerunners of the Therapeutic Farm sought to make
patients surveil *themselves* for signs of madness or religious transgres-
sion as well as engage in "self-restraint" that amounted—for Foucault,
at least—to using mental chains in place of physical ones.

Like many 1960s countercultural ideas, Foucault's interpretation
was iconoclastic and controversial. Helping people control themselves
and reflect on their own reactions is arguably assisting them in reach-
ing a key goal of human growth, and even contemporary readers may
be shocked by Foucault's suggestion that this moral treatment is a
form of domination. Many have challenged his cynical take,[7] though
it reminds us that care is often Janus-faced. Even well-intentioned
actions can *also* function as forms of control.

I first learned about the Therapeutic Farm when a young client of
the Actualization Clinic left for an extended stay there. Sheila was in
her early twenties and diagnosed with bipolar disorder, and she had
previously been in a residential treatment facility in Hawaii, a hospital in Ohio, and a partial-hospitalization program in Los Angeles.
Whereas she was once so depressed she couldn't perform daily tasks,
Actualization reported that she was now manic and acting out. The
case manager stated, "Her psychiatrist said she did her best while
catatonic for one year, depressed. Then she switched." Now Sheila
used drugs ranging from marijuana to crack cocaine and was purportedly "a sex addict" who "takes Uber everywhere and then screws the
Uber drivers."

At times, her problems appeared quotidian—a kind of struggle over independence and individuation from a worried family. Actualization case managers reported that Sheila's parents had very specific goals in mind, and some of the elements of her treatment at the clinic seemed to revolve around growing up more than managing serious mental illness. As noted previously, wealthy families often demanded attention to issues that wouldn't likely be prioritized in a public safety net clinic. One Actualization worker complained about being asked to monitor the young woman's college performance: "I didn't want to be, like, 'pull out your homework and let me see it.'" Because the parents continually asked Actualization about Sheila's sex life, another case manager began coaching her on dating. (Reportedly, she'd meet men on the dating app Tinder who feigned interest in order to sleep with her, then lost interest—hurtful behavior, but not unusual.)

Still, other more troubling issues arose. Although she was technically not "a danger to self or others," there were times when her drug use, mania, and purported hypersexuality put her in harm's way. A case manager said that Sheila went to a hotel to smoke crack cocaine with some men, who then took turns sexually assaulting her. While the care team and her family certainly didn't blame Sheila for having been raped, they nonetheless believed that her freedom in the community could put her in danger and that her choices needed to be constrained. Eventually, the family sent her to a wilderness camp for two months and then on to the Therapeutic Farm. Although I couldn't track Sheila's case directly, I reached out to the farm's director to learn more.

MEANINGFUL WORK AND LIVING IN COMMUNITY

The Therapeutic Farm sits on seven hundred acres of rural New England pasture. A day on the farm, I learned, includes communal meetings, various forms of group and individual therapies, and about five hours of work with the livestock, in the fields, or in the kitchen. Cheryl, the director, explained that the work was therapeutic. Clinical treatment was supplemental. "In broad strokes: meaningful work, living in community, with clinical supports." Note the language: Cheryl uses the phrase "living in community," which connotes communion with others, not "living in *the* community," which would imply only living outside an institution.

And what did she mean by "meaningful work"? Cheryl explained that working on the farm was intended to hold deep meaning for residents. "We're able to feel a sense of ownership and pride, and we're each contributing and creating continually that loop in what we do, and how it contributes meaningfully to our existence." In essence, she was describing what Marxists would call unalienated labor—people could see and enjoy the fruits of their work directly and work in concert for sustenance rather than toil as cogs in a faceless machine.[8]

Cheryl acknowledged the moral tension of putting people to work. Critics note that both this model and sheltered workshops for the disabled sometimes demand work without fair monetary compensation. There have been journalistic exposés of addiction centers that essentially treat residents as slave labor.[9] Nevertheless, in the careful practice of moral treatment, everyday work could indeed take on a higher purpose and bring meaning to patients.

Back in Los Angeles, the Actualization Clinic reported that Sheila truly enjoyed her six months at the Therapeutic Farm. I can't know, in any precise way, what effect the experience had on her. But my inquiries suggested that meaningful activity might effectively channel energy and constrain behavior in a way that helped cultivate the self. Even Foucault, that fiercest critic of moral treatment, expressed in later writings an admiration for various ascetic and spiritual practices of self-discipline—what he called "technologies of the self"—provided they were chosen freely.[10] What makes patients' experiences complicated in this regard is that they could fall into a gray area, neither legally coerced nor participating entirely of their own accord.

At the Actualization Clinic, meaningful work and activity didn't take place in fields or with livestock but throughout the city of Los Angeles. As patients' home visits and treatment days in the therapy groups decreased, Actualization insisted that they go to school, work, or volunteer. In some cases, helping clients start such new activities required enormous support or even going against people's initial stated choices. Since Actualization clinicians believed that a person's resistance might derive from mental illness, being spoiled, or fear, pushing them remained, in their eyes, a legitimate exercise of power.

Deirdre, the clinical supervisor, explained that it was a disservice to give sick people too much choice. Roy, a white man in his late thirties diagnosed as having schizophrenia, had refused to try any activities with his case manager. His father brought him to the clinic because he spent all day reading comics and watching TV. Asked what he wanted to work on, Roy was hesitant. Deirdre said not to give too much choice in such a case, revealing a logic drawn from parenting. "We don't want to infantilize our clients. But it's like with my kids: if I ask them what they want to do, they want to be on their phone. 'You want a bike ride or get something to eat?' If they want something else, [you say,] 'Sorry, that's not an option.'" Note that Deirdre warns against infantilization, then immediately suggests reducing choices the way she would with a stubborn child.

Roy was allowed choice from a narrowed range of acceptable options—none of which were reading comics and watching TV. The case manager began taking him to busy restaurants to increase his tolerance for discomfort. Roy would later tell me that this work, although difficult, was "better than any medication" he received, and he soon began to pursue more daily activities by himself. Although he didn't plan to work or move out of his father's house, he became more involved in visiting his sister and her small child. He could be a cool uncle instead of the strange man who didn't leave his room. Roy's achievements were real.

Even so, the pursuit of meaningful activity could be quite difficult for other clients. Kayvon, a Persian man in his sixties who lived at home with his mother, had been in treatment for schizophrenia for decades and now saw the case manager Dev on weekends. There was little expectation that he would become employed, but his family hoped he could still achieve small gains.

I sat with Kayvon and Dev one morning in a Starbucks after Kayvon played soccer, an activity he previously believed would cause a catastrophic event in his brain. Now Dev was insisting on additional uncomfortable activities, but Kayvon was scared that these would trigger a meltdown. "Dev," he pleaded, "I'm not going to risk my sanity for doing things that I *know*—"

Dev cut him off. "I would never put you at risk. You know that."

After some back-and-forth, Dev put his foot down. "It would be a disservice if I allowed this to continue, because it impacts the quality of your life."

Later, Dev explained his reasoning. In most public provision settings, case workers would accept Kayvon's refusal as a form of choice. "With the private [sector], I don't know if the right word is *you can get away with more*, but for instance, with Kayvon, we push through things, do things. But in the public [sector] I might not be able to do that. They could think that *that's not ethical*" [emphasis added]. To Dev, the truly unethical thing would be to allow people to live small lives, sitting at home and doing nothing all day.

GRANULAR BEHAVIORAL NORMALIZATION

Moral treatment has also inspired a variety of psychiatric rehabilitation techniques, many of which are now standardized interventions. The Actualization Clinic and Dev referred me to an ongoing social skills group run by a prominent academic psychiatrist, Dr. Schlessinger, who had designed trainings for people experiencing schizophrenia and social withdrawal. Participants had typically been through hospitalizations, were taking medication, and were working on the behavioral techniques needed for increased social interaction.

What struck me most was the granularity of behavioral intervention. It brought together speech therapy and role play and addressed the smallest elements of human interaction. Like the therapies addressed previously, such care is, in principle, widely available. Dr. Schlessinger's group had participants who weren't rich. And yet, pushing someone to engage in time-consuming and sometimes unpleasant therapies often required a case manager or highly involved family member to drive them around and conduct homework exercises in the community. That is, it was resource intensive if not always expensive.

Teaching these skills required an intense level of micromanagement. One participant called the doctor "a dragon" for the way he breathed down people's necks. For instance, I observed Dr. Schlessinger coach Riley, a young man who generally remained silent and seemed to suffer from "negative symptoms." His TV executive mother had reportedly sent him to the group to acquire skills with hopes of his getting a job.

Schlessinger enlisted a recent college graduate to accompany Riley out in the community and help him practice social and behavioral skills. In the classroom role-play session, Riley had to demonstrate his latest homework assignment, which was to thank the assistant for teaching him how to make the bed. The doctor said to show him exactly how he did the thanking. The young man hesitated, and Schlessinger modeled his version, saying, "Thank you for teaching me how to make my bed. Now I feel more independent. I don't have to rely on the housekeepers, and it makes me feel good."

Riley began to speak but stumbled. Schlessinger made him repeat each phrase. When the young man turned away, the doctor demanded that he look forward at his role-play companion. Riley broke eye contact again and looked at the ground, shaking. "Ugh, a nightmare," another participant whispered to me. Eventually, Riley finished the sentence.

This struggle shows how the doctor's group approach involves minute behavioral control of speech, bodily comportment, and eye contact. This is a form of disciplinary power used for psychiatric rehabilitation, and it is intended to prepare Riley for the job his mother insists on. In addition to the in-depth therapy that seeks answers in the past and the cognitive restructuring that rationalizes thoughts and emotions, here is an intensive behavioral conditioning that might scare clients yet truly be rehabilitative. After all, even the critical participant who called it a "nightmare" told me he appreciated the group because it made him more self-efficacious.

NOT BEING PUT OUT TO PASTURE

And what of those people who don't become so "independent"? In an earlier chapter, we learned of the surprising dearth of high-quality

Board and Care homes for wealthier clientele. This is due to the pecu-
liar economics of housing development, zoning, and adult residential
facility regulation. It's simply not as profitable to focus on long-term
custodial care as it is to sell families on a brief $50,000-per-month
residential treatment with the promise of recovery. That means, even
for families with money, that there are few high-quality, long-term
residential facilities for the profoundly impaired.

Actualization did have one place to which it could send clients
who, as Deirdre said, "really need the constant oversight. They might
be able to work a little bit, but they just can't make it on their own
in an independent living situation. They need the structure." The
Schizophrenia Institute wasn't in Los Angeles County, but it was close
enough that families could still visit, and it was an option beyond
giving up when a person wasn't succeeding with Actualization-style
outpatient services. "We value what they [the Institute] do. It's
not just, 'let's put them [severely disabled clients] out to pasture'
someplace."

Rather than allowing the metaphorical old horse to spend its final
days grazing out of sight—essentially what happens to poor people living in flophouse-type mental health facilities—the private care milieu
retained options for concerted constraint and cultivation. Technically
licensed as a Board and Care home, the Schizophrenia Institute was
a nonprofit organization with considerably more services than typical
adult residential facilities offer. Most residents retained their rights,
with about a fifth under guardianships (7 out of 36 had a legal conservatorship over them at the time). It had been in operation since
the late 1980s and cost approximately $3,500 a month for a shared
room—far less than a Malibu rehab or the Therapeutic Farm, but
nonetheless a great deal of money, especially for a family placing a
loved one in long-term care. People who only had government benefits
wouldn't be able to afford it.

On a bright Southern California morning, Dr. Xande, a clinical psychologist and the director, gave me a tour of the institute's grounds.
As we walked, several people approached to start conversations, some
using techniques I'd seen in Dr. Schlessinger's class. Indeed, Dr. Xande

explained to me, "You've already had a lot of people today say, 'Hey, how are you?' That's because they're practicing their social skills. They're trying and saying, 'Oh, a visitor! Let me try my skills out.'"

Compared with the Board and Cares with zero programming, the daily schedule here included a variety of activities ranging from group therapy to yoga to various workout regimens. Xande said people's activity and rest had to be controlled, and he was particular about daily scheduling and creating good sleep habits. "Otherwise, they end up staying up really late, staying up into the evening, really stressed and anxious, 'cause it can't calm their brain down 'cause they're tired. They can't stop. Almost like a child—not to mean to call adults with this illness 'children.'"

Dr. Xande caught and corrected himself when he used the phrase "like a child," and yet his facility engages in a level of intensive parenting-type intervention. Depending on the viewpoint, it could look either caring or excessively paternalistic. Then he expounded on the institute's approach to the physical and sensory environment.

Schizophrenia is known to have a lot of sensitivity towards certain stimuli. For example, too much visual movement can be really hard for the brain to filter out. In fact, vision is the number one way that we take in and process information, so if there's a lot of it, it can feel a little overwhelming. This is why we try to keep things lighter, dimmer, a little bit more casual. There's no major scents in the air, because olfactory activation also overstimulate . . . this is why we say no fragrances, no heavy lotions . . . the houses have an element of soundproofing.

As we walked through the treatment rooms and residential areas, I was indeed struck by the low level of noise and lack of smells. The air had a bit of a clinical scent, but not in the cigarettes-stifled-by-cleaning-chemicals way I'd noticed in the other Board and Care homes.

Overstimulation, I learned, extended to Dr. Xande's thoughts on diet. "Now the other thing here, love or hate it, the program is a sugar-free and caffeine-free program. It's not allowed here. If they had a

coffeepot, they would be going at it. And so we just say no to that."
Unlike the poor person's Board and Care home, where staff halfheart-
edly monitored crystal meth usage, the Schizophrenia Institute was
ever vigilant about mild stimulants like sugar and caffeine.

I marveled, too, at the attention paid here to organizing and moti-
vating people's Activities of Daily Living (their ADLs, skills for independent personal care). "Sometimes we take the week before and we
plan out the clothing for the whole week so they know what they're
going to wear that day when they wake up. Sometimes we set up
an alarm clock for them across the room. It's like a reward system.
Sometimes we say, '. . . we'll call your family, tell them not to pick you
up because you didn't brush your teeth.'"

Caring attentiveness and minute control, it seemed, had become
one and the same.

THE LIMITS OF LEVERAGE

All this presumes that plans get off the ground. In some cases, adults
who retain control of their own money may subvert concerted constraint by simply refusing to comply. In others, the reliance on the
involvement of families in the private sphere can become a weakness
when "noncompliant" families initially agree to leverage resources
available to their loved one, then recant and disrupt that incentive
structure.

First consider Witt, a white man in his forties who was a serious
alcoholic. He'd become successful in the movie industry, so he wasn't
financially beholden to anyone. He saw the Actualization Clinic team's
favored psychiatrist, Dr. Myrdal, and he enlisted two case managers
from the clinic as well as nonclinical "sober companions" to accompany him throughout the day and keep him from drinking. Treatment
was off to a good start, but once Witt decided to drink again, he simply
fired his providers.

After an alcohol-related scare sent Witt to the hospital, Dr. Myrdal
reached out to Actualization. Following residential rehab, Witt would
need community-based support, but Deirdre declined to take him on

again as a client. She pointed out that "he has his own money," and therefore he'd be immune to the case management team's attempts to leverage him into sobriety. Seeing him on TV some months later, she remarked, "I can't believe that guy is still alive." It was a remarkable difference from what I'd seen at the DMH, where staff is mandated to support clients, even those at risk of death due to serious addiction, and occasionally find such people dead. A private mental health-care provider like Actualization is less obliged to tolerate this risk and may refuse to help such a patient. When concerted constraint is rendered inoperable by a lack of leverage dynamics, clinics can simply say no.

Another unusual but revealing case is one in which a homeless woman briefly received services at Actualization. Carolyn, also in her forties, was diagnosed with schizophrenia and heroin dependence. Coming from a well-off family, she had been cut off and then had fallen through the cracks. Her brother, however, was now paying for private insurance through Breyer, the previously noted company that had contracted with Actualization in the wake of the Affordable Care Act and the ensuing influx of high utilizers. Carolyn was one of the initial cases.

Actualization didn't know what to do with Carolyn. Its staff couldn't figure out how to get her housed, for instance, because the insurer would not pay for nonmedical housing, and her brother wouldn't assist out of pocket. Spending hours at court hearings and tracking Carolyn down when she disappeared, the treatment team struggled to implement their therapeutic procedures. In the end, Deirdre decided that the clinic couldn't help her, and she asked the insurance company not to send Actualization any more homeless people. This case reveals how concerted constraint is reliant on a baseline of financial resources and family involvement; elite therapeutic expertise may not translate without those structures in place.

TOLERANCE AS FAILURE

Some of the most frustrating cases, from the Actualization Clinic's perspective, were those in which families repeatedly claimed they would use leverage with their loved one but then would tolerate unmedicated psychosis and drug usage in the home. I tracked one such case. The client was a woman in her early fifties named Kaye. Her elderly parents were at their wits' end—but unwilling to put their daughter out of the house.

Diagnosed alternately as having bipolar disorder and schizophrenia, Kaye had been in and out of psychiatric facilities for much of her life. Her father was a prominent physician, and the family had come to the Actualization Clinic many times over the years. They arranged for Kaye to live outside the family home, but she refused to stay there. She would frequently show up and ask to be let in, and the family would resume their long-standing dynamic. Inconsistent in taking her primary psychiatric medications, Kaye abused her anxiety pills and amphetamines.

Actualization case manager Greg met with Kaye and attempted to "align" with her, taking her to museums and sitting with her in the family home. He described her as a six-year-old in an adult's body. When the case management team coached the family to kick her out and push her toward a residential treatment center, Kaye's mother would agree, then quickly fold. "They might agree to it at first," Greg said. "But what about if she shows up and it's raining and she has a black eye?" In this case, he thought Kaye should enter a long-term dual-diagnosis setting that could attend to both the substance use and the psychiatric symptoms.

> It became really clear that just visits from Actualization was not nearly enough, that she really needed some heavy psychiatric care. She needed to get on the right medicine and consistently, and she really was in a position where she was gonna benefit from long-term care.
>
> But she wouldn't do it. She threw a temper tantrum and wouldn't do it, so we were coaching the family, like, "You have to have this be an either/or situation. You don't have to be angry or mean about it, but you have to say, 'It's not good for you to live here. It's not good for us, so you can't live here anymore.'"

But Kaye's family wouldn't stick to the plan. The team scheduled a collaboration with an interventionist who would help the parents be strong. In the end, though, the family gave up and stopped visiting the Actualization Clinic. Note that affluent people may be in a different position from poorer families, as there is always money to be given, always a room in the house, and the adult child knows it.

As Greg joked at team meeting, "It's not like the good old days when you can just stick someone in the state hospital." Today, the family couldn't even get an emergency hold. "They tried to take her into treatment, and she would run away and then come back. And then they'd have the police come try to 5150 her, and she would calm down and tell them what they needed to hear, so they wouldn't take her."

RE-CREATING HOUSING FIRST

Sometimes, whether as a last resort or because they feared that leverage would backfire, privileged families created something akin to the harm-reduction and Housing First models in the public sector. They used different language, and they did not justify it via the goal of street clearance, cost savings, or a patient's right to self-determination. They just couldn't bear to see their child homeless and had ceased to see any other options.

As Zara from the National Alliance on Mental Illness explained, leveraging resources normally works with privileged people because they are "so accustomed to being taken care of, they acquiesce and go get to the doctor and start taking the meds so they can move back home." When we spoke, however, she was currently assisting two families for whom it had not worked. One mother had kicked her son out, and he simply became a homeless person. She visited him on the street, bringing him food and supplies, but he would not enter care. The second family couldn't bear to put their son on the streets and had essentially developed a harm-reduction housing plan.

As Zara explained to me, "[Their son] . . . went to Stanford, brilliant. He's always been a bit odd and mentally ill, and [his family pays] for an apartment for him and he's doing heavy drugs and won't give up the heavy drugs to have a life."

"And have they threatened to take away the apartment or—"

Zara cut me off. "No, this couple can't do that. They've taken away everything else. He has no money. Nothing. They buy him a gift card from Trader Joe's and stuff like that to get food."

For Actualization and other private mental health-care providers, securing simple stable housing and harm reduction were not considered successes. I observed this judgment with the case of a wealthy white woman in her fifties. She came to the Actualization Clinic on a legal conservatorship that required she accept an antipsychotic injection and meet with a psychiatrist. At the end of the yearlong order, however, she was exercising her right to go off meds. She also regained access to her substantial trust fund with $12,000 a month in disbursements. Had the family worked with the Actualization Clinic and its lawyers earlier in her life, they might have put together a "spendthrift trust" that made the money contingent on treatment or other obligations. But her brother explained that all the family elders were dead, and their wills were finalized.

"What will make her better is pulling the twelve grand," seethed Deirdre, who believed that this maneuver could leverage the woman into taking the injection and continuing therapy. "She'll have all the money in her own place *just being crazy.*" There was no legal remedy, however. The case manager nodded and sighed, "We kind of lost her." Although the woman was arguably very comfortable and had previously lived on her own without medication, and although such an outcome might be viewed as success at the DMH, here in the elite setting her situation was deemed a disaster.

LIVING AND DYING LIKE THE POOR

At the end of the line, there is the nightmare scenario—one that ties affluent families to poorer ones. Despite using every available resource and making every best effort, some families watched their adult relative wind up dead on the street. Eric, a white man in his early sixties and brother to a lifelong patient, told me that his family's story showed why money doesn't make a difference. He promised to care for his brother, Todd, after their parents' deaths. Eric secured a property, but Todd abandoned it and disappeared. Soon he was in and out of brief hospital stays, and Eric managed to become his conservator and send him to a locked facility.

A few months later, however, Todd returned to court, lucid and advocating for himself, and the judge ended the conservatorship. Now Eric lacked legal control, and the sibling relationship was damaged. When money was not disbursed immediately, Todd got angry and set his room on fire. He was arrested and moved to a mental health wing of the Los Angeles County Jail. Eric spent tens of thousands of dollars on lawyers' fees to obtain a plea bargain for his brother.

After Todd's release, Eric didn't know what to do besides dole out his brother's monthly portion of the family trust. Todd spent it, as near as anyone could tell, on crystal meth. A lawyer told Eric that he could not misrepresent the arson situation to landlords, and so rather than apartments he housed his brother in unlocked Board and Care homes and hotels. Indeed, as Eric rattled off the names, I recognized some as the "flophouses" where I met county clients. He said that these Board and Care homes were overrun with drugs and lacked monitoring, adding that his brother began to run with "street people."

Todd died while wandering naked in the streets. The police car dispatched to the scene accidentally ran him over. Eric blamed the mental health laws for his brother's death. "If there's a parent or a sibling or any kind of person who's a genuine guardian who's interested in the welfare of that person, they should be able to keep that person in a hospital like they're a child," he said. Unlike those who corrected themselves when they likened adult patients to children, Eric had no such reservation.

Identifying as a former California counterculture liberal, Eric had come to regard the mental health system as propounding a false notion of freedom: "How in the world can a civil libertarian advocate argue that letting someone live on the street, where there's no idea what's going on in their head or how dangerous they are, it's somehow freedom? What [way] are they free? They're free to defecate in public. That's not freedom. They're not making a choice. In order to make a free choice, you have to have the ability to have a rational thought." Here he echoed classical liberal theorists who believed that freedom required rationality. Like John Locke, who said, "Lunaticks and ideots are never set free from the governance of their parents," it didn't make sense to him to give his brother rights.

In another era, Eric might have had Todd committed long term. In this one, his brother had his freedom, and Eric tried but failed to control and protect him. Ultimately, Todd lived and died a strange, highly resourced version of street life.

•   •   •

Here, in a *family systems governance project* that aims to craft *a viable identity*, the Actualization Clinic and its collaborators leverage people into intensive treatment that will putatively generate healthy choices. The approach, which I've called *concerted constraint,* involves incentivizing action, not just by giving and retracting money, but by offering a real promise of a future. Clinicians want people to choose to take meds and refuse drugs, to learn to enjoy meaningful work, to live in community, to communicate effectively, and to engage in activities such as eating with their families in restaurants. The intervention takes place on a significantly more granular level than what we saw at the DMH, including a variety of psychotherapies to address behavior, thoughts, habits, and desires. Here care *is* control, and immediate freedom is constrained to generate a more substantive future freedom.

We can learn a great deal by contrasting concerted constraint with tolerant containment. When a person ends up living on their own while psychotic, perhaps because their trust fund has made it difficult to leverage them, the Actualization Clinic considers it a failure. From this perspective, a person who remains highly symptomatic or bizarre should either be in the hospital or sent to a place like the Schizophrenia Institute to be monitored and therapeutically engaged.

This can lead to strange and uncomfortable ironies, as when a person prefers the idle time of jail to expensive, intensive treatment.

Ultimately, there are still instances in which the concerted constraint model falls apart—whether due to lack of resources (the unusual case of a homeless person in elite care) or because of fear that leverage will backfire. Families may then improvise a harm-reduction model, lose their relatives to the street or public systems, or funnel them money until they die. In exasperation, some affluent people claim that wealth doesn't solve the problem, and then they advocate a return to the asylum era.

CONCLUSION

On a chilly afternoon in March 2021, I stood at the fenced-off edge of Echo Park Lake. Located three miles northeast of Skid Row, the once-beatific area had become the site of a large homeless encampment. Police officers stood guard as city workers broke down the tent community. When I inquired about their plan, one officer said, "We're cleaning up the place"—a jarring euphemism for displacing people the city found undesirable. Some camp residents gathered up their things and bid goodbye to their home, cautiously hoping the city would make good on promises of a hotel room. Others stayed to fight.

Protestors gathered in solidarity and asserted that campers—whether victims of California's housing crisis, addicted, seriously mentally ill, or all the above—should be cared for, not criminalized. The activists clashed with police through the evening and into the next day, drawing on a powerful new framework formed during the summer 2020 demonstrations against police violence and mass incarceration. Holding signs that read House Keys, Not Handcuffs and Care Not Cages, they demanded that the city "defund the police" and invest instead in communities. During the world-altering COVID-19 pandemic, there was a profound reckoning with a host of social inequalities, and a new public attention had been drawn to abusive law enforcement.

I shared the activists' outrage at the heavy-handed policing. Still, I felt a sense of unease. My fieldwork had taught me that to focus on the policing and on eviction days was to see only part of the problem. The fact was that Los Angeles, in the name of "rights" and "health," had tolerated the encampment for more than a year. Much as I had seen the *Jones v. City of Los Angeles* decision and the *Lavan* injunction delay the uprooting of the Spring Street encampment in 2013, a more recent Ninth Circuit Court ruling, *Martin v. City of Boise*, had deemed it cruel and unusual punishment to arrest or fine homeless people if there was no shelter or housing available.[1] Bolstered by a temporary directive from the Centers for Disease Control and Prevention to avoid encampment dispersal for fear of spreading coronavirus, the city's "tolerance," with occasional "public health cleanings," had become standard procedure.[2]

To understand such situations, we must analyze the long stretches of acceptance as much as the moments of eviction. Although the city hadn't been helping people adequately—indeed, it lacked the resources to house or treat everyone in the many encampments—it had also largely left people alone. Protestors were demanding care instead of cages, but the urban policy response was increasingly to offer neither. The city was engaged in *tolerant containment*. Police no doubt still harass homeless people, if only to drive them to de facto city-sanctioned encampments. Most are then tolerated on the street, their "rights" intact; a handful might be left idle in flophouse hotels; and fewer still, the most psychiatrically disabled and disruptive, might become eligible for harm-reduction programs and placement in Housing First apartments.

Although better than criminalization or incarceration, the temporary right to be left alone is not without cruelties. Moreover, it has spillover effects for the broader community—as in Echo Park, where even sympathetic, left-leaning residents came to demand police action. And once the city could make credible claims to have offered enough shelter in compliance with the law (not to the entire homeless population but to those in a targeted camp), it simply displaced people to other areas, where they would be temporarily tolerated again.

THE FRANKENSTEIN'S MONSTER OF
CIVIL LIBERTIES AND AUSTERITY

The situation at Echo Park Lake was explosive but hardly unique. It represents one instance of a profound transformation in the public management of social deviance. Instead of trying to fix social problems, we have come to simply accept them, so long as they are in the "right place." In the wake of *Martin v. City of Boise*, other West Coast jurisdictions have learned to temporarily tolerate encampments. Once-radical ideas like harm reduction have entered the mainstream—and far beyond Los Angeles. For instance, Housing First programs that eliminate treatment compliance requirements are now considered a standard best practice across much of the nation.

Drug decriminalization provides another example. In California in 2014, Proposition 47 remade many previous drug possession felonies into misdemeanors.[3] The state's prisons released thousands of inmates who'd been arrested on drug charges, and some police departments deprioritized drug arrests.[4] In 2020, Oregon adopted even broader decriminalization laws. And city-level experiments have gone further still.[5] During the initial COVID-19 wave in 2020, San Francisco offered unhoused people hotel rooms, even delivered drugs and alcohol to keep them from wandering outside.[6] Activists across the nation have demanded the release of nonviolent offenders from jail and prison, and some municipalities have elected progressive prosecutors who promise not to pursue such cases. Cities have begun to take seriously the idea that behavioral health specialists might replace police as the first responders for certain forms of public disturbance.

There is much to admire in these developments, and they signal a possible break with the moral and policy disasters of mass incarceration and mass criminalization. Yet California, so often a bellwether state for legislative change, has failed to generate the revenue and public infrastructure to effectively serve people in crisis, much less get at the root causes of homelessness and addiction, or deliver preventive mental health services. The aforementioned Prop 47, for one, repeated a number of mistakes from psychiatric deinstitutionalization.

Prisoners were released, but the reentry services and drug rehabilitation treatment promised to them were nowhere to be found. Many were left to the streets.[7] In the absence of robust solutions, merely tolerating social problems is frequently tantamount to the state abdication of responsibility.

Conservatives blame these outcomes on permissive liberal governance,[8] but the truth is that neither left nor right would intentionally design a system this dysfunctional. It's a Frankenstein's monster created by mating civil libertarianism with austerity.[9] When cities can neither enforce behavioral norms in public space nor provide meaningful help to people, they seem to acquiesce, accepting unacceptable outcomes through dubious tolerance. This helps explain why, even in liberal areas primed for police scrutiny, we see a countermovement to "refund the police" in order to clear city streets of visible suffering and chaos.[10]

Still, as cities like Los Angeles enact encampment bans near schools and pursue street sweeps, activists will respond with lawsuits and protests to block them. The battle continues, but in effect the struggle for positive rights to housing and health care has been eclipsed. What remains is the negative liberty to be left alone—the right to be homeless, to use drugs, and to be psychotic. It is this strange situation that much of this book has sought to explain.

THE HYPER-UNEQUAL MARKET FOR CARE AND CONTROL

Alongside these public struggles are the less visible private ones taking place within families. Here the fight is to access care and control before loved ones end up on the street or in jail. In a 2021 *Los Angeles Times* op-ed, Jasmin Iolani Hakes describes the struggle to assist her twenty-something daughter who was diagnosed with serious mental illness. The young woman had voluntarily engaged in an intensive outpatient mental health program with apparent success, but when her private insurer downgraded her to minimal services, she disintegrated. She was hospitalized after a suicide attempt. As Hakes writes, "Why do we make it so hard to find a place for those who are mid-fall, who need more than once a week with a therapist, less than an intervention on the street? Why do we wait for them to hit rock bottom?"[11] This is the public versus private insurance trap: only the wealthy will receive intensive care before "rock bottom." Hakes's daughter will have to become a public issue to be prioritized for treatment. It is unlikely private insurers will step up because our current system essentially allows Medicaid to subsidize their failure.[12]

Money, as we have seen, can sometimes offer the well-to-do a different pathway to care. Affluent families spend enormous sums to avoid both punishment and tolerant containment in the public sector. This elite market in *concerted constraint* (with programs that promise therapeutic micromanagement and clinical transformation) has emerged precisely because families deem the other systems so undesirable—not just for the inability to deliver care but for the inability to exert control. Of course, even among the most privileged are those patients who will still use their freedoms to say no, get arrested, run away, or die.

At the intersection of such dynamics—the housing crisis, the criminalization of mental illness, the failure of private insurance, and parental heartbreak—we see a renewed interest in coercion. Paralleling social movements that fight mass incarceration and criminalization by demanding liberties, attempts have been made to help by *revoking* certain rights. These include, for instance, changing the definition of "grave disability" to make it easier to force people into psychiatric treatment, or expanding mandated rehab for drug-related arrests. New York mayor Eric Adams proposes to remove homeless people with psychosis from the streets, whether or not they seem to pose a public threat,[13] while Sacramento mayor Darrell Steinberg has called for a right and an obligation to shelter, meaning a person would have a guaranteed shelter bed—and no ability to refuse it.[14] Others argue that it is time to "bring back the asylum."[15] As I write in 2023, three California counties are piloting Governor Gavin Newsom's new CARE (Community Assistance, Recovery, and Empowerment) Courts, which paradoxically will court-order people with psychosis into "voluntary" psychiatric services under threat of legal guardianship. All these approaches aim to end criminalization and ameliorate home-lessness, addiction, and mental illness—but by stripping people of certain rights.

WHERE DO WE START?

My research has convinced me that we can't truly address these over-lapping crises without profound structural change to our society. This would include rights to housing, whether through public provision, expanded private housing production, or likely both.[16] A real solution would also involve universal health-care coverage and perhaps work or basic income guarantees. In short, we need a strong social safety net and rights to sustenance.

Yet we are a long way off from developing such a robust welfare state or appropriate housing supply in many areas. Furthermore, there are dilemmas of mental illness and freedom that are not reduc-ible to poverty. Studying wealthy families has taught me that material resources, unto themselves, can only clarify, not resolve such dilem-mas. So, where do we start?

In 2022, the *New York Times* editorial board published "The Solution to Our Mental Health Crisis Already Exists."[17] Reflecting on the history of deinstitutionalization, the authors argue that the country delivered on the promise of hospital closure without creating access to community care. Therefore, they suggest that the federal government finally develop something resembling President Kennedy's proposed Community Mental Health Center System.

I agree completely that we must expand access. But to focus on access merely leads to the comparative question: What "community mental health care" are we talking about? My research has shown rad-ically different versions of what an outpatient clinic does, what ther-apy involves, what proper housing looks like, what "recovery" consists of, what kinds of futures can be dreamed, and what "client choice" means. Consider the differences discussed in this book.

In part 1, "Community Care for Different Communities," we saw the problems of serious mental illness play out in different ways for contrasting types of mental health-care providers and patients. Public safety net care only makes sense given municipal government's need to manage visible urban poverty and the homelessness crisis. Street-based outreach serves as an initial point of entry, where mental health workers labor alongside police to determine who qualifies for what services. The goal is to clear space and identify a subset of the street population that is ostensibly disabled and therefore "deserving" of care. Here, "mental illness" is not only an individual experience or social issue but also a bureaucratic resource, since diagnosis can trigger access to medical, housing, and cash benefits. Possible actions for treatment are shaped by, among other things, the infrastructure and facilities at hand, like shelters, supportive housing, jails, and Board and Care homes.

Elite private services, on the other hand, only make sense given privileged families' goal of reforming wayward relatives. Here care is shaped by love, fear, and embarrassment on the part of families and by the profit motive and the need for professional satisfaction on the part of providers. Possibilities for treatment are shaped by the available infrastructure of residential settings, beachside sober living homes, intensive outpatient programs, and therapeutic farms. Diagnostic specificity matters in this realm, where there are highly specialized treatments available for different conditions, rather than because diagnosis might be used to secure government benefits. Thus, the meanings of both *community care* and *mental illness* may be divided along class lines as well as goals related to the politics of urban space versus privileged family systems.

Part 2, "Unequal Treatments, Unequal Recoveries," showed that these contrasting worlds have radically different definitions of being disabled and of getting better. Whether treatment providers might say someone's mental illness has improved depends in large part on a *social prognosis* of the lives people can expect to live. The goals of care are radically different across types of clinics. For public safety net settings, "recovery" is a state in which people stay housed and no longer trigger emergency response calls. The practical problems at hand are the risk of recurrent homelessness or criminalization. This means that "treatment" beyond medication consists not of specialized psychotherapies but of processing Section 8 housing vouchers, dealing with landlords to avoid evictions, negotiating with probation officers, and helping clients acquire skills for living indoors.

For elite providers, clients typically have their baseline needs met by family money. The practical problems in this sphere are tied to individuals' failures to achieve the benchmarks of their age, becoming "stuck," or lacking viable identities. Thus, "recovery" is defined as a future in which people return to college, work, have meaningful activities, or at least participate in respectable society. Case managers provide various therapies for their patients or connect them to specialty clinics, get them to go outside, find them part-time jobs, or help them craft identities such as "artist" or "responsible uncle." With their divergent definitions of recovery, both the public safety net and elite private treatment can credibly claim to practice the ideal of recovery-oriented care.

Part 3, "The Paradox of Client Choice," showed how the very meanings of *freedom* and *client empowerment* are relative to context. Public providers for the formerly homeless or criminalized mental patient offer choices in terms of the noninterventionist approach I call *tolerant containment*. Because clients have been treated harshly and abandoned in the past, the first step is lowering clinical and societal expectations. As a form of generalized harm reduction, providers concede a degree of medication noncompliance, drug usage, and idleness as inevitable. Below a hospitalization threshold, overworked, understaffed, and underfunded providers default to framing client choice as a matter of people doing whatever they want. Since the key issue is keeping people housed, out of jail, and out of the ER, being psychotic or high is acceptable, so long as it occurs in the right place.

Elite private providers, on the other hand, attempt to reengineer choices in a process I call *concerted constraint*. Having leveraged financial resources or otherwise coaxed people into treatment, these facilities are positioned to discipline behavior, heal relationship wounds, generate self-efficacy, and help clients choose among new futures.

With their sufficient staffing and resources, clinics can attempt to transform people so that they are not symptomatic, idle, addicted, or bizarre. The goal is making people behave in class-appropriate ways, and unlike in the public programs, remaking the self seems possible in this setting. The only choices not allowed here are the ones offered the poor: to be an idle body in a Board and Care home or psychotic and high on the street or in an independent apartment. Ironically, disadvantaged clients left to their own devices can appear "freer" than the privileged ones, whose families invest in "fixing" and constraining them.

Stark divergences in philosophy and practice leave a lot of ambiguity. In other words, a new federal community care system *might* mean one that helps cities keep their jail or homeless stats down, or one that appeases family members and their needs; one that consists of harm reduction and guerrilla social work, or one that uses intensive psychiatric rehabilitation to build identities; one that defines freedom in terms of maximum autonomy, or one that defines freedom in terms of the right and obligation to upper-middle-class respectability.

Or we could work to build something new.

In what follows, I consider three broad problems for US mental health policy, each corresponding to a part of the book:

1. How to create a housing and treatment infrastructure that addresses the needs of patients, their families, and their communities
2. How to give psychiatrically disabled people of different social classes lives of dignity and hope
3. How to honor client choice (even when we inevitably try to constrain it)

Only after we've addressed these community care dilemmas can we tackle the question that has haunted mental health debates since deinstitutionalization: *Should we bring back the asylum?*

BUILDING BETTER TREATMENT INFRASTRUCTURES:
WORKING WITH WHAT WE HAVE

Much of our existing infrastructure for the poor patient is awful. It is oriented toward goals like saving the government money and maximizing profit for private actors. I have been tempted, at times, to think in terms of a revolutionary or abolitionist approach, tearing down the system to build something new. However, given the history of psychiatric hospital closure and the failed movement for community care, I remain wary of slash-and-burn tactics. What we need instead is harm reduction at the institutional level.

Taking a cue from the harm reductionists, who advocate for keeping drug users safe until change is possible (even when that means enabling destructive behavior), we need to keep our frayed safety net from ripping apart entirely. From there we can enlarge and improve it.

Consider a key issue for both the city and the privileged family in Los Angeles: where to place people who don't require hospitalization but have difficulty with independent living. Given the homelessness crisis, cities like Los Angeles have come to celebrate even the worst housing, like Board and Care homes, while acknowledging their inadequacy. The elite private sector, surprisingly, has not provided better. Recall from chapter 3 that even high-socioeconomic-status families struggle to find quality, long-term placements for their loved ones, because private industry focuses on short-term, high-expense treatment facilities that promise transformation (and profit). Thus, we have two dynamics at play: the city's need to keep its homelessness numbers down and save money in a constrained housing market, and the family's need to find quality long-term care in a private sector that doesn't regard such care financially worth its while.

What's the pragmatic approach, given the gridlock on housing construction in states like California and the reality of the profit motive in the private mental health sector? We must temper our ideals, for we'll be building out our new system atop existing infrastructure. This means accommodating projects unrelated to mental health issues, such as urban politics, family demands, and the profit motive. There's nothing inherently illegitimate about cities wanting to get people off the streets, families wanting a place to put loved ones outside the home, and private actors asking for fair compensation for their service. The key is not to let these dimensions dictate care.

As an example of institutional harm reduction, take the Board and Care system. Despite some compassionate operators, these flophouses are so poorly reimbursed that they are unable to offer much "care" or a sense of "home." In some cases, they aren't even oriented toward their residents. Recall in chapter 8 how Mr. Daniels framed his operation less in terms of service to residents than in terms of service to the state: keeping people off the streets and out of expensive hospitals. I've met activists who told me these facilities were beyond reform, so they advocated for the elimination of the Board and Care system. Ironically, this is finally happening, but not because better housing is available. Operators are losing money and finding it easier to sell than maintain their properties in California's inflated real estate market. More closures would be disastrous, leading yet more people to homelessness. Bad as they are, we must save the Board and Care homes to keep people housed—then we remake the facilities.

As the sociologist Alex Barnard and I have argued, doing so will require short-term and long-term interventions.[18] In the near term, we stem closures by reimbursing Board and Care homes at a higher level, as some counties have begun to do. This will only slow the tide, as some owners will still sell the properties and get out of the business if real estate prices continue rising. That is why, in the longer term, state or municipal governments will need to purchase or develop facilities such that at least some portion is publicly owned; this will allow the safety net to remain intact if not ideal. We could finance the endeavor using existing funds from the California Mental Health Services Act, or through property tax reforms to stabilize municipal funding more generally (see chapter 4).[19]

But it's still not enough to keep the system in place just to warehouse people. Board and Care homes must be transformed so that their residents have dignified living conditions. We do this by tying funding increases to expectations that homes facilitate access to educational and vocational services, offer recreation, and let residents share in decision-making, as seen in peer support and clubhouse models. Life in these settings might, in theory, present a context of interdependence and community building rather than the boredom and isolation of a flophouse. We could look to Geel, Belgium, a town with a tradition of housing disabled "boarders" from surrounding communities, for cues on how to create meaningful integration.[20] No doubt it will take money as well as a system of accountability and a different vision of the facilities' roles within the safety net to achieve it. The effort will benefit not only the city but also the better-off families who struggle to find appropriate placements in the private market. Moving toward a publicly run, high-quality system of Board and Care homes need not disrupt the parallel long-range goals of building permanent housing with intensive support services, high-quality clinics and hospitals, peer-run respites, and residential treatment centers.

The principles of working with what we have and understanding—without bowing to—the needs of various actors' projects will apply across different instances. For example, the state of California and its cities began to rent and then purchase run-down motels for the homeless during the early phases of the COVID-19 pandemic, when travel restrictions left the businesses empty and at risk of bankruptcy. Like the better Board and Care homes I envision, facilities like underused hotels or office space left empty by remote work could also be rented or purchased, rezoned, remade, and staffed with appropriate services while being operated in democratic fashion. In the long run, addressing the broader homelessness crisis will require a substantial expansion of housing supply, and the state of California is finally taking steps to speed development.[21] But until we can build enough real housing and create high-quality service centers, we must do the best with existing infrastructure and a clear sense of the existing need.[22]

MAKING LIVES WORTH LIVING:
VALUING A VARIETY OF FUTURES

My research has shown two vastly different social prognoses and recovery orientations in the clinical worlds of the poor and the rich: the promise of a life off the institutional circuit versus the promise of a new viable identity. Each setting succeeds at times but just as often fails in ways difficult for clinicians to see. This is because the vision of care in each setting is constrained by institutional prerogatives. The public settings may get people off the street—no small feat—but without a plan to move beyond this, they de facto treat poor people with mental illness as though they have no future. The elite private settings, on the other hand, have material abundance but value systems that can lead people to despair for a different reason: recovery is predicated on individualistic benchmarks that are not necessarily appropriate or fulfilling. Making something better, on each side, will require both policy and cultural change.

On the public side, the Los Angeles County Department of Mental Health (DMH) and contracted nonprofits are evaluated with quantitative measures of homelessness, jail, and hospitalization reduction. Although these are all reasonable goals in the hierarchy of immediate needs, such priorities inevitably skew mental health-care providers' approaches. People typically stabilize in terms of housing because at the public safety net level, treatment is basically equated with housing intervention. Consider what care and recovery mean, in concrete terms, for DMH clients featured in chapters 4 and 5: Delilah can look forward to moving from a mental-illness-related apartment complex to subsidized senior housing, but therapeutically speaking, her trauma remains unaddressed. Gillian receives crucial help with her probation and housing. But what about her goals with her children? And Jeremiah, who is described as "what hope looks like," is grateful that he's off the street, but he believes "there should be more." He dreams of gaining computer skills and working again, or reconnecting with his wife, but those dreams feel out of reach. All these clients come up against a tragic waste of human potential that transcends mental illness—it's about our society's failure to create social opportunities and real roles for the vulnerable.

In essence, there is a risk that urban political dynamics dictate the clinical focus of care or limit the horizon for individuals' futures. A benevolent kind of dehumanization occurs, even among genuinely caring staff who believe in the mission of serving the poor. Without connections to patients' families and a sense of life narrative, providers can come to see people as essentially ahistorical—a problem in the present but lacking a past or a future. In reacting to the real social crises of their patients, mental health workers have little room to share in what might appear to be unrealistic dreams. And even if the clinical mind-set changed, the existing system presents patients with concrete disincentives to getting better. Hard-won survival resources are predicated on disability, so many fear losing medical, housing, and cash benefits should they "graduate" from a program or fully return to work.

Consider the following scenario: someone like Jeremiah finds employment. Right now, it may not be worth it. If he makes too much money, he risks losing his public insurance coverage and housing support. And when he looks to his mentally healthy peers struggling to survive in the Southern California economy, taking three buses to a minimum-wage job, he may decide, quite rationally, that the life of a professional mental patient is better. If people want to pursue things like employment, we need to ensure they can do so without fear of losing the stability they have. This can come through further tweaks to Supplemental Security Income and Medicaid policy for higher income allowances. Ideally, we would have universal health care and housing rights so that access to survival isn't predicated on staying sick. Until we improve the life prospects of everyday working people as well, it will make little sense for psychiatric service users to leave patient status.

In the elite private world, I found different constraints on the future. These can't be solved by an infusion of resources, for these people are already rich. These constraints instead require shifts in culture and values. In some cases, money is part of the problem. Elite providers and affluent families must reckon with how *individualized* treatment may become too *individualistic* and therefore eschew the *community* integration that providers aspire toward. Recall in chapter 6 how Shelly's wealth allowed her to hire therapists, masseuses, and psychics, an affordance that may also prevent her from venturing into the world to make nonpaid friends.

Similarly, the Actualization Clinic case managers take Sherman to community college classes and the museum, and they build him a website to house his essays. He says, however, that he has no one in his life beyond those who work at Actualization. Sherman never suffered the traumas of the street, but his experience of loneliness, in the end, is not that different from Delilah's at the DMH. Here rich peoples' values and ideals of high-class achievement can prevent opportunities for community building and social integration. Anthony, for instance, decided not to go back to the Painted Brain art workshop because it felt "low class," and he instead planned to rent out space in an art gallery. His money means he can do so—but this individual-level intervention means he misses out on creating community with other artists who share his disability.

In sum, there is a risk that privileged families dictate narrow meanings of the good life, constraining possibilities for their loved one's future. Providers in this system construe patients very differently than at the DMH—as complex people who are only temporarily debilitated. Sometimes this optimism is quite helpful. Perversely, though, some of the wealthy clients lead small lives not because of deprivation but because of privileged family expectations. Think of the man with schizophrenia whose family made him quit his job at P.F. Chang's because they thought it was beneath them. As William, the director of one of Actualization's sister programs, explained, the privileged patient may also suffer from intense internalized stigma because they are being compared to siblings and relatives who are seen as extremely successful. This leads to people fighting for unrealistic dreams that may, in some cases, cause them more harm than good.

There's nothing wrong with people having conventional dreams of success. Surely, RJ and Brandon should have a chance to return to college if that's what they want, but it's also OK if they don't make it. Not everyone will be like Leonard, Dev, or Geraldine, talking about pursuing their graduate degrees at the National Alliance on Mental Illness speaker series. When our culture can't validate people for their simple worth as humans, as siblings, as friends, apart from jobs or keeping up appearances, it's both harmful to those individuals and a waste for the communities around them. Disability justice activists have long argued that recovery discourse is too often bound to an individualistic ideal of participation in contemporary capitalism: work, get married, seem normal, and don't ask much of others.[23] That's fine, but it's also fine if people use benefits, have different forms of friendship and kinship, ask for help, and are a little weird.

This means policy changes for accommodation and material assistance to achieve dreams, as well as changes to combat what disability studies scholars call the "hegemony of normalcy" and the pervasive social pressure to conform.[24] We must truly integrate people into their communities, give them concrete roles through which to contribute, and recognize that these things can happen outside formal jobs and careers. Often the communities must change too. Some of the above improvements are about mental health policy, yes—and some are about the broader social issue of how we value human beings beyond educational and market performance.

HONORING CLIENT CHOICE: BALANCING TOLERANCE AND CONSTRAINT

We can't discuss freedom without accounting for power. I just said that we must accept people as they are and combat the "hegemony of normalcy," but at the extremes these actions present problems. How can we still honor people's choices while seeking to restrict them? This is the inherent tension in a liberal society that wants to both care for, and empower, people with psychiatric disabilities.

The philosopher Michel Foucault famously argued that the eighteenth-century Quaker moral treatment of madness evidenced the most insidious form of social control.[25] The Quakers had rejected older approaches to confinement that merely beat people or chained them to the wall. Instead, they pushed patients to work in the asylum gardens and monitor their own thoughts for sin or insanity, rewarding those who learned to exhibit "proper" behavior. By replacing physical chains with intensive surveillance and the internalization of norms, these pastoral programs seemed to control people with psychological chains and therapeutic micromanagement. For Foucault and other critics of the asylum, attempts to normalize the poor social deviant through this "disciplinary power" became as suspect as brute domination.

My research has revealed, however, that there is little disciplinary power involved in managing the public mental patient. Poor people with disabilities may be "free" on the street, where they are ignored until they cause trouble; warehoused in jail, where no one monitors their behavior; or tolerated and contained in subsidized housing, where they smoke meth and yell. In fact, I found that disciplinary power is now reserved for the privileged: only the wealthy can afford the concerted constraint of sending their children to elite private rehabs and places like the Therapeutic Farm, a descendant of that Quaker moral treatment system. We can accept Foucault's insight that intensive treatment may act as control while acknowledging it can genuinely be care too. The question becomes how tolerance and constraint should be balanced. My comparative ethnographic observations show us the range of possibilities.

For the public sector, the key lesson is that generalized harm reduction is not nearly enough. When programs lack the means to provide clients with consistent attention, otherwise suitable interventions like Housing First can become mere tolerant containment.[26] We need substantially more resources so that mental health-care providers can truly attend to people and cultivate them through care. Occasionally, there is "natural growth" to be celebrated, as in chapter 8, when Janey feels safe in housing and reduces crack usage on her own. But the system also tolerates things that should not be tolerated, like people drinking themselves to death in subsidized housing or harassing their neighbors. I'm not naïve. There is no easy fix. Cultivating people and altering their behavior, without turning to overt force, is expensive and difficult. Sometimes such cultivation is impossible, because care is coming so late in life after so many years of neglect, or because people's disabilities are so profound that therapeutics might not be viable. If so, focusing on keeping people safe and out of trouble might be the best that providers can do. But we must ensure that this is genuinely the case, not a way of rationalizing the fact that our public clinics are understaffed.

For the private sector, the lessons are the opposite. Many elite private providers are simply unprepared for long-lasting serious mental illness and continued addiction. Lacking a harm-reduction model, they're unsure what to do with people who don't rapidly get better or become sober. Although places like Actualization meet the ethical standard of referring such clients elsewhere, there aren't many referral options, because the elite world isn't good at this. Some clients may end up in the public safety net eventually, as with the young man who drove away in his car. Or they may end up dead. As it stands, private providers too often wash their hands of such "difficult" cases.

Recall from chapter 9 how the concerted constraint model can fall apart, and how leverage can create new crises. The reliance on financial dependence as a means of engagement also means that providers don't know what to do without it. Consider when Actualization declined to work with the alcoholic Hollywood writer again after he came out of the hospital because he had his own money and therefore couldn't be leveraged. Or when its employees balked at working with a homeless, heroin-addicted woman diagnosed with schizophrenia because there wasn't family money at play, and she presented more risks than they were used to. Rather than develop capacity to manage risk and connect with her, the clinic simply told the insurance company not to send it more homeless clients. I watched public safety net providers continue to engage people in risky situations and slowly work to build therapeutic connection. The private mental health treatment agencies ensure that no one dies on their watch, but only because they refuse to watch over anyone who seems likely to die.

If high-risk clients express interest in care, elite providers should have a strategy in place to help them. Such people might make use of the therapeutics, but this requires keeping them alive and building trust until they are ready to do so. These actions, of course, are what the harm reductionists from the public sector and nonprofit worlds are experts in. The key question will be how to carry these out correctly in the private sphere so that the periods of tolerance are about safety and relationship building, rather than the kind of destructive indulgence some families perform by funneling cash to drug-addicted, disabled loved ones.

Finally, there must be real regulation of concerted constraint to ensure that normalizing practices are legitimately therapeutic. Recent exposés of elite private facilities, especially in the "troubled teen industry," have shown how therapeutic centers force people to work in demeaning conditions to "break" spoiled patients.[27] Work requirements can be exploitative when a poor person is used to generate profit, or abusive when a rich young adult is made to do repetitive tasks to break his or her spirit. Yet scheduled activity and work can indeed be therapeutic, even if the physical task looks like a problematic form of labor. Whether something is "good" or "bad" normalization is hard to judge from afar; we will need to develop both regulatory and enforcement capacity to recognize and intervene in abusive practices.

BRING BACK THE ASYLUM?

I have addressed ways to improve community care along three dimensions: infrastructure, futures, and choices. But even presuming we can, it's not a given that freedom in the community is appropriate for everyone experiencing mental illness. Current pessimism over the mental health and homelessness crises has led people throughout this book, rich and poor alike, to wonder whether we should "bring back the asylum." Desperate care workers dreamed of a place resembling an animal shelter or "jail forever" for a subset of mental patients, and wealthy families claimed that money for voluntary care was not enough—they need legal changes to allow for permanent conservator-ship and more locked facilities.

Let me start by saying that the asylum question is too blunt. We are, in a sense, haunted by the ghost of the state hospital, imagining a caricature rather than its true history. People like nurse Vic have a romantic view of that system, whereas many patient advocates imag-ine every large hospital as equally terrible. A more nuanced discussion must take seriously the differences among individuals and institu-tions. Most people we met in this book didn't require formally coer-cive care, but others simply weren't successfully enrolled in any sort of voluntary assistance. Some stayed on the street, some were arrested, and some died, including some with family and money. An asylum system—alongside court-ordered community-based care—could offer safe harbor. The risk remains, however, that this could turn into the kind of dumping ground of old.

Addressing the asylum question in good faith means considering its components: First, given real resource constraints, what would its relationship be to voluntary outpatient services? Second, what *type* of asylum would we create? I'm glad that there are staunch civil libertar-ians who condemn all forced treatment, for they will keep attention on the many ways that "care" becomes a ruse for the exercise of power. Yet this needed perspective must be balanced with concerns of safety, health, and the preservation of possible futures. In some cases, force may be a violation—*and* the lesser of evils. Once again, I return to the idea of institutional harm reduction: the goal is to make necessary coercion less bad.

TIMING AND PRIORITIZATION

The first issue is how to balance the needed expansion of both vol-untary and involuntary settings, outpatient and institutional. Recall that Harry Brickman, director of the Los Angeles County DMH in the 1960s, complained that the then governor Ronald Reagan had emptied the state hospitals before the DMH could develop the com-munity care sector. It has been playing catch-up ever since. Consider what might happen if we reversed this state of affairs and now poured most of our resources into resurrecting an asylum system and changing legislation in order to ease forced treatment before expanding the voluntary community services. In this vein, some conservative policy writers have argued as much, insisting that we lift the 1965 Medicaid exemption that prevents federal money from flowing to larger-scale facilities[28] and prioritize spending on long-term hospitalization for the most seriously mentally ill.[29]

I am sympathetic to these arguments. There is a dire need for expanded inpatient and residential care, including some coercive services geared toward the neediest. Still, timing matters, and if poorly done this reprioritization of resources could backfire tremendously. As they say, when you're holding a hammer, everything looks like a nail. If asylums become an available and reputable resource, many people who might otherwise be well served by compassionate voluntary care or low-barrier housing might instead be institutionalized. Families may decide that their best bet is to dump a difficult relative in a facility rather than explore a range of better-suited options. Recall the point made by Laura, leader of the DMH intensive treatment team, that when a person's first experience with psychiatry is domineering, getting confined and "punched in the face" with a high dose of an injectable antipsychotic, he or she might then be turned off from treatment forever. If we lean into institutional coercion at the expense of voluntary care, we risk unnecessary force and the creation of a whole new group of treatment-resistant people.

Now imagine instead that we finally put adequate resources into excellent voluntary services—community-based programs with housing guarantees and case management, mainstream psychiatry alongside alternatives like peer-run respites, early psychosis intervention, job and education assistance, drug rehab on demand, and voluntary hospitals. As you've read, rich people might say they wouldn't go back to a hospital but, in crisis, will voluntarily go to a beautiful private rehab overlooking the ocean. We tend to associate hospitalization with involuntary care, but this is often because the facilities are terrible and we only have space for those who have been deemed dangerous or a legal liability. Not all our facilities can be oceanside sites in Southern California or the Therapeutic Farm of New England, of course, but there's no reason we can't create safe, decent, and caring hospitals that people choose to utilize.

In such a system, some people may exhaust every possible high-quality voluntary option and require long-term hospitalization. But rather than inappropriately "solving" social problems by disappearing a mass of people, we will have winnowed that confined group to only those we truly cannot serve in the community.

PEER-DESIGNED HOSPITALS AND PROCEDURAL JUSTICE

Any new coercive system must contend with two unpleasant truths. First, advocates of forced treatment are correct that some people will self-destruct or harm others without coercive intervention to address their mental health needs. Second, activists who fight forced treatment are correct that our coercive services have a bad track record and often fail spectacularly. Research demonstrates that people placed on emergency holds or processed through mental health court routinely find these experiences traumatizing,[30] which can lead to treatment disengagement and even increased suicide risk.[31] Given these two truths, polarized advocates on each side have dug in their heels. But there is room for compromise and even collaboration.

As Professor Alex Barnard and I have argued in the press, if there is an expansion of forced care, the people who have the most intimate knowledge of how coercion goes wrong—that is, patient representatives—should have the power to design it.[32] We must ask why people want out of our existing hospitals or other treatment so badly and then use that information to guide improvements. We might think broadly, hiring architects who themselves have been hospitalized to make less alienating psych wards; recruit user interaction design engineers (like those who create shopping or technological interface experiences) to work with ex-patients to remake emergency intake procedures; and bring people with lived experience into research and evaluation.[33] We could also utilize peer respites staffed by people with lived experience of mental illness instead of using hospitalization as a default. We could employ psychiatric advance directives, in which people describe their wishes for how they are to be treated should they become extremely manic or psychotic, as a safeguard to help protect patients' rights and preferences.[34]

Coercion need not automatically lead to alienation. Researchers have found that people often put less weight on their technical legal status of voluntary/involuntary than on whether they have been treated with dignity.[35] Ultimately, the meaning of forced care is different when we're talking about high-quality settings, like a pastoral farm offering activities or a beautiful hospital unit, versus a dungeon-like ward or building. The moral calculus changes too, if we have provided for people's basic needs, given them at least partial say in their treatment, and provided enough resources so that they have true options at discharge.

California's new CARE Courts and similar programs in other states present an opportunity to try such a compassionate and just approach. Many activists have argued that these court procedures, which connect people to voluntary services under threat of possible conservatorship, are oppressive and have taken a hard-line stance against such courts.[36] There is certainly a risk of abuse, and I, too, am wary of CARE Courts as they have been outlined. That's why the state should mitigate such risk by bringing in patient activists to ensure due process and improve the care and court procedures. Activists, for their part, should see that such programs will be developed with or without them, and theirs is the crucial missing voice. Disability rights proponents have long argued that there be "nothing about us without us" and that they deserve a true seat at the table rather than tokenistic inclusion. It is incumbent on authorities and legislators to give them that seat and on activists and advocates to use it.

Even in those rare cases that do lead to guardianship or long-term hospitalization, there is tremendous room for improvement in what legal scholars call procedural justice. Research shows that a legal decision itself is only part of what matters to people; equally important is whether the procedure is legitimate. This goes beyond the legal safeguards that formally protect rights. It matters that people feel their voices are heard and that these are not kangaroo courts. A fair process is both the right thing to do and crucial for ensuring that coercion doesn't lead to patient cynicism and disengagement. In short, we must listen to people who have been hospitalized, not write them off as crazy.

Taking these steps will require a great deal of humility. Inevitably, there will be "false positives" of people who are inappropriately forced into treatment, and "false negatives" of people who should have been assisted but were left alone. Treatments like antipsychotic medication can be lifesaving in some cases, profoundly damaging in others, or both—and it can be impossible to know before trying.[37] A willingness to acknowledge harm, then course-correct, will be key for developing a system people can trust.[38]

FREEDOM AS AN INFERIOR GOOD

In 1894, the poet and journalist Anatole France wryly observed, "The law, in its majestic equality, forbids the rich as well as the poor to sleep under bridges, to beg in the streets, and to steal bread."[39] He likely envisioned a more just world that gave poor people resources, keeping them from sleeping rough, panhandling, or stealing. Another response is to allow people to sleep under bridges and yell on side streets. I have described this as tolerant containment, and it's a de facto form of public policy that offers rights to be homeless, to use drugs, or to refuse psychiatric services, so long as people stay relatively unobtrusive. It speaks the language of freedom but acts like abandonment, and it's becoming the predominant form of social control in cash-strapped cities which can neither police away, nor solve, their social problems.[40]

Such tolerance is hardly effective public policy. It makes a mockery of rights. Still, it is compatible with one version of "freedom"—what the philosopher Isaiah Berlin called negative liberty to avoid external coercion. This type of liberty is dear to Americans, and it is an important value to be wrestled with. There are good arguments for and against radical free speech rights, property rights, and the like. But the right to be homeless or psychotic can become a cruel joke if not accompanied by real assistance.

Economists speak of inferior goods, mostly consumed by the poor, and superior goods, mostly consumed by the rich. As a society, we have collectively made the structures and support that cultivate an orderly life into a superior good, only available to the few, and freedom into an inferior good. If you can consume nothing else, you can consume the freedom to smoke meth, sleep in a tent, and behave chaotically.

We need a better response to Anatole France's aphorism than leaving people alone under bridges or free to experience psychiatric breakdown—we need housing, health care, and the freedom to pursue a viable life. Robust social rights are crucial if we ever hope to meaningfully honor people's choices and personhood. Sometimes those social rights and positive liberty will mean harm reduction and peer-delivered voluntary services. Sometimes they will require tempering people's choices in the here and now, to bring them self-control and long-term choice-making ability. Both require a significant investment of resources such that "freedom to" becomes a reality and coercion is done with appropriate care.[41]

The bioethics of behavioral health is rife with ambiguities. Social policy is too blunt an instrument to settle existential dilemmas, and it cannot generate the cultural change we will need to fully honor different forms of personhood. But if ethical choices regarding freedom and treatment have been predetermined by disinvestment in the care and housing infrastructure, or by whether a person has been deemed an embodied social problem versus a beloved child, well, that is both a moral and a policy failure. Good social policy can ensure that ethical questions are not decided by inequality. From that baseline, we can begin to grapple with the complexity of peoples' freedom and dreams—whether they are strangers on the sidewalk, our loved ones, or ourselves.

ACKNOWLEDGMENTS

I am deeply indebted to the people who helped me over the decade it took to research and write this book. First and foremost, I thank the psychiatric service users, mental health-care providers, family members, activists, officials, folks on the street, and many others who shared their lives and perspectives with me. I do not thank them all by name, given concerns with privacy, but in an obvious sense this book would not have been possible without their participation. More than that, they were generous and open about often difficult experiences, and for this I am eternally grateful.

At UCLA, Stefan Timmermans gave me more time and careful cultivation than any graduate student could expect. Beyond his brilliance as a sociologist and methodologist, he kept me on track and believed in me at times when I almost threw in the towel. It was only when I began to mentor graduate students myself that I saw just how special this level of commitment is. Hannah Landecker, Rogers Brubaker, Joel Braslow, and Aaron Panofsky joined Stefan to create a group of mentors second to none. They sent me back to the drawing board more than once, frustrated, tired, but also exhilarated. Thanks to both the National Science Foundation and UCLA for financial support during this period.

At the University of Michigan, the Society of Fellows pulled me out of my disciplinary myopia into a broader intellectual world. What a

pleasure and privilege to talk with biologists about what I meant by
"care ecology," to learn about evolution, architecture, and literary theory, and to in turn make my research legible to scientists and human-
ists. The sociology department provided a wonderful intellectual base
and the chance to hone my craft as a teacher, and I learned much in
my time among sharp thinkers and kind people. Special thanks to my
dear friends Heath Pearson and Bridget Purcell for taking me into
their home when COVID-19 arrived and left me isolated. Fabulous
minds, top-notch Vanagon travel companions.

At UC San Diego, I was welcomed into a wonderful community in
the sociology department. Amy Binder has been an amazing faculty
mentor, always ready with good fiction recommendations. Current
chair Kwai Ng has kindly helped me navigate the early days of profes-
sorhood with ease. Arriving during pandemic times was strange, and
I thank Dan Navon, David FitzGerald, Kevin Lewis, Abigail Andrews,
Richard Pitt, Vanesa Ribas, and Michel Estefan for inviting me to
hang and making me feel welcome. Outside the department, I thank
Lilly Irani and Keolu Fox for conversations about politics, design, and
making the work matter beyond the academy.

For mentorship away from my official institutional home bases,
Corey Abramson provided a model of social scientific rigor and intellectual honesty—my transitioning from his research assistant to his
collaborator was when I felt like a real sociologist. Bradley Lewis at
NYU, Sascha Dubrul, and others from the Icarus Project shaped this
project years before it started. Martin Sanchez-Jankowski, Deborah
Lustig, Christine Trost, and Philip Fucella at the UC Berkeley Center
for Ethnographic Research set me on the path to becoming a social
scientist.

And then there are the many, many people who have thought with
me: my grad crew of Eleni Skaperdas, Chris Rea, Alex Holmstrom-
Smith, Yewon Lee, Kyle Nelson, Michael Siciliano, Edwin
Everhart, Phi Su, Jeremy Levenson, Zach Griffin, Wisam Alshaibi,
Eli Wilson, Emily Yen, Forrest Stuart, Anthony Ocampo, David
Trouille, Carmella Stoddard, Phung Su, Lauren Textor, and all who
attended the Ethnography Working Group; my fellow California

book-writing club members Chris Herring, Alex Barnard, and Josh Seim; my fellow Michigan book-writing club members Alexandra Murphy, Jeremy Levine, Dan Hirschman, and Jacob Lederman; the Princeton Ethnography group led by Mitch Duneier and Matt Desmond; the Boston Medical Sociology group; the Michigan Social Theory Workshop; the anonymous peer reviewers at the *American Sociological Review*; Gabe Rossman and Charles Fain Lehman for conservative perspectives that kept me honest; Philippe Bourgois, Marcia Meldrum, Laurie Hart, and the rest of the UCLA Social Medicine reading group; Ching Kwan Lee, Jeffrey Prager, Bill Roy, Jack Katz, and other UCLA faculty who shaped my thinking; Xiaohong Xu, Charlotte Cavaille, Paige Sweet, Roi Livne, Luciana De Souza Leão, Carson Byrd, Rob Manduca, and Roseanna Sommers, who made A2 feel like home, if only a temporary one; and a bunch of others whose feedback or thinking made its way into the book: Grace Rainier Long, Jessica Feldman, Zsuza Berend, Adaner Usmani, Margaret Kelly, Anthony Dimario, Liam Ecker, Andy Scull, Laura Van Tosh, Amelia Dmowska, Iddo Tavory, Gil Eyal, Beth Bromley, Belinda Johns, Drew Oldham, David Benesty, and Hannah Reiss. I'm sure there are others whom I've unintentionally missed, and I hope they know my gratitude extends to them as well.

For help with the craft of writing, high praise goes to Elizabeth Jean Bailey. After she read the first page of the introduction and suggested how to restructure it for clarity, I knew I had to have her help me with the manuscript. Reggie Hui took a novelist's eye to the text and saw how I might enliven my prose. Michael Bakal, the person I trust most with draft ideas in both writing and life, always seemed to know what to cut. Finally, Letta Page did a fabulous job with copyediting and honing turns of phrase.

At the University of Chicago Press, I thank Elizabeth Branch Dyson for her work in turning this manuscript into an actual book. She gave me detailed reading and sharp feedback, and she put a first-time author at ease, all while stepping into her editorial role in the middle of the publication process. The three manuscript reviewers—two anonymous, and David Snow, who revealed his identity when I asked for further thoughts—made the book substantially stronger. Sandy Hazel helped tighten everything in the last round of copy edits. And I thank the late Douglas Mitchell, who believed in this project when he signed me; I wish I'd had the chance to show him the final product, then talk jazz and philosophy.

Finally, I thank my parents, Joyce Hee and Kelvin Gong, for their love and support. My mother gave me my affection for literature and reminded me of the human story I wanted to tell. My father was always there to listen, remind me to laugh, and help me get out of my head by taking me busking at Berkeley BART or singing at senior homes. Without my family I'd be lost; I love them more than I can say.

RESEARCH APPENDIX

Ethnographic research often unfolds in unpredictable ways. Since fieldwork is less standardized than some other social science methods, it helps to know how the researcher collected their information and analyzed it. My comments here should help readers better evaluate the book and help other ethnographers prepare for issues that may arise in their own projects.

First, I discuss the logic of comparison and how I selected my cases. Second, I give a more in-depth description of the main clinics. Third, I describe my approach to data collection and interpretation. Fourth, I offer a visualization of the overarching argument. Fifth, I explain how I selected individual people and stories to illustrate my general claims. Sixth, I describe how my presence and identity shaped the study. Finally, I explain my approach to empirical and theoretical generalizability.

LOGIC OF CASE COMPARISON AND CASE SELECTION

To understand how social inequality shapes the management of mental illness, I engaged in comparative ethnography—that is, I spent time at psychiatric clinics for the poor and those for rich people and immersed myself in the contrasting worlds. The research project was not originally comparative, however. I had only planned to study public safety net care and began with the Los Angeles County Department of Mental Health clinic for practical reasons. I had worked as an interviewer on a federally funded evaluation project of the California Mental Health Services Act and had therefore already visited treatment teams throughout the state. When I moved to Los Angeles to pursue my PhD at UCLA, I contacted the DMH to see whether I could follow one of its programs. There were difficulties, such as going through a research bureaucracy and getting live-scanned to see whether my fingerprints matched anyone's in a criminal database. Yet the process was also straightforward because of my previous connection—the staff knew I'd worked in community mental health services after college, so they thought I could be a useful volunteer, or at least not get in the way.

As I took more classes during my PhD program, I became interested in comparative sociological research. Many of sociology's major ideas come from comparing societies, such as the historical development of capitalism or the evolution of legal systems in different parts of the world. I thought I could better understand what I saw in Downtown LA by going to, say, Sweden, or another European country with a strong welfare state. But my advisor, Stefan Timmermans, dissuaded me from my original plans to jump into international comparison. For one thing, he wasn't convinced I knew Los Angeles's public system yet. He saw I was interested in how resources shape care, but he said to wait until I had identified my focal points. Eventually, I suspected that there was something interesting going on with how resource constraints shaped ideals of client choice, and my advisor agreed that a contrasting case of a wealthy clinic could help illuminate this. After being referred to elite private mental health-care providers in Los Angeles, I saw that my comparative ethnography could best be conducted locally.

Early on I had envisioned my comparison as like a laboratory experiment where I looked at how the variable "social class" impacted otherwise identical cases. When I found the Actualization Clinic, I thought I'd identified my perfect comparison: the clinic's case management team saw people in the community, had shared roots in the

1970s model of "hospitals without walls," and appeared to share organizational characteristics (see below), so I could "control" for these factors and observe a single difference. Of course, the real world is not a laboratory, and social class is not a single isolated variable.

When I moved from the public to the elite private settings, I encountered differences in racial demographics, jail histories, family involvement, and even how people talked about mental illness. I was jarred by the fact (obvious in hindsight) that so many things I had taken for granted at the DMH were simply irrelevant—the homelessness crisis, for instance, and the attendant focus on things like Section 8 housing vouchers. And when elite providers complained about overinvolved families, I suddenly realized how many clients in the Skid Row clinic were disconnected from relatives. The comparison was revealing things but not what I'd expected.

Although originally frustrated that I didn't have a "perfect comparison," I came to see this as useful in a different way: each clinical world helped me look at the other one through fresh eyes. Rather than isolate a variable to establish causality, I was using comparison to better understand how contrasting worlds made sense of mental illness, and how mental illness shaped people's lives in different settings. I learned from forms of comparison other than those based on the logic of variables as found in statistics and experiments—instead, these compared entire worlds of meaning to better understand each case. Such an interpretive comparison can "clarify particularities through contrasts" and let cases "form a kind of commentary on one another's character."[1] As is common in ethnographic research, my conceptualization of the study itself changed over time. For instance, while I initially envisioned the comparison as one purely of social class, I came to see it was also about mental illness as a public problem of the city versus a private one of the family. Thus, what I saw as a research difficulty—no obvious singular outcome variable—was itself a finding, not a study design problem.

Ultimately, my approach to comparison evolved throughout the research process in what Tavory and Timmermans have since called "sequential comparison."[2] The researcher begins with one case study and slowly develops both a research question and an answer. If there are key puzzles in the initial site that cannot be answered without comparison, then it is time to find the appropriate next case study— for me, it was moving from the poor to the rich clinics and then getting to know middle-class people trying to access each. For further reflections on comparison in field research, see my 2020 book coedited with Corey Abramson, *Beyond the Case: The Logics and Practices of Comparative Ethnography*.[3]

COMPARISON OF THE MAIN CLINICS

The primary clinics exist in very different organizational ecologies, serve clients who have different backgrounds, and use vastly different resources to process and treat those clients, but the clinics are also in some ways directly comparable. In organizational terms, the DMH and Actualization clinical teams share important structural similarities, because they both are variations on the Assertive Community Treatment team model—the so-called hospital without walls—that emerged in the 1970s. This model is known as the gold standard of community-based mental health services, as it provides wraparound services and staff who can meet people in their homes or elsewhere. It aims to provide comprehensive psychosocial care alongside medical-psychiatric intervention.

Both clinics feature an interdisciplinary team of case managers who provide recovery-oriented service provision in the community. Each team includes a licensed clinical social worker and a PhD-level psychologist in supervisory roles. With such community-based care, providers aim to move beyond the simple "medical model" to whole-person treatment. From a distance, clients, too, may appear clinically similar in terms of diagnosis, such as schizophrenia, bipolar disorder, or major depression. In each setting, people may have a history of hospitalization and the difficulties associated with freedom and medication and/or treatment "noncompliance."

Yet there are also significant differences. The DMH team model is set up to be largely self-contained, a sort of one-stop shop. With a doctor, nurses, and social workers along with staff members without an advanced education, the DMH team covers the gamut of health-care provision. With about 9 workers for around 140 served, the client-to-staff ratio is approximately 16:1, far lower than in the regular outpatient clinics. Moreover, the team includes workers certified to write psychiatric holds for when they decide coercion is called for.

The Actualization Clinic, on the other hand, acts in conjunction with providers such as outside medical care, psychotherapists, and treatment centers. Most of its clients come in with a private psychiatrist, with whom it maintains contact. Serving around 80 people at a time with 10 workers and with a client-to-staff ratio of approximately 8:1, the clinic offers a level of potential individualized care typically unavailable to the public mental patient. Additionally, its line-staff members all have master's degrees, primarily in either psychology or marriage and family therapy, and a handful in social work. Rather than initiating psychiatric holds in house, Actualization has these handled by the client's private psychiatrist or with a call to the DMH Psychiatric Emergency Team.

The client populations differ as well. The DMH's formal criteria prioritize those who have a diagnosis of serious mental illness *and* a history of jail, homelessness, or repeat hospitalizations. In terms of age, its team treats clients from 26 to 59 years old. More than half the clients have a schizophrenia diagnosis of some type, with others typically diagnosed as having bipolar disorder or major depression. The majority of the Downtown team clients are nonwhite and socially disconnected, and they have little to no family involvement. Note that these characteristics hang together: people with privilege and family support are less likely to have the jail and homelessness records that trigger qualification for DMH services. Ironically, many of the middle-class family activists who lobbied for the 2004 California Mental Health Services Act, which taxed millionaires to fund case management teams, found that their own relatives were ineligible for the mental health programs, because these prioritized "underserved" and "unserved" people with the most social need.[4]

The Actualization Clinic, in contrast, has no explicit criteria that potential clients must meet. They serve clients aged 18 years and older and are open to people of a variety of diagnoses. Thus, while records indicate that roughly 30 percent of its clients are diagnosed as having a schizophrenia-related disorder and approximately 20 percent with a bipolar disorder diagnosis, it serves a greater number of people diagnosed with depression, anxiety, or an eating disorder. Furthermore, its clients skew younger. Most are white, although there are privileged families of color who contract the services as well. Many clients have histories of hospitalization, but there is far less criminal justice involvement and almost no homelessness. Thus, the Actualization Clinic serves a clientele with differences in terms of race, social class, and institutional trajectory. At a glance (and as an estimate over the time I observed, because client numbers changed, and staff came and left):

SNAPSHOT OF PRIMARY CLINICS

	DMH Full Service Partnership	Actualization Clinic
Client-to-staff ratio	~16:1 (140:9)	~8:1 (80:10)
Master's degree held by field workers	4 of 9	10 of 10
Funding	Medicaid/Medicare, county/state funds	Family out-of-pocket payments ~$6K/month
Client classification requirement	Serious mental illness + homeless/jail/ hospital discharge	None

DATA COLLECTION AND INTERPRETATION

In the tradition of urban ethnography, I immersed myself in the daily rhythms of my research subjects' lives and tried to see things from their perspectives. I took notes by hand on paper and sometimes in my smartphone. At treatment meetings and case conferences, I was allowed to write notes in real time, and I recorded these as verbatim quotations. While out and about, I'd take "jottings" of behavioral observations and key phrases and write these up as narrative field notes when I got home. I paraphrase statements from these field observations, representing phrases as quotations only if I was confident about their accuracy. I prioritize firsthand observation of social interaction as my primary data, and then I supplement this with commentary from the relevant actors. Often this meant observing a striking interaction in the field, then following up with conversation or interviews.

In some cases, I was a participant-observer with a concrete role to fulfill (e.g., as a homeless outreach volunteer), in others a somewhat obtrusive observer (e.g., sitting on the street corner or in group therapy), and in still others a conversation partner (e.g., hanging out and informal interviews). I carried out fieldwork primarily between 2013 and 2017 and conducted interviews throughout and in the subsequent years, for a total of fifty-five recorded interviews. (*Two notes:* First, I did some preliminary fieldwork in 2012 as I figured out what would become my focal points. Second, fieldwork across those five years was not fully continuous—I took periodic breaks when holidays, travel, and other work obligations necessitated.)

As a volunteer at the Los Angeles County Department of Mental Health clinic, each week I observed team meetings, client-provider interaction at the clinic, home visits, and therapeutic groups. During the first year, I volunteered multiple times a week with DMH workers assigned to a homeless outreach project, which brought me in contact with new clients, potential clients who were screened out, and other social service and law enforcement agencies doing street work. Through a recurring homeless task force, I observed meetings between business owners and local government officials as they debated the proper tactics for the removal of a small tent city. Apart from my formal time with agencies, I participated broadly in this social world. For instance, I shared meals with subjects, attended concerts and social events with DMH workers, spent a few nights in homeless encampments, marched with activists fighting street sweeps of unhoused people, participated in the US Department of Housing and Urban Development's annual "homeless count," and drove people to appointments or other engagements.

With the Actualization Clinic, I observed weekly case conferences at which case managers discussed clients, co-ran a social group, attended group therapy, and participated in events for private agencies in a referral network. Owing to privacy concerns, I was rarely able to accompany staff on home visits, and Actualization limited my access to clientele it selected or those I had met in therapy groups. To triangulate case conference discussion, I observed the field services of a private-practice case manager who had once been an Actualization client and was now affiliated with the clinic. Furthermore, I visited the rehabs, sober living homes, and therapeutic residences that Actualization worked with, to observe daily life and speak with both clients and staff. Outside my formal time with agencies, I participated in everyday social life to understand people's experiences more broadly. For instance, I had meals with staff and clients, became a doubles partner for an Actualization psychologist who used tennis as therapy, celebrated birthdays, and joined clients in healthy Los Angeles lifestyle activities like workouts.

To interpret my field notes and interviews, I approached my materials with, as Timmermans and Tavory put it, "the broadest theoretical base possible."[5] Neither being a "blank slate" nor trying to test a favorite theory, I read everything that felt relevant. I'd entered the field with some general ideas in mind, given research literature in the sociology of medicine, the history of psychiatry, recent books on homelessness, and theories of social control, but soon found I had to widen my reading list. Colleagues and teachers directed me to research on policing, urban politics, and fiscal policy, which helped me understand what was happening in Downtown. In line with Timmermans and Tavory's "abductive" approach, I used some coding and memo-composing procedures from the grounded theory tradition, but I always had in my mind various theories and literature rather than working purely from the data.

As noted above, the puzzling finding regarding the ostensible "freedom" of poor clients in safety net services made me curious about the comparative case, so I extended my fieldwork to include the Actualization Clinic and the private mental health agencies. There the issue of family dynamics was so prominent that I began to read sociological work on families. During my earliest presentation of preliminary findings, several audience members suggested I focus on the literature about class and parenting. Reading my cases against each other, and in conversation with a good deal of the social scientific literature, I theorized my core concepts of social prognosis, tolerant containment, and concerted constraint.

This use of local puzzles that emerged from fieldwork and comparison also drove my approach to interviews. Rather than aim for a randomly selected, representative sample of patients, parents, mental health-care providers, and other stakeholders (certainly appropriate in some types of studies), I sought out people who could help me understand issues that came up as I spent time on the ground. Typically, I'd encounter some dynamic and get curious, but I'd need data from another location or type of person to fill in the gaps. This theoretical sampling took me to meet with many different types of people, and my interview questions might vary depending on the topic of interest.

An example: after observing how important families were at the Actualization Clinic, I visited support meetings at the Westside Los Angeles chapter of the National Alliance on Mental Illness (NAMI). To understand that organization, I interviewed a leader about both her own experience and available support for relatively privileged parents. This in turn made me curious: what kinds of support were there for less affluent families of color, and were their problems different? To answer this, I sought out a leader at the NAMI Urban Los Angeles affiliate, which primarily serves this other demographic. He explained that his group was in fact much more concerned about criminalization and housing insecurity than was the Westside Los Angeles chapter, and so it had support workshops devoted to these issues. Since I was trying to map out how systems and organizations work rather than understand the general experience of some group (e.g., as in a study on parental experience, which would require a broad data set devoted to many parents), my interview sampling proceeded thus.

As with most in-depth, qualitative studies, a combination of data is presented that I observed directly, along with statements from participants about things that happened outside my view. Because of a variety of barriers—patient privacy laws that prevented me from seeing records, access issues when clinics only shared certain information, and so on—some stories rely on one person's recollection. When possible, I tried various ways to triangulate, such as searching for news reports or asking others who were involved. If a person reported a story of things I could not witness, I note it as such, for example "according to the case manager, the patient had this experience." The law professor Steven Lubet has pushed ethnographers to be more adversarial with their evidence, to fact-check and to separate out what people say from what they do—an important corrective to playing it fast and loose with data.[6] At the same time, as Michael Burawoy has argued, the merits on which ethnographies should be judged are not particular isolated facts but theoretical statements about how the world works.[7] The latter includes mechanisms, cultural frames, patterned behavior, and people's understanding of their worlds. Good ethnography will accomplish both tasks.

ANALYTICAL TABLE AND SUMMARY

Below is a visualization of the book's overarching argument. Although I present the framework in narrative form in the main text, I could not have written it without using such a table for analytical reduction and clarification.

ANALYTICAL SUMMARY

	DMH and public safety net care	Actualization and elite private care
Governance project	Urban poverty governance— managing social problems for the city Example: client who is homeless, at risk of reincarceration, or otherwise a disturbance	Family systems governance— managing relational issues, family emotions, and reputation Example: client who is a "failure to launch," embarrassing, or at risk of becoming like the poor
Ecology of services	Homeless outreach, ER, welfare, Board and Care, shelters, Housing Authority office, probation, police/jail	Specialist hospital, residential therapy program, beachside sober living home, boarding school, college disability services
Social prognosis	A place to live outside the "institutional circuit," e.g., housed and not in jail or the hospital	A viable identity—robust personhood. Either work and school or at least a respectable role (uncle, eccentric artist, etc.)
Logic of care and control	Tolerant containment and neutralization of public nuisance— keep people indoors to avoid criminalization. Reduce harm of "noncompliance," drug use, and strange behavior	Concerted constraint and normalization through intensive therapeutic investment and activities. Control without punishment, and the power to keep people on track
Type of freedom	Freedom from normalization. Freedom to be a "crazy," drug-using person, within the constraints of poverty	Freedom from the life of the poor patient. Developmental freedom to recover, exert choosing capacity, and become respectable

DATA PRESENTATION AND GENERALIZATION

One of the most vexing and intriguing parts of studying psychiatric practice is that its categories are in flux. There is ongoing debate as to whether two people diagnosed as having schizophrenia even have the same illness. This makes it difficult to compare treatment for the rich and the poor in a straightforward manner. Unlike studies of diabetes clinics for the rich and the poor, I can't be sure that two people diagnosed as having schizophrenia are experiencing the same illness. In some sense, it is also impossible, then, to know whether a given person was representative of the average patient with that illness. In what follows, I give some background on this issue and then explain my approach, which focuses less on representative patients than on comparing dilemmas and problem solving across clinics.

In the 1960s, radical sociologists claimed that mental illness diagnoses were socially constructed, with labels like *schizophrenia* serving as catchall categories that likely described many different illnesses or experiences. In response, the American Psychiatric Association worked to standardize the categories in its *Diagnostic and Statistical Manual of Mental Disorders*. This led to better reliability, in that two doctors would likely see a person exhibit a set of characteristics and diagnose the same illness, but it did not necessarily lead to construct validity—people still debated whether *schizophrenia* referred to a singular underlying illness. Today, the latest neurological and genetic research confirms the once-radical sociological critique: rather than identify shared biomarkers for illnesses, the geneticists think that the existing categories lump many different illnesses together, or that ostensibly different categories have shared genetic roots. Contemporary scientists suggest that the current diagnostic categories are likely to be replaced in the future with genetically derived ones, and we can't assume that people with the same diagnosis today in fact share the same underlying condition.[8]

Psychiatric epidemiologists struggle with this—if they can't objectively diagnose an illness, how do they know they are accurately tracking its rises and falls across time and place? What if some people have been inaccurately diagnosed? As noted previously, it is well known that overall rates of distress are associated with socioeconomic status, but the diagnostic question remains. This makes comparative sociological research on mental illness tricky as well, *if the goal is explaining illness severity outcomes.*

My solution became to focus on similar problems and dilemmas for the clinical worlds rather than solely on diagnoses. In other words, the unit of analysis is not the patient with a given illness but the clinics in their respective ecologies. The question at hand is how the clinical worlds respond to similar problems, and this is how I select cases for presentation. My outcomes focus less on psychiatric prognosis than on social prognosis—the kinds of lives-with-illness people can expect to live. I can most clearly explain this with the comparative vignettes that open the three parts of the book.

In chapter 7, for instance, Hugo Castile and Tom Burton are both young men who become psychotic and use drugs but refuse treatment, utilizing legal rights developed during the deinstitutionalization period. The men have different diagnoses—schizophrenia and bipolar disorder—but their illness is less important than the shared dilemmas. It is quite possible, given the vagaries of psychiatric diagnosis, that each could have received the other's label or even the diagnosis of drug-induced psychosis. The key issue is the dilemma *for the clinical regimes* between respecting civil liberties and pursuing treatment when a person is occasionally psychotic. The young men present a way to see how it plays out in different settings—namely, tolerating and containing Hugo versus constraining and cultivating Tom. Hugo is not precisely an average DMH client, for he is younger than most people in the clinic. But the dilemma he presents to the clinic is extremely common: psychosis plus treatment refusal and risk of a return to homelessness. The solution outlined of low-barrier housing and harm reduction is also quite representative of the DMH clinic. Tom's tech-related delusions and goals are somewhat unique to him, but the approach to managing his behavior is quite general in his milieu.

Throughout the body chapters, I illustrate a range of common issues the clinics deal with—in chapters 5 and 6, for instance, I offer observations of a case conference in each setting. From there, I choose patients to illustrate the clinics' tasks. I do not claim that each one of them is representative of a person having that diagnosis. The practical problems and responses are my object of study. Sometimes I track shared issues, as just noted. Other times, the issues are different: for instance, getting people back to college is a common activity at places like Actualization but not at the DMH. These differences are *research findings* related to social prognosis rather than a problem of research design. This is simply a different type of study from one that tries to show how social class shapes traditionally defined mental illness outcomes.

This approach also leads to an important question about focusing on the poor and the rich and how I learned about the middle class. Rather than "average" mental health-care providers representative of all public versus private care, I view the DMH and Actualization clinics (and their collaborators) as "critical cases" that make the differences in care stark and therefore visible for analysis, and "represent with special clarity phenomena which exist widely but in more diluted form elsewhere."[9] Public safety net care in Downtown and elite private care in West Los Angeles are at the extreme poles of social inequality. Using these contrasting cases helped me identify their most important features and develop theoretical categories (tolerant containment and concerted constraint)—but at the same time I risked obscuring what falls in between them.

During my earliest presentations on the research, I was asked about the middle class and why I was focusing on these poles of inequality. I went looking for an intensive clinic for middle-class people but struggled to find one. This, it turned out, was also not a methodological problem but an empirical research finding. Much of the private insurance typically utilized by middle-class people is inadequate for serious mental health needs. Soon I heard many complaints from care providers and families about, for instance, Kaiser Permanente in California for its failure to provide mental health care. Indeed, the health provider's own therapists went on strike, claiming that they could not do their job and help people unless Kaiser changed its practices.[10]

Without a good option in the middle, many people are forced to either give up private insurance and enter the public safety net or go into debt in their efforts to finance elite private care. Thus, I found that I was already inadvertently studying the middle class. By following how people entered, left, and sought or failed to gain access to public safety net and elite care, I also learned a great deal about the plight of the people in the middle. As I spoke with them, and especially as I followed their trajectories over time, I could also better understand how the same person might be processed through different clinical systems.

IMPACT OF RESEARCHER POSITION

In ethnography, the field worker is the research instrument, and their social position necessarily influences what they see and how they make sense of it. Much has been written about the advantages and disadvantages of "insider" versus "outsider" status for cultivating rapport and understanding. Doing comparative work in urban Los Angeles across class lines as an upper-middle-class, highly educated, Asian American man meant I sometimes was "studying up," sometimes "studying sideways," and other times "studying down." Racially speaking, I was not an insider in spaces that were primarily Black, Brown, or white (although there are certainly many Asians in the city, and some appear in this book). Nor do I identify as a patient, a clinician, or a close family member. This has both advantages and drawbacks.

In Skid Row, people seemed to assume that I was a social service provider, a Little Tokyo resident, or perhaps a voyeur or drug purchaser. In the DMH clinic, I was introduced as a volunteer, and people nearly always shrugged with indifference when I asked whether I could observe and take notes for school. Since I'd worked in mental health care after college, it was easy enough for me to assist with basic tasks like driving people around. At the time, I had a large Mohawk and didn't look professorial or like an authority figure. No doubt, some clients saw me as aligned with staff, but most consented to participation once they saw I mostly just stood around and made small talk. Some people had been involved in research before, since LA's Skid Row has been studied by social scientists and reformers for generations. Some of the street-based observations took place in public settings.

The elite world presented a different dynamic. Although not white, I had the class bearing and educational credentials to fit in. Here I could take multiple roles in the setting. For instance, when at the beachside treatment home Namaste Gardens, I blended in when I wore board shorts and a tank top and draped my long hair like a surfer's (the Mohawk since grown out). In such settings, some young clients asked for my advice about colleges. When I went to treatment meetings among elite professionals, I might change into a collared shirt and put my hair in a "man bun" like a typical young LA hipster. The access issues, however, were profound and telling. For instance, one Malibu dual-diagnosis rehab made me sign extra paperwork on nondisclosure, so what I observed there serves only as background. More generally, rich people are paying for privacy. Some of these clinics are not subject to oversight, because they are all direct pay, not insurance covered. Thus, I visited organizations that didn't even keep records on outcomes, let alone have experience with a social scientist.

My own subjective and affective reactions played an important role in analysis. For instance, when I moved to study the elite clinics, I realized I was impacted in a different way watching young upper-middle-class patients lose their career dreams than when I observed DMH clients' suffering and material precariousness. The tragedies among the former were emotionally relatable in that they seemed like something that could happen to me, while I viewed the hardships of the latter as more like a public policy issue—I'd get fired up about the right to housing, for instance, but less so about the loss of the DMH clients' dreams. Suddenly I realized that even though I'd come to think of some DMH clients as my friends, I was viewing them through a lens of abstraction. This embarrassed me, but it also alerted me to the gestalt switch that happens when a person has become marked as a sidewalk psychotic, thereby shaping the kinds of possible lives "we" (including middle-class providers) imagine for "them"—all part of what I would later call social prognosis. Soon I questioned whether I would accept the public safety net definition of a "good outcome" (not in jail, not on the street) for a loved one, which helped me understand families. And it also made me far more concerned about the hopes and dreams of the people I knew Downtown.

THEORETICAL GENERALIZATION

Finally, I'd like to address the generalizability of the knowledge that comes from this study. Although I believe that elements of the findings should apply across mental health clinics in other places, there may be important differences related to contrasting state laws, funding schemes, and the like. My theoretical categories are oriented more toward general dynamics in care and control. Rather than a question of whether my sample generalizes to the population of mental health clinics at large, I argue that my concepts help us explain different types of cases that share dynamics and mechanisms (the difference between so-called statistical and theoretical generalizability). Allow me to illustrate this with two of my main concepts.

Tolerant containment is a general strategy to mitigate harm and manage deviance when corrective social control is ineffective or too expensive. It comes from a mix of civil libertarianism and budget austerity. In psychiatric care, we see this in the harm reduction, Housing First logic that essentially accepts noncompliance, drug usage, and idleness. We see it elsewhere in attempts to decriminalize drugs without funding rehab (California Proposition 47), attempts to secure people's rights to be homeless without providing them rights to housing (*Martin v. City of Boise*), and early release for prisoners without the crucial reentry services that help ex-offenders reintegrate. Sanctioned homeless encampments and safe injection sites no doubt have important differences from tolerant containment for the housed psychiatric patient, but elements of the underlying logic are the same. In a moment when Americans across the political divide are questioning mass incarceration and hyperpolicing, the compromise of tolerant containment—essentially civil liberties without social rights—may become increasingly prominent.

Concerted constraint, on the other hand, is a general strategy to reform elite actors, maintain their privilege, and keep them out of public circuits of social control. Rather than being opposed to luxury, concerted constraint may call for therapeutic discipline for generating self-efficacy and respectability. The key idea is to reform elite deviance rather than merely tolerating or punishing it. In psychiatric care, we see this with in-depth therapeutics that seek to reform thoughts and behavior in "bubble" facilities offering respite from the regular world. We might see this also in boarding schools for teenagers, residential therapy for celebrity sexual predators, or any other effort to keep affluent people from criminal responsibility or downward mobility.

NOTES

INTRODUCTION

1. Chronic homelessness is generally defined as occurring when a homeless person with a disability lives in a place not meant for human habitation, in a safe haven, or in an emergency shelter and has been unhoused continuously for more than a year, or at least four instances across the last three years, totaling at least one year. See US Department of Housing and Urban Development 2015.

2. Grave disability is officially defined as "a condition in which a person, as a result of a mental health disorder, is unable to provide for his or her basic personal needs for food, clothing, or shelter." See California Welfare and Institutions code 5008. In practice, there is continual debate about whether a person qualifies or not. For instance: is a person who eats out of a dumpster providing for his or her basic personal need for food? Some evaluators determine the answer is yes, and therefore the person is not gravely disabled. Alex Barnard (2023) has argued that the interpretation of the criteria is highly sensitive to resource availability—that is, when hospital beds are available, clinicians are more likely to declare that a marginal case in fact presents as grave disability.

3. Freud 2008; Sacks 1985; Black and Andreasen 2011.

4. The literature on psychiatric deinstitutionalization is vast and contested. I draw on summaries from Scull 1977; Brodwin 2013; and Grob 2014.

5. US Department of Housing and Urban Development 2022. These numbers are notoriously tricky, since psychiatric diagnosis itself is imprecise, and some research uses self-reporting without access to official records. Estimates tend to put the rate of serious mental illness at between 20 and 25 percent of the homeless population. Many more people, of course, experience general psychological distress from the difficulties of the situation. The California Policy Lab's 2021 research from Los

Angeles found that 20 percent of street-outreached clients in Los Angeles had a formal diagnosis of serious mental illness entered in Los Angeles County Department of Mental Health records (see Hess et al. 2021). As we'll see in chapter 2, however, there are reasons to be skeptical of even these data sources.

6. Bronson and Berzofsky 2017. Note that this was based on data from the previous decade.

7. There were less than forty thousand state hospital beds in 2016. See Fuller et al. 2016.

8. I took periodic breaks from fieldwork, such as during holidays, travel, or particularly challenging teaching duties. A strength of the data collection process was that I observed the treatment centers longitudinally, across several years in each setting, allowing me to check for changes in both people and institutions. Still, I do not want to imply that I was continuously in the field throughout this entire period.

9. Rose 1999, 4.

10. Berlin 2017 (from the original 1958 essay). There is an extensive literature interpreting Berlin's two notions of freedom. To be clear, Berlin didn't simply mean freedom from *government* coercion when discussing negative liberty, but this is how it is often interpreted by civil libertarians, who tend to focus on avoiding state coercion.

11. As Elizabeth Davis (2012) argues in her study of Greek psychiatric care, Rose's theory of neoliberalism is in general poorly suited to thinking about serious mental illness. By writing from the "we" of society and neoliberal subjects at large, Rose's theory of government neglects a major part of the Foucauldian project: how modern institutions use the pathological to define the normal.

12. See Mossakowski 2014 for a review.

13. The term *social prognosis* appears occasionally in the medical literature, but in a different sense from my use of it. Typically, it refers to the general social outcomes of a given illness—for instance, "Social Prognosis of Patients with Ulcerative Colitis," Hendriksen and Binder 1980, investigates the kinds of marital and employment outcomes of people who suffer from this illness compared with the general population. My use of *social prognosis* refers to how individuals with the same set of symptoms or the same diagnosis may be processed differently through different clinical systems, and how social inequality then patterns the possible experiences and futures available to them. It is also different from the Global Assessment of Functioning used in psychiatric evaluation, in that the social prognosis resides less in the individual than in the clinical regime. There are both high- and low-functioning clients (to use that imperfect language) in both public safety net and elite settings—the point is that the clinics will likely process them differently.

14. Foucault 1977.

15. See Wacquant 2009 on policing and incarceration, and Beckett and Herbert 2008 on urban banishment. The assumption, often well founded, is that privileged people get kid-glove treatment when it comes to policing. But there's also a dearth of

research on other methods of social control, so the theoretical predictions are often quite speculative.

16. Lareau 2011.

17. This took extra time because Rick's housing voucher was a "project-based" one tied to the building, rather than a "tenant-based" voucher that he could take on the open market to any landlord. Thus, the DMH providers had to go through an additional process to help him move.

18. Scull 1990.

19. Morrison 2013.

20. As defined by the National Institute of Mental Health 2022.

21. Frances 2012.

22. Foucault 1965; Schrader, Jones, and Shattell 2013; Scull 2015.

23. DuBois, Bante, and Hadley 2011; Skultans 2005.

CHAPTER ONE

1. Jones v. City of Los Angeles, 444 F.3d 1118 (9th Cir. 2006); Lavan v. City of Los Angeles, 693 F.3d 1022 (9th Cir. 2012).

2. Stuart 2016.

3. See Gong 2017 for a history of the term and debate. My finding is that the understanding of "lack of insight" has shifted over time relative to institutional arrangements. In premodern theories of madness, it was essentially definitional: a person who was delusional could not know that he or she was delusional. There was, in a sense, no reason to debate his or her insight. In the later asylum era and under the dominance of psychoanalysis, clinicians tried to make sense of lack of insight and "postpsychotic depression." Institutionalized people would be in "denial" of mental illness, doctors believed, because it was a threat to the ego, and once they exited psychosis, they would become sad. Finally, during the post-deinstitutionalization era and in the turn to biological/neurological psychiatry, *insight* suddenly took on a new meaning related to legal capacity. This was because patients had the right to refuse care, which was creating problems for other actors. Family activists and clinicians began to agitate for civil commitment reform so they could more easily hospitalize people. A neurological theory of anosognosia, akin to stroke victims who cannot recognize partial paralysis, offered a better legal argument for overriding rights than the vague "denial" posited by earlier psychoanalytic theories.

There is, however, no clear objective measurement of impaired insight for psychosis akin to that seen in many neurological cases. This helps explain why arguments based on "anosognosia for psychosis" have been only partially successful in overriding rights. As I note in this book, however, whatever its scientific validity, the concept is important, because it offers a practical shorthand for what seems experientially obvious: some people indeed *seem* to lack awareness of the situation and *seem* too psychotic to understand their own experience and rights. Thus, the thinking goes, should such people really be entitled to treatment decision-making? Of course, for many patients and advocates, this is an insulting way of disregarding a person's views.

4. Morrissey and Goldman (1984) argue that there have been "cycles of reform" rather than any sort of linear progress.

5. Sisti, Segal, and Emanuel 2015.

6. Scull 2015.

7. Locke 1980, 350.

8. Mill 1999, 10.

9. Foucault 1965.

10. See Parry 2006.

11. Quoted in Scull 2015, 305.

12. Deutsch 1948.

13. Hollingshead and Redlich 1958.

14. Laing 1968.

15. Goffman 1961.

16. Kesey 1962.

17. Szasz 1964.

18. See Scull 1977 for an attempt to adjudicate the relevant causes.

19. Scull 1977.

20. See Eide and Gorman 2021. Some general hospital settings, like Bellevue in NYC, can skirt this issue because the psychiatric beds comprise less than half the facility, which is primarily dedicated to physical health.

21. As Alex Barnard (2023, 4) puts it, government "abdicated authority" over care and control for the most severely disabled. If the state hospital represented a kind of centralized, quasi-socialist model of authority, the subsequent system was heavily dispersed and left up to market forces. By delegating duties to myriad actors (municipal, nonprofit, and for-profit) and granting considerable discretion at the local level, states like California created a situation in which there seemed to be no one in charge. For an early critique of the antipsychiatry and deinstitutionalization movements from a socialist perspective, see Peter Sedgwick's 1982 *Psycho Politics*. He argued that seeming radicals like Foucault, Laing, and Goffman were providing ideological cover to conservatives, who would cut services to the vulnerable. Sedgwick understood the need to rethink the idea of mental illness, but he also insisted that the category was needed by patients and communities to make demands on the state.

22. Friedman 2020, 41.

23. Marx 2004, 119.

24. Treffert 1973, 49.

25. Gilmore 2008, 32.

26. Some authors (e.g., Alexander 2010) argue that purported crime spikes were fabricated to justify the war on drugs, target Black and Brown men, and maintain

racial hierarchy. Yet the best available data suggest in fact a rise in crime, likely explained by deindustrialization and disinvestment in public goods (see Clegg and Usmani 2019). Hyperpolicing and mass incarceration, for all their drawbacks, likely did help reduce violence, although the precise causes of the great crime decline remain hotly debated (see Sharkey 2018).

27. Gilmore 2007; Wacquant 2009.

28. Alexander 2010.

29. Dear and Wolch 2014, 95.

30. Hopper et al. 1997.

31. See Abramson 2009 on how this plays out in elder care.

32. Although the academic literature on privileged families navigating these systems is scant, there is a burgeoning genre of parent memoirs that is extremely illuminating and helped me better understand familial perspectives. Two books that received considerable attention—perhaps because the parents in question were also already prominent journalists—are Pete Earley's 2007 *Crazy: A Father's Search through America's Mental Health Madness* and Ron Powers's 2017 *No One Cares about Crazy People.*

33. McLean 2000.

34. Padwa et al. 2016.

35. NAMI tends also to emphasize biopsychiatric explanations of mental illness and sideline alternative perspectives. Some critics imply this may be because most of the organization's funding comes from the pharmaceutical industry (see Rothman et al. 2011). Another likely explanation is that a biological model frees families from the kind of blame previously visited on them, when psychoanalytic theories suggested that poor parenting induced schizophrenia.

CHAPTER TWO

1. This is Wacquant's (2010, 75) description of jails, but I find this to be an evocative phrase to describe the safety net institutions similarly acting as "dams" alongside the penal ones.

2. See Stuart 2016.

3. For a useful review on homelessness in California, see Streeter 2022.

4. Colburn and Aldern 2022.

5. Padwa 2009, oral history interview. Note, however, that this is a gloss on a longer and more complicated story—increased patient discharge had begun in the earlier waves of deinstitutionalization before Reagan's tenure, and many California hospitals weren't fully closed until the 1990s. Furthermore, although Ronald Reagan is often blamed for decimating the mental health system, first in California and then nationally, he could hardly do it alone. When it comes to cuts to mental health funding or hospital closure, the historical record often shows bipartisan action.

6. See Snow and Mulcahy 2001 on types of space and homelessness.

7. Mathieu 1993.

8. Duneier 1999, 60.

9. Snow and Anderson 1993.

10. Luhrmann 2007.

11. Lipsky 2010.

12. See Garfinkel 1956 on degradation ceremonies.

13. See Dobransky 2009; Hansen, Bourgois, and Drucker 2014.

14. See Whooley 2010 on workaround diagnoses.

CHAPTER THREE

1. Quoted in Meares 2019.

2. Las Encinas Behavioral Healthcare n.d.

3. In an analysis of health care reform measures, Goldman (2010) notes that for the most part, people diagnosed as having schizophrenia would only have been eligible for public services in the past. This was because many people would have been excluded from private insurers based on preexisting conditions. Although some of these insurability rules have changed, it's still an open question as to how many people will be able to stay on private plans, or whether those plans will deliver quality care.

4. To be sure, there are white and class-privileged families who also navigate the struggles of homelessness and criminalization, and who fear that police will harm their loved ones. In later chapters, you will meet some of them. Such stories can also be found in the memoirs of white middle-class parents, as in Ron Powers's 2017 *No One Cares about Crazy People*. But, at least according to my interactions with NAMI representatives, these dimensions are treated as more salient at chapters like NAMI Urban Los Angeles.

CHAPTER FOUR

1. See for instance Davidson et al. 2006; Deegan 1988.

2. Luftey and Freese 2005.

3. Tanya Luhrmann (2000, 242) notes that in the days before managed care, unethical psychoanalytic psychiatrists would sometimes exploit wealthy patients and families, seeing patients for daily therapy sessions even if the person was too sick to benefit from them. I don't proclaim to know whether this was the case at a place like Resolve and if care was driven by profit or a genuine belief in the efficacy of psychodynamic therapy for psychosis. The key point is that this is an option only for more privileged people. From my vantage point as a sociologist comparing clinical regimes, whether it "worked" or not for Gwen in some official sense, it gives her a narrative for making sense of her experience, and it shaped her psychosocial care more broadly.

4. See for instance Rothschild 2013.

5. Luftey and Freese 2005; see Abramson 2015 for an analysis of differential access to medical care for the aged as well as an analysis of how cultural dispositions shape elders' responses. I focus primarily on what is offered and deemed appropriate for psychiatric patients in different worlds; but future research, in the vein of Abramson's book, should focus more attention on how and why similarly situated people make different psychiatric health decisions.

6. See Ridgeway 2019.

7. See Mossakowski 2014 for a review.

CHAPTER FIVE

1. Hopper et al. 1997.

2. Los Angeles County Department of Mental Health 2011.

3. When Reagan signed the Omnibus Budget Reconciliation Act of 1981, it not only lowered federal funding—it also converted money earmarked for community mental health into block grants. This block grant structure gave states broad discretion to use the federal mental health dollars for other purposes. See Bell 2022.

4. Estroff 1981.

5. Hopper et al. 1997.

6. See Martin 2008 for an analysis. Contrary to many who viewed the tax revolt as a nefarious conservative plan, Martin argues that things like Proposition 13 were relatively populist in origin—local home value assessors had previously underassessed property values. Therefore, home owners had previously been given favorable tax rates relative to true value, and they fought new assessments that would substantially increase their tax bills.

7. Cannon and Kotkin 1979.

8. See Barnard 2022.

9. Rhodes 1991.

10. Desjarlais 1994, 897.

11. See Deegan 1988; Davidson et al. 2006.

12. Davidson et al. 2006.

13. Braslow 2013. 184.

14. Myers 2015.

15. Sapien 2018.

16. Dobransky 2009.

17. Brodwin 2013, 184.

18. Scheffler and Adams 2005.

19. See for instance Scheff 1966.

20. See Baldessarini et al. 2013.

21. See Aviv 2019 for an in-depth analysis of both prescription cascades and patient experiences.

CHAPTER SIX

1. Goffman 2009.

2. William had worked previously in California, but here he is describing his work with county services in a northeastern state. He has operated private services on the East and West Coasts. Although I do not address it here, he also drew an important distinction within the private sector: that between agencies that were provider owned and operated (like his and the Actualization Clinic) and those that were being bought up by venture capital firms. Such firms began investing in behavioral health services in the wake of the Affordable Care Act, as more people became eligible for mental health insurance coverage. William suggested to me that clinician-owned facilities are more likely to be patient centered and only secondarily profit oriented, whereas the externally owned facilities are pushed to focus almost entirely on the bottom line. I've heard others in the field make similar claims, and it seems plausible. The counterargument is that there is a drastic deficit in care supply, and the business-minded firms may drive innovation, fix inefficiencies, and deliver services to more people. It is an important area for future research.

3. William referenced in this conversation, among others, the radical peer support network the Icarus Project. For this group, the language of "mental illness" is inadequate to describe people's experience. Instead, the Icarus Project uses the language of "dangerous gifts." See the 2013 zine, *Navigating the Space between Brilliance and Madness.* The group celebrates the importance of different viewpoints and sensibilities tied to "bipolar disorder" that might facilitate creativity in the arts, politics, and human problem solving, but are potentially "dangerous" and require care. Like the myth of Icarus, the group suggests to its members that they cultivate their gifts but not fly too close to the sun. Having previously worked with the Icarus Project activists, many of whom are anarchists and socialists, I'm certain they'd find it encouraging but also ironic that their ideas show up in care for the most privileged.

4. Luhrmann 2000.

5. Hansen 2019.

6. See Altomonte and Bagnall Munson 2021 for an in-depth treatment of how caregivers for the elderly and the developmentally disabled understand the project of restoring or creating autonomy. The authors note the importance of temporality and expectation: how client dependence in the moment can still be construed as part of independence because of its orientation toward an independent future.

7. See for instance Swanson et al. 1998 in *Biological Psychiatry* on the general association of higher education with lower psychotic symptomology. Koutsouleris et al. (2016) more recently found that unemployment, lower level of education,

and unmet social needs are associated with worse outcomes in first-episode psychosis.

8. Ussher 2013.

9. Bateman and Fonagy 2008, 181.

1. O'Connor v. Donaldson, 422 U.S. 563, 95 S. Ct. 2486, 45 L. Ed. 2d 396 (1975).

2. Riese v. St. Mary's Hospital and Medical Center, 209 Cal. App. 3d 1303, 243 Cal. Rptr. 241 (Ct. App. 1987).

3. Foucault 1977.

4. Cited in Foucault 1965, 266.

5. Scull 2015.

6. Foucault 1965, 257.

7. Wacquant 2009.

8. Soss, Fording, and Schram 2011.

9. Feeley and Simon 1992. Analyzing the psychiatric realm, Robert Castel (1991) similarly suggested that focus on individual humans was being replaced by managerial assessment of "risk" in community treatment. In a new "post-disciplinary model," authorities would not confine the dangerous individual but instead attempt to manage madness at the population level.

10. Wacquant 2009, 296.

11. Herring 2019.

12. Seim 2017.

13. See Biehl 2013 on such a human dumping ground in Brazil.

14. See Tsemberis, Gulcur, and Nakae 2004.

15. See Willse's incisive 2010 critique of this as a case of "neo-liberal biopolitics."

16. Lareau 2002, 749.

17. Lareau 2011, 238, 748.

18. Solomon 2012, 36–37.

CHAPTER EIGHT

1. See Ashwood et al. 2018.

2. See McCoy 2015. I worked with the Pathways to Housing organization in the late 2000s.

3. Although Housing First has an excellent track record for getting and keeping people housed, there is a weaker evidence base for improvements in mental health, addiction, or social outcomes. See Tsai 2020 for a review.

4. See Scull 1981, 741.

5. Wolpert and Wolpert 1974.

6. Smith 1975, 54.

7. Emerson, Rochford Jr., and Shaw 1981, 783.

8. See Lecher and Varner's 2023 investigation for the *Los Angeles Times* and the Markup, which found that white homeless people are consistently ranked higher on the vulnerability measures than Black or Latino people and are therefore likely to be prioritized for housing. There is debate as to how and why this is happening. The authors also report on individual cases where people appear to be quite vulnerable in lay terms, but the Vulnerability Index Service Prioritization Decision Assistance Tool does not rank them as such. See also Osborne 2019 for a sociological analysis of how these vulnerability measures and apparent objectivity entrench ideals of deservingness and render some categories of people undeserving, leaving them in limbo.

CHAPTER NINE

1. Solomon 2012, 295.

2. Sandoval 2019.

3. See Szalavitz 2006 on the weak evidence base for harsh, confrontational rehab and boot-camp-style programs.

4. As the political scientist C. Fred Alford (2000) found after visiting an American prison, the Foucauldian theory of surveillance and disciplinary power does not align with the reality of contemporary carceral systems. Far from Foucault's famous image of a panopticon (a hypothetical surveillance tower design where inmates are always visible but never know whether they are being watched, leading them to eventually police themselves), the real prison is one in which the guards look away. Rather than a form of power where an inmate's every move is watched and corrected, American penality is marked primarily by physical segregation and abandonment. Perhaps prisoners brutalize one another, lose their minds, or merely sit there bored—the state seems to shrug.

This disjuncture between Foucault's famous imagery and reality is, at least in part, an issue of method: Foucault analyzed penologists' texts about the design of facilities rather than empirically observed how caging really plays out. For Alford, this means Foucault mistakes an ideology for reality and therefore mischaracterizes how power functions. In the contemporary LA County jail setting, Channing's observation of medication noncompliance and workers' seeming acceptance of the drug trade speaks to the fact that even our punitive institutions can be marked by what I call tolerant containment.

5. Foucault 1965, 243.

6. Foucault 1965, 250.

7. Scull 1989.

8. Marx and Engels 2009.

9. Walter 2020.

10. Foucault 1988.

CONCLUSION

1. Jones v. City of Los Angeles, 444 F.3d 1118 (9th Cir. 2006); Lavan v. City of Los Angeles, 693 F.3d 1022 (9th Cir. 2012); Martin v. City of Boise, 920 F.3d 584 (9th Cir. 2019).

2. What is new is the degree to which these court cases make the encampments in some sense legally sanctioned, so long as appropriate resources are not available. Cities have long chosen not to enforce in certain areas, if only so they had somewhere to send homeless people encountered in more desirable zones. See Herring 2014 on unofficial administrative strategies for managing encampments.

3. See California Courts 2017.

4. Castellano et al. 2016.

5. See Selsky 2020.

6. See Fracassa and Fagan 2020.

7. Castellano et al. 2016.

8. See Stephens 2021; Shellenberger 2021; and a host of *City Journal* articles, like Sandberg 2022.

9. I owe this phrasing to the late Chris Shea of the *Washington Post*, who pushed me to transform my academic jargon into readable prose. Many of the ideas in this conclusion were made legible through his editing of my 2021 and 2022 *WaPo* Sunday Outlook pieces (the latter with Alex Barnard), and I am tremendously grateful for his keen eye. As clarification, I use the language of "austerity" regarding the repeated budget cuts to services and general disinvestment in public goods. This is clearest when it comes to the history of community mental health care and how it was starved both federally and in California after the Great Tax Revolt. Services provided have never been enough relative to need, and many municipal services have seen cuts precisely when they needed expansion, such as following hospital closure. As we saw in chapter 4, systems like the Los Angeles County DMH have seen continual budget and service cuts. In the context of expanded civil liberties (e.g., the perfect storm of Proposition 13 and deinstitutionalization), this can become especially problematic. On the other hand, some conservatives (as well as so-called supply-side progressives) will argue that the issue isn't budget austerity but bad regulation. This is clearest with homelessness in California, where the story of cuts (e.g., disinvestment in public housing) must be complemented by a broader supply-side story: neighborhood dissent and long environmental review processes (often weaponized by those established residents) make it extremely difficult to build. Los Angeles learned a lesson with HHH, the bond measure that funds supported housing, where each unit

took years and upwards of $500,000 to produce (see Klein 2022). If there aren't enough units to rent and constructing the new affordable developments balloons in price, even a large pot of money won't go far.

10. See Wall Street Journal Editorial Board 2021 on San Francisco mayor London Breed's reversal on the issue.

11. Hakes 2021.

12. Despite widespread acknowledgment that insurance companies inappropriately deny mental health coverage, regulators have been slow to police or fine them. Reporting for NPR in 2022, Yuki Noguchi notes that this may be because there is little good data available—on either the level of patients' struggles or the extent of insurer noncompliance with parity laws. Families, often isolated and confused, are in no position to fight back. This must be addressed. In the long run, I would like to see a single-payer, universal health care system in the United States. But in lieu of this, private health insurers should be compelled to deliver mental health care in compliance with the law.

13. Fitzsimmons and Newman 2022.

14. Mayor's Office of Community Engagement, City of Sacramento. 2021.

15. Sisti, Segal, and Emanuel 2015.

16. I'm in general agreement with those conservatives and "supply-side progressives" who argue that to achieve housing abundance, we must change some regulations that have slowed housing production. California's Environmental Quality Act is a notorious example of how well-intentioned environmental protections can be weaponized, as when NIMBY neighbors claim in bad faith that a new development poses possible environmental threat. See Gray 2021. We need to reform such laws to allow for both legitimate reviews and appropriate building. Even among those fighting for increased production, however, there is considerable debate over the appropriate balance of public versus private market rate construction. "Yes in my backyard" (YIMBY) activists often suggest that increased private housing supply will, on its own, benefit the poor through filtering. The idea is that as wealthy people move into new luxury developments, their former residences will be occupied by middle-class people, who themselves will have moved from elsewhere, making room for poorer people in their previous neighborhoods. Simply having more supply will, in theory, drive down overall rents. But others counter that "trickle-down" housing policy is an inefficient way to help poor people (perhaps wealthy people from outside the city will move in if desirable new units are built, so the filtering might never happen), and that as soon as it's not profitable, private capital will move elsewhere—this is what happened with housing construction during the Great Recession (see Dayen 2023 for an analysis of why this can't be solely left to the private sector). At the other end of the spectrum, then, is the suggestion to build a massive amount of social housing. Singapore, a capitalist nation that nonetheless treats housing as a social rather than a financial asset, provides one model. Some 80 percent of the populace

lives in high-quality public housing, while the private housing market still exists on a smaller scale. See Bryson 2019 on Singapore and for a general analysis of these dynamics. I'll leave it to others with the relevant expertise to adjudicate the proper balance of different types of public and private development.

17. New York Times Editorial Board 2022.

18. See Gong and Barnard 2019.

19. Here I'm referring to the continued legacy of Proposition 13, as described in chapter 4, which slashed and froze California property taxes in the late 1970s. Since then, the state has relied more on income taxes, which means coffers boom and bust with the economy, and especially tech. The recent results are tragicomic: for instance, in early 2022 California governor Gavin Newsom bragged about a $97.5 billion surplus for fiscal year 2022–23. But by November, the legislature's budget advisor projected that revenues would fall short by $41 billion, leaving the state in a deficit of $25 billion in 2023–24. (See Walters 2022). This level of unpredictability makes it extremely difficult for municipalities to rationally plan services. The state should rebalance its tax base with a heavier emphasis on property taxes.

20. See Chen 2016.

21. See Dougherty and Karlamangla 2022 on California's fight against NIMBYism. The state has made important strides here, such as getting rid of single-family zoning, shepherding affordable developments through the approval process, and suing counties that fight housing.

22. Absent robust funds and changes to regulations, there will be hard choices and prioritizations. Building supportive housing in California is extremely expensive; in Los Angeles, for instance, the HHH-bond-measure units are costing upwards of $500,000 each. In the spirit of Housing First and a commitment to real solutions, cities have deprioritized shelter in favor of investment in real units. This is well intentioned, but building individual units simply can't keep pace with the level of unsheltered homelessness. In addition to repurposing hotels, perhaps California will have to build a shelter system like New York City's. The danger is stopping there rather than developing the real housing long term. Los Angeles mayor Karen Bass's signature homelessness program, Inside Safe, has been utilizing hotels to move thousands off the street (see Fajardo, Becenti, and Bang 2023)—all to the good, but there is a real question as to where people will go permanently. Ultimately, I'm fighting against either/or; I'm saying we need to build shelter and real housing as well as consider things like "tiny homes," all while also using what we have available to us now as stopgap measures.

23. Howell and Voronka 2012.

24. Davis 1995.

25. Foucault 1988.

26. Housing First has become a political football in the contemporary culture wars, with some conservatives suggesting that it is ineffective and even to blame for

growing homelessness (see DeParle's 2023 *New York Times* coverage of the fracas). In fact, recent studies confirm previous findings that low-barrier permanent supportive housing is highly effective at ending homelessness for people with co-occurring psychiatric disabilities and addiction (see Raven, Niedzwiecki, and Kushel 2020 for a randomized study that found that 86 percent of participants in the treatment group were successfully housed, and 92 percent of them stayed housed through the study period, compared with only 36 percent assigned to typical services). Thus, Housing First remains an important tool for this population. Yet proponents must remain clear eyed about two things. First, as I argue throughout this book, low-barrier housing might offer a base for clinical improvement and social recovery if it is accompanied by robust care resources and persistent case managers. In reality, however, providers are often under-resourced and understaffed relative to client need in this regard, meaning that the approach can easily descend into tolerant containment— housing first, housing only. Second, even if that impressive 86 percent success rate from the Raven, Niedzwiecki, and Kushel study is correct, that leaves 14 percent for whom the model is apparently not working. These people may require an alternative intervention beyond Housing First.

27. See for instance Kingkade's (2022) reporting on a Wyoming Christian rehabilitation program that forced teens to perform hard labor on the farm. For a more general critique of the Troubled Teen industry and tough-love therapeutics that lack an evidence base, see Szalavitz 2006.

28. Stephen Eide and Carolyn Gorman (2022) of the Manhattan Institute, for instance, focus on the financial barriers to inpatient hospitalization. Therefore, they say we must repeal the Medicaid Institutions of Mental Disease (IMD) exclusion and alter the structure of block grants so that more of our federal dollars can flow to hospitalization rather than focus primarily on community care. As discussed in chapter 1, the exemption was meant to discourage patient warehousing and encourage quality community facilities, but critics contend it has made it virtually impossible to create and sustain hospitalization for the indigent.

29. Should we focus funds on "mental illness" instead of "mental health," as the late D. J. Jaffe often put it? This means taking funds used for relatively minor mental health struggles and redirecting them to treatment for serious illness. Jaffe made fair points scrutinizing budgets that spend as much on school "consultants" as on clinicians who treat children in schools (see his 2020 article in the *New York Post*). I agree that we should prioritize care resources for the more seriously disabled in the short term, but I also want long-term investment in preventive care and early intervention. We must expand the pie, not simply take away from mental health services for the minor cases. Note that although much of Jaffe's later work was with the right-leaning Manhattan Institute, he would object to being called a conservative per se.

30. Meyer et al. 1999.

31. See Jones et al. 2021; Ward-Ciesielski and Rizvi 2021.

32. See Gong and Barnard 2022.

33. People who have lived experience of the hospital system have already made crucial contributions in the research and evaluation dimensions. The health policy scholar Morgan Shields, for instance, has shown how the performance metrics used to evaluate inpatient settings don't reflect patient-centered outcomes—and her analysis is at least partially informed by her own experience as an inpatient. See Lejeune's (2022) interview of Shields in *Mad in America*.

34. The psychoanalyst and law professor Elyn Saks, herself diagnosed as having schizophrenia, has written elegantly about a variety of possible ways to maximize autonomy while being paternalistic. See for instance her 2010 book *Refusing Care*. Informal variants of advance directives hold much promise, such as those developed by the now-defunct peer network the Icarus Project. People work with close friends to map out their warning signs, authorize certain people to speak to them when they begin to act strangely, and lay out precise plans for crisis, for instance "If it's not so bad, take me to this hotel. If it is really bad, take me to this hospital, but never that other one." See Icarus Project 2013.

35. Shields and Beidas 2022.

36. Levin 2022.

37. The literature on antipsychotic medication is contentious. Most studies show clear utility in the short term, although the benefits are often accompanied by serious metabolic and neurological side effect. Things get trickier, however, with long-term use. For instance, in a much-discussed twenty-year longitudinal study of patients who continued versus discontinued medication, Harrow and Jobe (2013) find that some people who withdraw from antipsychotics have more relapses early on, but then this drug-free group seem to do better long term. The causality is hard to establish, since it may be that people with more minor forms of illness can more easily discontinue medication; on the other hand, it may be that the medication is indeed harmful because it induces "dopamine supersensitivity" in the brain and increases chronicity. Either way, it suggests that not all people diagnosed with schizophrenia or other psychotic disorders should be on these medications forever. The trick remains figuring out if, when, and for whom acute or long-term use is appropriate. For a highly critical take on antipsychotic medication, see Whitaker 2010. For a mainstream psychiatric interpretation of the controversy surrounding long-term antipsychotic use, see Frances 2016.

38. Alex Barnard makes two further points in his 2023 book *Conservatorship*: First, a new or improved coercive system will require some central authority that can coordinate the many local state, nonprofit, and for-profit actors involved. Of the current chaos, Barnard writes, "Police officers cannot convince ER doctors to admit people in crisis into the hospital. Public guardians cannot make inpatient psychiatrists apply for conservatorship for individuals who might benefit from it. Judges struggle to get basic information out of doctors necessary to rule on

whether someone is gravely disabled. And county mental health departments are overruled by private providers of long-term care" (16). If the state doesn't step up to the task of coordination and use its authority, people will continue to fall through the cracks.

Second, making any better system will also require much better data to ensure accountability. In the case of California, "the state's data are so poor in quality, inconsistent, and incomplete that it does not even know how many LPS conservatees there are, where they are, or what happens to them" (Barnard 2023, 18–19). Without such information, government obviously cannot properly evaluate whether its new initiatives are functioning.

39. France 1894.

40. To be clear, I am not claiming that tolerant containment has fully replaced other modes of social control and urban governance. Still, it is a major development, and one not well accounted for by existing theories. Allow me to situate it alongside dominant social scientific concepts and images of control.

Followers of Michel Foucault often invoke the panopticon to describe how governments and institutions discipline the populace. Recall that the panopticon is a type of prison where inmates never know whether they are being watched, leading them to eventually police themselves (see Foucault 1977). This tradition predicts ever-increasing attempts to normalize social behavior through surveillance, scheduling, or therapeutic micromanaging—both in and out of prison. But, as I've shown in the case of Los Angeles, there is an astonishing tolerance of deviance so long as it stays on the "right" streets; an absence of normalization in public psychiatric clinics; and nonsurveillance in housing for the indigent. Ironically, sometimes it is only the privileged who may be monitored and normalized in panoptic settings.

Another powerful image is the sociologist Loïc Wacquant's (2009) centaur state, which imagines the government as resembling the creature of Greek mythology that has a human head and a horse's body: civil on top with laissez-faire economic freedom for the rich, while harsh below with paternalistic social policy (e.g., workfare) and prison for the poor. In Wacquant's telling, the contemporary social control of marginal people isn't about behavioral correction and internalization as in the panopticon so much as it is about brute confinement and stinginess. This hyperpunitiveness is a functional component of neoliberal societies that have outsourced jobs and cut welfare benefits, and now need a way to control the resulting social problems.

Surely these images capture something about mass incarceration, the weak American welfare system, and our intuitive sense that the wealthy get away with things like financial crimes. But they also risk obscuring changes on the ground. Incarceration has been on the decline for more than a decade, with prosecutors less likely to pursue minor offenses and people increasingly being granted early release. Furthermore, social service providers have begun to complement paternalism and abstinence-based logics with harm reduction. The centaur state image, then, also can't account for the massive tolerance of social disorder in urban space.

Next, consider another attempt to think beyond the panopticon: Gilles Deleuze's use of the highway image. For Deleuze, the disciplinary societies which enclosed people in spaces like schools, prisons, and asylums had given way to a new dispersed form of human management in "societies of control." Instead of the panopticon, he offers the image of driving: people speed around, feeling as though they are freely choosing their actions, but they in fact are making these choices on a track already laid out for them. "You do not confine people with a highway," he said. "But by making highways, you multiply the means of control . . . people can travel infinitely and 'freely' without being confined while being perfectly controlled. That is our future" (2007, 322).

This is an intriguing way to think about the governance of free people, and it surely says something about our experiences of choice and constraint on the information superhighway and social media algorithms. Perhaps it explains control for the healthy middle-class people in the mainstream of society, who will freely do what is expected of them. But (and forgive me for being too literal) on the streets of Los Angeles, not everyone is freely driving on the highway: some are living under it as shelter. Far from being "perfectly controlled," they are left alone—free, perhaps, to create their own governance structures and challenge dominant actors, to engage in radical lifestyle experiments, or, more likely, to see their life options drastically reduced and to die prematurely. That is a different governance through freedom.

Now imagine if alongside the panopticon, the centaur state, and the highway we add this image (at once an empirical fact and a metaphor) to our conceptual imagination: the tolerated homeless encampment. A man in the throes of psychosis stands in a public park. A city outreach worker offers him housing and care, which he refuses. His healthy homeless neighbors ask whether they can have the services, but the outreach providers ignore them. A group of protestors stand chanting, demanding that the city leave the unhoused alone. This image of tolerant containment may help illuminate many developments in the years to come.

41. Note that there is also a danger in mandating rights to care without ensuring the proper investment to deliver it. Armando Lara-Millán (2021) has shown how legal demands to provide services when institutions lack the resources (as in mandating medical care to prisoners) can merely lead to "redistributing the poor"—relabeling people and shuffling them to other settings or bringing in certain categories of patients/prisoners that will deliver more revenue, to both provide the illusion that services were delivered and keep organizations alive. If the collision of negative liberties and budget austerity leads to tolerant containment, positive rights to resources in a context of disinvestment may simply lead to redistribution and organizations juking the stats.

RESEARCH APPENDIX

1. Skocpol 1984, 370; Geertz 1971, 4.
2. Tavory and Timmermans 2020.
3. Abramson and Gong 2020.
4. Yanello 2011.
5. Timmermans and Tavory 2012.
6. Lubet 2018.
7. Burawoy 2019.
8. See Insel et al. 2010.
9. Katz 2012, 259.
10. Mensik 2022.

REFERENCES

Abramson, Corey. 2009. "Who Are the Clients? Goal Displacement in an Adult
   Day Care Center for Elders with Dementia." *International Journal of Aging and
   Human Development* 68 (1): 65–92.
———. 2015. *The End Game*. Cambridge, MA: Harvard University Press.
Abramson, Corey, and Neil Gong, eds. 2020. *Beyond the Case: The Logics and
   Practices of Comparative Ethnography*. Global and Comparative Ethnography,
   edited by Javier Auyero. New York: Oxford University Press.
Alexander, Michelle. 2010. *The New Jim Crow: Mass Incarceration in the Age of
   Colorblindness*. New York: New Press.
Altomonte, Guillermina, and Adrianna Bagnall Munson. 2021. "Autonomy on the
   Horizon: Comparing Institutional Approaches to Disability and Elder Care."
   Theory and Society 50 (6): 935–63.
Ashwood, J. Scott, Sheryl H. Kataoka, Nicole K. Eberhart, Elizabeth Bromley,
   Bonnie T. Zima, Lesley Baseman, F. Alethea Marti, et al. 2018. *Evaluation of
   the Mental Health Services Act in Los Angeles County: Implementation and
   Outcomes for Key Programs. Rand Health Quarterly* 8 (1).
Aviv, Rachel. 2019. "The Challenge of Going Off Psychiatric Drugs." *New Yorker*,
   April 8, 2019.
Baldessarini, R. J., G. L. Faedda, E. Offidani, G. H. Vazquez, C. Marangoni,
   G. Serra, and L. Tondo 2013. "'Switching' of Mood from Depression to Mania
   with Antidepressants." *Psychiatric Times* 30 (11): 9.
Barnard, Alex. 2022. "From 'the Magna Carta' to 'Dying on the Streets': Media
   Framings of Mental Health Law in California." *Society and Mental Health* 12 (2):
   155–73.
———. 2023. *Conservatorship: Inside California's System of Coercion and Care for
   Mental Illness*. New York: Columbia University Press.

Bateman, A., and P. Fonagy. 2008. "Comorbid Antisocial and Borderline Personality Disorders: Mentalization-Based Treatment." *Journal of Clinical Psychology* 64 (2): 181–94.

Beckett, Katherine, and Steve Herbert. 2008. "Dealing with Disorder: Social Control in the Post-Industrial City." *Theoretical Criminology* 12 (1): 5–30.

Bell, Katherine. 2022. "The Mental Health Systems Act of 1980." *Documents to the People* (50) 4: 12–15.

Berlin, Isaiah. 2017. "Two Concepts of Liberty." In *The Liberty Reader*, edited and introduced by David Miller, 33–57. London: Routledge.

Biehl, Joao. 2013. *Vita: Life in a Zone of Social Abandonment.* Berkeley: University of California Press.

Black, Donald W., and Nancy C. Andreasen. 2011. *Introductory Textbook of Psychiatry.* 5th ed. Washington, DC: American Psychiatric Publishing.

Braslow, Joel Tupper. 2013. "The Manufacture of Recovery." *Annual Review of Clinical Psychology* 9 (1): 781–809. https://doi.org/10.1146/annurev-clinpsy -050212-185642.

Brodwin, Paul. 2013. *Everyday Ethics: Voices from the Front Line of Community Psychiatry.* Berkeley: University of California Press.

Bronson, Jennifer, and Marcus Berzofsky. 2017. *Indicators of Mental Health Problems Reported by Prisoners and Jail Inmates,* 2011–12. Special Report, US Department of Justice, Bureau of Justice Statistics, 1–16. https://bjs.ojp.gov/ content/pub/pdf/imhprpji1112.pdf.

Bryson, John. 2019. "A Century of Public Housing: Lessons from Singapore, Where Housing Is a Social, Not Financial, Asset." *Conversation*, July 31, 2019. https:// theconversation.com/a-century-of-public-housing-lessons-from-singapore -where-housing-is-a-social-not-financial-asset-121141.

Burawoy, Michael. 2019. "Empiricism and Its Fallacies." *Contexts* 18 (1): 47–53.

California Courts. 2017. "Proposition 47: The Safe Neighborhoods and Schools Act." https://www.courts.ca.gov/documents/Prop-47-Information.pdf.

California Welfare and Institutions Code, Section 5008. https://leginfo .legislature.ca.gov/faces/codes_displaySection.xhtml?lawCode=WIC& sectionNum=5008.

Cannon, Lou, and Joel Kotkin. 1979. "Crisis Grows in Calif. Mental Hospitals." *Washington Post*, April 16, 1979.

Castel, Robert. 1991. "From Dangerousness to Risk." In *The Foucault Effect: Studies in Governmentality*, edited by Graham Burchell; Colin Gordon, and Peter Miller, 281–98. Chicago: University of Chicago Press.

Castellano, Jill, Brett Kelman, Kristina Hwang, Brian Indrelunus, and Christopher Weddle. 2016. "Two Years after Prop. 47, Addicts Walk Free with Nowhere to Go." *Desert Sun* (Palm Springs, CA), December 14, 2016. https://www.desertsun

.com/story/news/crime_courts/2016/12/14/prop-47-california-addiction/
94083338/.

Chen, Angus. 2016. "For Centuries, a Small Town Has Embraced Strangers with
Mental Illness." National Public Radio, July 1, 2016. https://www.npr.org/
sections/health-shots/2016/07/01/484083305/for-centuries-a-small-town-has
-embraced-strangers-with-mental-illness.

Clegg, John, and Adaner Usmani. 2019. "The Economic Origins of Mass
Incarceration." *Catalyst* 3 (3): 9–53.

Colburn, Gregg, and Clayton Page Aldern. 2022. *Homelessness Is a Housing
Problem: How Structural Factors Explain US Patterns.* Berkeley: University of
California Press.

Davidson, L., M. O'Connell, J. Tondora, T. Styron, and K. Kangas. 2006. "The
Top Ten Concerns about Recovery Encountered in Mental Health System
Transformation." *Psychiatric Services* 57 (5): 640–45.

Davis, Elizabeth. 2012. *Bad Souls: Madness and Responsibility in Modern Greece.*
Durham, NC: Duke University Press.

Davis, Lennard J. 1995. *Enforcing Normalcy: Disability, Deafness, and the Body.*
London: Verso.

Dayen, David. 2023. "A Liberalism That Builds Power." *American Prospect*, May 25,
2023. https://prospect.org/economy/2023-05-25-liberalism-that-builds
-power/.

Dear, Michael J., and Jennifer R. Wolch. 2014. *Landscapes of Despair: From
Deinstitutionalization to Homelessness.* First published 1987. Princeton, NJ:
Princeton University Press.

Deegan, Patricia E. 1988. "Recovery: The Lived Experience of Rehabilitation."
Psychosocial Rehabilitation Journal 11 (4): 11–19.

DeParle, Jason. 2023. "Federal Policy on Homelessness Becomes New Target of the
Right." *New York Times*, June 20, 2023.

Desjarlais, Robert. 1994. "Struggling Along: The Possibilities for Experience among
the Homeless Mentally Ill." *American Anthropologist* 96 (4): 886–901.

Deutsch, Albert. 1948. *The Shame of the States.* New York: Harcourt, Brace.

Dobransky, Kerry. 2009. "The Good, the Bad, and the Severely Mentally Ill: Official
and Informal Labels as Organizational Resources in Community Mental Health
Services." *Social Science and Medicine* 69 (5): 722–28.

Dougherty, Conor, and Soumya Karlamangla. 2022. "California Fights Its
NIMBYs." *New York Times*, September 1, 2022. https://www.nytimes.com/
2022/09/01/business/economy/california-nimbys-housing.html.

DuBois, James M., Holly Bante, and Whitney B. Hadley. 2011. "Ethics in
Psychiatric Research: A Review of 25 Years of NIH-Funded Empirical Research
Projects." *AJOB Primary Research* 2 (4): 5–17.

Duneier, Mitch. 1999. *Sidewalk.* New York: Farrar, Straus and Giroux.

Earley, Pete. 2007. *Crazy: A Father's Search through America's Mental Health Madness*. New York: Penguin.

Eide, Stephen, and Carolyn Gorman. 2021. *Medicaid's IMD Exclusion. The Case for Repeal*. Manhattan Institute, February 23, 2021. https://www.manhattan -institute.org/medicaids-imd-exclusion-case-repeal#notes.

———. 2022. *The Continuum of Care: A Vision for Mental Health Reform*. Manhattan Institute, September 2022. https://media4.manhattan-institute.org/ sites/default/files/the-continuum-of-care-vision-for-mental-health-reform.pdf #page=14.

Emerson, Robert M., E. Burke Rochford Jr., and Linda L. Shaw. 1981. "Economics and Enterprise in Board and Care Homes for the Mentally Ill." *American Behavioral Scientist* 24 (6): 771–85.

Estroff, Sue E. 1981. *Making It Crazy: An Ethnography of Psychiatric Clients in an American Community*. Berkeley: University of California Press.

Fajardo, Tony, Kaitlyn Becenti, and Annie Bang. 2023. "Despite Controversies, Mayor Bass' Homeless Initiative Receives Support from Experts and Non-profits." USC Annenberg Media, April 18, 2023. https://www .uscannenbergmedia.com/2023/04/18/despite-controversies-mayor-bass -homeless-initiative-receives-support-from-experts-and-non-profits/.

Feeley, Malcolm M., and Jonathan Simon. 1992. "The New Penology: Notes on the Emerging Strategy of Corrections and Its Implications." *Criminology* 30 (4): 449–74.

Fitzsimmons, Emma, and Andy Newman. 2022. "New York's Plan to Address Crisis of Mentally Ill Faces High Hurdles." *New York Times*, November 30, 2022.

Foucault, Michel. 1965. *Madness and Civilization: A History of Insanity in the Age of Reason*. Translated by R. Howard. Abridged ed. New York: Vintage.

———. 1977. *Discipline and Punish: The Birth of the Prison*. New York: Random House.

———. 1988. *Technologies of the Self: A Seminar with Michel Foucault*. Amherst: University of Massachusetts Press.

———. 2008. *Psychiatric Power: Lectures at the Collège de France, 1973–1974*. New York: Macmillan.

Fracassa, Dominic, and Kevin Fagan. 2020. "San Francisco Gives Methadone, Alcohol, and Cannabis to Some Addicts and Homeless Isolating in Hotels." *San Francisco Chronicle*, May 6, 2020. https://www.sfchronicle.com/bayarea/ article/SF-providing-medications-alcohol-cannabis-to-15251350.php.

France, Anatole. 1894. *Le lys rouge* [The red lily]. Paris: Calmann-Lévy.

Frances, Allen. 2012. "Why Are There No Biological Tests in Psychiatry?" Streams of Consciousness. *Scientific American*, May 11, 2012. https://blogs .scientificamerican.com/streams-of-consciousness/why-are-there-no-biological -tests-in-psychiatry/.

———. 2016. "Setting the Record Straight on Antipsychotics." Commentary, *Psychiatric Times*, February 17, 2016. https://www.psychiatrictimes.com/view/setting-record-straight-antipsychotics.

Freud, Sigmund. 2008. *Three Case Histories*. New York: Simon and Schuster.

Friedman, Milton. 2020. *Capitalism and Freedom*. Chicago: University of Chicago Press. First published 1962.

Fuller, Doris A., Elizabeth Sinclair, Jeffrey Geller, Cameron Quanbeck, and John Snook. 2016. "Going, Going, Gone: Trends and Consequences of Eliminating State Psychiatric Beds, 2016." Arlington, VA: Treatment Advocacy Center.

Garfinkel, Harold. 1956. "Conditions of Successful Degradation Ceremonies." *American Journal of Sociology* 61 (5): 420–24.

Geertz, Clifford. 1971. *Islam Observed: Religious Development in Morocco and Indonesia*. Chicago: University of Chicago Press.

Gilmore, Ruth Wilson. 2007. *Golden Gulag: Prison, Surplus, Crisis, and Opposition in Globalization California*. Berkeley: University of California Press.

———. 2008. "Forgotten Places and the Seeds of Grassroots Planning." In *Engaging Contradictions: Theory, Politics, and Methods of Activist Scholarship*, edited by Charles Hale, 31–61. Berkeley: University of California Press.

Goffman, Erving. 1961. *Asylums: Essays on the Social Situation of Mental Patients and Other Inmates*. New York: Doubleday Anchor.

———. 2009. *Stigma: Notes on the Management of Spoiled Identity*. New York: Simon and Schuster. First published 1963.

Goldman, Howard H. 2010. "Will Health Insurance Reform in the United States Help People with Schizophrenia?" *Schizophrenia Bulletin* 36 (5): 893–94.

Gong, Neil. 2017. "'That Proves You Mad, Because You Know It Not': Impaired Insight and the Dilemma of Governing Psychiatric Patients as Legal Subjects." *Theory and Society* 46:201–28.

———. 2021. "California Gave People the 'Right' to Be Homeless, but Little Help Finding Homes." *Washington Post*, May 20, 2021, Sunday Outlook.

Gong, Neil, and Alex Barnard. 2019. "Save San Francisco's Board and Care Homes: Then Fix Them." *San Francisco Chronicle*, September 17, 2019.

———. 2022. "Forcing Homeless People into Treatment Often Backfires. What about a Firm Nudge?" *Washington Post*, May 11, 2022, Sunday Outlook.

Gray, M. Nolan. 2021. "How Californians Are Weaponizing Environmental Law." *Atlantic*, March 12, 2021. https://www.theatlantic.com/ideas/archive/2021/03/signature-environmental-law-hurts-housing/618264/.

Grob, Gerald N. 2014. *From Asylum to Community: Mental Health Policy in Modern America*. Princeton, NJ: Princeton University Press.

Hakes, Jasmin Iolani. 2021. "My Daughter Fell off the Mental Health Care Cliff, and I Have to Jump after Her." *Los Angeles Times*, June 7, 2021.

Hansen, Helena. 2019. "Substance-Induced Psychosis: Clinical-Racial Subjectivities and Capital in Diagnostic Apartheid." *Ethos* 47 (1): 73–88.

Hansen, Helena, Philippe Bourgois, and Ernest Drucker. 2014. "Pathologizing Poverty: New Forms of Diagnosis, Disability, and Structural Stigma under Welfare Reform." *Social Science and Medicine* 103:76–83.

Harrow, Martin, and Thomas Jobe. 2013. "Does Long-Term Treatment of Schizophrenia with Antipsychotic Medications Facilitate Recovery?" *Schizophrenia Bulletin* 39 (5): 962–65.

Hendriksen, C., and Vi Binder. 1980. "Social Prognosis in Patients with Ulcerative Colitis." *British Medical Journal* 281 (6240): 581–83.

Herring, Chris. 2014. "The New Logics of Homeless Exclusion: Homeless Encampments in America's West Coast Cities." *City and Community* 13 (4): 285–309.

———. 2019. "Complaint-Oriented Policing: Regulating Homelessness in Public Space." *American Sociological Review* 84 (5): 769–800.

Hess, Nathan, Colin Capara, Robert Santillano, and Janey Rountree. 2021. "Unsheltered in Los Angeles: Insights from Street Outreach Service Data." California Policy Lab, February 24, 2021. https://www.capolicylab.org/wp -content/uploads/2021/02/Unsheltered-in-Los-Angeles.-Insights-from-Street -Outreach-Service-Data.pdf.

Hollingshead, August B., and Frederick C. Redlich. 1958. *Social Class and Mental Illness*. New York: Wiley.

Hopper, Kim, John Jost, Terri Hay, Susan Welber, and Gary Haugland. 1997. "Homelessness, Severe Mental Illness, and the Institutional Circuit." *Psychiatric Services* 48 (5): 659–65.

Howell, Alison, and Jijian Voronka. 2012. "Introduction: The Politics of Resilience and Recovery in Mental Health Care." *Studies in Social Justice* 6 (1): 1–7.

Icarus Project. 2013. *Navigating the Space between Brilliance and Madness: A Reader and Roadmap of Bipolar Worlds*. 10th anniversary ed. N.p.: Icarus Project.

Insel, Thomas, Bruce Cuthbert, Marjorie Garvey, Robert Heinssen, Daniel S. Pine, Kevin Quinn, Charles Sanislow, and Philip Wang. 2010. "Research Domain Criteria (RDoC): Toward a New Classification Framework for Research on Mental Disorders." *American Journal of Psychiatry* 167 (7): 748–51.

Jaffe, D. J. 2020. "Thrive Hasn't Been Fixed, Will Still Fail to Focus on Those Who Need Help." *New York Post*, March 9, 2020.

Jones, Nev, Becky K. Gius, Morgan Shields, Shira Collings, Cherise Rosen, and Michelle Munson. 2021. "Investigating the Impact of Involuntary Psychiatric Hospitalization on Youth and Young Adult Trust and Help-Seeking in Pathways to Care." *Social Psychiatry and Psychiatric Epidemiology* 56:1–11.

Katz, Jack. 2012. "Ethnography's Expanding Warrants." *Annals of the American Academy of Political and Social Science* 642 (1): 258–75.

Kesey, Ken. 1962. *One Flew over the Cuckoo's Nest.* New York: Viking Press.

Kingkade, Tyler. 2022. "Teens Were Sent to Wyoming Ranches for Therapy. They Say They Found a Nightmare of Hard Labor and Humiliation." NBC News, September 7, 2022. https://www.nbcnews.com/news/us-news/wyoming-christian-troubled-teen-ranches-abuse-rcna46112.

Klein, Ezra. "The Way Los Angeles Is Trying to Solve Homelessness Is 'Absolutely Insane.'" *New York Times*, October 23, 2033. https://www.nytimes.com/2022/10/23/opinion/los-angeles-homelessness-affordable-housing.html.

Koutsouleris, Nikolaos, René S. Kahn, Adam M. Chekroud, Stefan Leucht, Peter Falkai, Thomas Wobrock, Eske M. Derks, Wolfgang W. Fleischhacker, and Alkomiet Hasan. 2016. "Multisite Prediction of 4-Week and 52-Week Treatment Outcomes in Patients with First-Episode Psychosis: A Machine Learning Approach." *Lancet Psychiatry* 3 (10): 935–46.

Laing, Ronald David. 1968. *The Politics of Experience.* New York: Ballantine Books.

Lara-Millán, Armando. 2021. *Redistributing the Poor: Jails, Hospitals, and the Crisis of Law and Fiscal Austerity.* New York: Oxford University Press.

Lareau, Annette. 2002. "Invisible Inequality: Social Class and Childrearing in Black Families and White Families." *American Sociological Review* 67, no. 5 (October): 747–76.

———. 2011. *Unequal Childhoods: Class, Race, and Family Life.* Berkeley: University of California Press.

Las Encinas Behavioral Healthcare. N.d. Program brochure. Accessed June 11, 2023. https://www.lasencinashospital.com/sites/default/files/attachments/Program%20Services%20Brochure.pdf.

Lecher, Colin, and Maddy Varner. "Black and Latino Homeless People Rank Lower on LA's Housing Priority List." *Los Angeles Times.* February 28, 2023. https://www.latimes.com/california/story/2023-02-28/black-latino-homeless-people-housing-priority-list-los-angeles.

Lejeune, Julia. 2022. "Breaking Academia's Silence on Inpatient Psychiatry: An Interview with Researcher Morgan Shields." *Mad in America*, November 9, 2022. https://www.madinamerica.com/2022/11/breaking-academias-silence-about-harms-in-inpatient-psychiatry-an-interview-with-researcher-morgan-shields/.

Levin, Sam. 2022. "California Proposal Would Force Unhoused into Treatment." *Guardian* (US ed.), March 3, 2022. https://www.theguardian.com/us-news/2022/mar/03/california-proposal-forced-unhoused-treatment.

Lipsky, Michael. 2010. *Street-Level Bureaucracy: Dilemmas of the Individual in Public Service.* 30th anniversary expanded ed. New York: Russell Sage Foundation.

Locke, John. 1980. *Locke: Two Treatises of Government.* London: Cambridge University Press. First published 1690.

Los Angeles County Department of Mental Health. 2011. *Mental Health Services Act Annual Fiscal Update Year 2011–2012*. https://file.lacounty.gov/dmh/cms1_179197.pdf.

Lubet, Steven. 2018. *Interrogating Ethnography: Why Evidence Matters*. New York: Oxford University Press.

Luhrmann, Tanya Marie. 2000. *Of Two Minds: The Growing Disorder in American Psychiatry*. New York: Alfred A. Knopf.

———. 2007. "Social Defeat and the Culture of Chronicity: Or, Why Schizophrenia Does So Well Over There and So Badly Here." *Culture, Medicine and Psychiatry* 31:135–72.

Lutfey, Karen, and Jeremy Freese. 2005. "Toward Some Fundamentals of Fundamental Causality: Socioeconomic Status and Health in the Routine Clinic Visit for Diabetes." *American Journal of Sociology* 110 (5): 1326–72.

Martin, Isaac William. 2008. *The Permanent Tax Revolt: How the Property Tax Transformed American Politics*. Stanford, CA: Stanford University Press.

Marx, Karl. 2004. *Capital*. Vol. 1. Penguin Classics. London: Penguin. First published 1867.

Marx, Karl, and Friedrich Engels. 2009. *The Economic and Philosophic Manuscripts of 1844 and "The Communist Manifesto."* New York: Prometheus Books.

Mathieu, Arline. 1993. "The Medicalization of Homelessness and the Theater of Repression." *Medical Anthropology Quarterly* 7 (2): 170–84.

Mayor's Office of Community Engagement, City of Sacramento. 2021. "Mayor Introduces Right to Housing, Obligation to Accept for Unhoused Residents." November 15, 2021. Updated November 16, 2021. https://engagesac.org/blog-civic-engagement/2021/11/15/t5fwjeigk8hhm57yh82u5jbgi8cyyp.

McCoy, Terrence. 2015. "Meet the Outsider Who Accidentally Solved Chronic Homelessness." *Washington Post*, May 6, 2015.

McLean, Athena. 2000. "From Ex-patient Alternatives to Consumer Options: Consequences of Consumerism for Psychiatric Consumers and the Ex-patient Movement." *International Journal of Health Services* 30 (4): 821–47.

Meares, Hadley. 2019. "The Sunshine Cure." LA Curbed. Last updated June 17, 2019. https://la.curbed.com/2015/9/30/9916132/southern-california-rehab-capital-sanitariums.

Mensik, Hailey. 2022. "10-Week Kaiser Strike Ends with Deal Aimed at Improving Mental Health Access." Healthcare Dive, October 25, 2022. https://www.healthcaredive.com/news/kaiser-strike-mental-health-california-hawaii-deal/634917/.

Meyer, Harriet, Tero Taiminen, Toni Vuori, Aki Äijälä, and Hans Helenius. 1999. "Posttraumatic Stress Disorder Symptoms Related to Psychosis and Acute Involuntary Hospitalization in Schizophrenic and Delusional Patients." *Journal of Nervous and Mental Disease* 187 (6): 343–52.

Mill, John Stuart. 1999. *On Liberty, and Other Essays*. Oxford: Oxford University Press. First published 1869.

Morrison, Linda J. 2013. *Talking Back to Psychiatry: The Psychiatric Consumer/ Survivor/Ex-patient Movement*. New Approaches in Sociology: Studies in Social Inequality, Social Change, and Social Justice, edited by Nancy Naples. New York: Routledge.

Morrissey, Joseph P., and Howard H. Goldman. 1984. "Cycles of Reform in the Care of the Chronically Mentally Ill." *Psychiatric Services* 35 (8): 785–93.

Mossakowski, K. N. 2014. "Social Causation and Social Selection." In *The Wiley-Blackwell Encyclopedia of Health, Illness, Behavior, and Society*, edited by W. C. Cockerham, R. Dingwall, and S. Quah, 2154–60. Chichester, UK: Wiley-Blackwell.

Myers, Neely Laurenzo. 2015. *Recovery's Edge: An Ethnography of Mental Health Care and Moral Agency*. Nashville, TN: Vanderbilt University Press.

National Institute of Mental Health. 2022. Mental illness statistics. https://www .nimh.nih.gov/health/statistics/mental-illness.

New York Times Editorial Board. 2022. "The Solution to Our Mental Health Crisis Already Exists." *New York Times*, October 4, 2022.

Noguchi, Yuki. 2022. "Paying for Mental Health Treatment Leaves Families Isolated and in Debt." National Public Radio, October 19, 2022. https://www.npr .org/sections/health-shots/2022/10/19/1125446666/debt-mental-health-care-u -s-families.

Osborne, Melissa. 2019. "Who Gets 'Housing First'? Determining Eligibility in an Era of Housing First Homelessness." *Journal of Contemporary Ethnography* 48 (3): 402–28.

Padwa, Howard. 2009. Interview with Harry Brickman. Oral Histories, UCLA Public Health. https://hpmh.semel.ucla.edu/wp-content/uploads/2021/02/ 07c9dc72_Harry_Brickman.pdf.

Padwa, Howard, Marcia Meldrum, Jack R. Friedman, and Joel T. Braslow. 2016. "A Mental Health System in Recovery: The Era of Deinstitutionalisation in California." In *Deinstitutionalisation and After: Post-war Psychiatry in the Western World*, edited by Despo Kritsotaki, Vicky Long, and Matthew Smith, 241–65. Mental Health in Historical Perspective. Cham, Switzerland: Springer International. https://doi.org/10.1007/978-3-319-45360-6_12.

Parry, Manon S. 2006. "Dorothea Dix (1802–1887)." *American Journal of Public Health* 96 (4): 624–25. https://doi.org/10.2105/AJPH.2005.079152.

Porter, Roy. 2003. *Madness: A Brief History*. Oxford: Oxford University Press.

Powers, Ron. 2017. *No One Cares about Crazy People: The Chaos and Heartbreak of Mental Health in America*. New York: Hachette Books.

Raven, Maria C., Matthew J. Niedzwiecki, and Margot Kushel. 2020. "A Randomized Trial of Permanent Supportive Housing for Chronically Homeless

Persons with High Use of Publicly Funded Services." *Health Services Research* 55:797–806.

Rhodes, Lorna. 1995. *Emptying Beds: The Work of an Emergency Psychiatric Unit.* Berkeley: University of California Press.

Ridgeway, Leslie. 2019. "Author Esmé Weijun Wang Shares Hope at Saks Institute Distinguished Fall Lecture; Writer of 'The Collected Schizophrenias' Discusses Stigma and Self-Advocacy with Prof. Elyn Saks." USC Gould School of Law, November 27, 2019. Accessed June 11, 2023. https://gould.usc.edu/about/news/?id=4632.

Rose, Nikolas. 1999. *Powers of Freedom: Reframing Political Thought.* Cambridge: Cambridge University Press.

Rothman, S., V. Raveis, A. Friedman, and D. Rothman. 2011. "Health Advocacy Organizations and the Pharmaceutical Industry: An Analysis of Disclosure Practices." *American Journal of Public Health* 101 (4): 602.

Rothschild, Anthony J. 2013. "Challenges in the Treatment of Major Depressive Disorder with Psychotic Features." *Schizophrenia Bulletin* 39 (4): 787–96.

Sacks, Oliver. 1985. *The Man Who Mistook His Wife for a Hat, and Other Clinical Tales.* New York: Summit Books.

Saks, Elyn R. 2010. *Refusing Care: Forced Treatment and the Rights of the Mentally Ill.* Chicago: University of Chicago Press.

Sandberg, Erica. 2022. "San Francisco's 'Housing First' Nightmare." *City Journal,* April 28, 2022.

Sandoval, Edgar. 2019. "Princeton Graduate Killed Father over Allowance. He Got 30 Years to Life." *New York Times,* September 27, 2019.

Sapien, Joaquin. 2018. "After Years in Institutions, a Road Home Paved with Violence, Hunger, and Death." ProPublica, March 14, 2018. https://features .propublica.org/supported-housing/new-york-mentally-ill-supported-housing -nestor-bunch/.

Scheff, Thomas. 1966. *Being Mentally Ill: A Sociological Theory.* Chicago: Aldine.

Scheffler, Richard M., and Neal Adams. 2005. "Millionaires and Mental Health: Proposition 63 in California; What It Is, and Why It Passed." *Health Affairs* 24, no. Suppl. 1: W5-212–W5-224.

Schrader, Summer, Nev Jones, and Mona Shattell. 2013. "Mad Pride: Reflections on Sociopolitical Identity and Mental Diversity in the Context of Culturally Competent Psychiatric Care." *Issues in Mental Health Nursing* 34 (1): 62–64.

Scull, Andrew T. 1977. *Decarceration: Community Treatment and the Deviant; A Radical View.* Englewood Cliffs, NJ: Prentice-Hall.

———. 1981. "A New Trade in Lunacy: The Recommodification of the Mental Patient." *American Behavioral Scientist* 24 (6): 741–54.

———. 1989. *Social Order/Mental Disorder: Anglo-American Psychiatry in Historical Perspective.* Berkeley: University of California Press.

———. 1990. "Deinstitutionalization: Cycles of Despair." In "Challenging the Therapeutic State: Critical Perspectives on Psychiatry and the Mental Health System," special issue, *Journal of Mind and Behavior* 11 (3/4): 301–11.

———. 2015. *Madness in Civilization*. Princeton, NJ: Princeton University Press.

Sedgwick, Peter. 1982. "Psycho Politics: Laing, Foucault, Goffman, Szasz and the Future of Mass Psychiatry." New York: Harper and Row.

Seim, Josh. 2017. "The Ambulance: Toward a Labor Theory of Poverty Governance." *American Sociological Review* 82 (3): 451–75.

Selsky, Andrew. 2020. "Oregon Leads the Way on Decriminalization of Hard Drugs." Associated Press, November 4, 2020. https://apnews.com/article/oregon-first-decriminalizing-hard-drugs-01edca37c776c9ea8bfd4afdd7a7a33e.

Sharkey, Patrick. 2018. *Uneasy Peace: The Great Crime Decline, the Renewal of City Life, and the Next War on Violence*. New York: W. W. Norton.

Shellenberger, Michael. 2021. *San Fransicko: Why Progressives Ruin Cities*. New York: Simon and Schuster.

Shields, Morgan C., and Rinad S. Beidas. 2022. "The Need to Prioritize Patient-Centered Care in Inpatient Psychiatry as a Matter of Social Justice." *JAMA Health Forum* 3 (2): e214461.

Sisti, Dominic A., Andrea G. Segal, and Ezekiel J. Emanuel. 2015. "Improving Long-Term Psychiatric Care: Bring Back the Asylum." *JAMA* 313 (13): 243–44. https://doi.org/10.1001/jama.2014.16088.

Skocpol, Theda. 1984. "Emerging Agendas and Recurrent Strategies." In *Vision and Method in Historical Sociology*, edited by T. Skocpol, 356–85. Cambridge: Cambridge University Press.

Skultans, Vieda. 2005. "Varieties of Deception and Distrust: Moral Dilemmas in the Ethnography of Psychiatry." *Health* 9 (4): 491–512.

Smith, Christopher. 1975. "Being Mentally Ill—in the Asylum or the Ghetto." *Antipode* 7 (2): 53–61.

Snow, David A., and Leon Anderson. 1993. *Down on Their Luck: A Study of Homeless Street People*. Berkeley: University of California Press.

Snow, David A., and Michael Mulcahy. 2001. "Space, Politics, and the Survival Strategies of the Homeless." *American Behavioral Scientist* 45 (1): 149–69.

Solomon, Andrew. 2012. *Far from the Tree: Parents, Children and the Search for Identity*. New York: Simon and Schuster.

Soss, Joe, Richard C. Fording, and Sanford F. Schram. 2011. *Disciplining the Poor: Neoliberal Paternalism and the Persistent Power of Race*. Chicago: University of Chicago Press.

Stephens, Bret. 2021. "A Letter to My Liberal Friends." *New York Times*, February 1, 2021.

Streeter, Jialu. 2022. "Homelessness in California: Causes and Policy Considerations." Stanford, CA: Stanford Institute for Economic Policy Research.

Stuart, Forrest. 2016. *Down, Out, and Under Arrest: Policing and Everyday Life in Skid Row*. Chicago: University of Chicago Press.

Swanson, Charlie L., Jr., Ruben C. Gur, Warren Bilker, Richard G. Petty, and Raquel E. Gur. 1998. "Premorbid Educational Attainment in Schizophrenia: Association with Symptoms, Functioning, and Neurobehavioral Measures." *Biological Psychiatry* 44 (8): 739–47.

Szalavitz, Maia. 2006. *Help at Any Cost: How the Troubled-Teen Industry Cons Parents and Hurts Kids*. New York: Riverhead Books.

Szasz, Thomas S. 1964. *The Myth of Mental Illness: Foundations of a Theory of Personal Conduct*. New York: Harper and Row.

Tavory, Iddo, and Stefan Timmermans. 2020. "Sequential Comparisons and the Comparative Imagination." In *Beyond the Case: The Logics and Practices of Comparative Ethnography*, edited by Corey M. Abramson and Neil Gong, 185–208. Global and Comparative Ethnography, edited by Javier Auyero. New York: Oxford University Press.

Timmermans, Stefan, and Iddo Tavory. 2012. "Theory Construction in Qualitative Research: From Grounded Theory to Abductive Analysis." *Sociological Theory* 30 (3): 167–86.

Treffert, D. A. 1973. "Dying with Their Rights On." *American Journal of Psychiatry* 130 (9): 1041.

Tsai, Jack. 2020. "Is the Housing First Model Effective? Different Evidence for Different Outcomes." *American Journal of Public Health* 110 (9): 1376.

Tsemberis, Sam, Leyla Gulcur, and Maria Nakae. 2004. "Housing First, Consumer Choice, and Harm Reduction for Homeless Individuals with a Dual Diagnosis." *American Journal of Public Health* 94 (4): 651–56. https://doi.org/10.2105/AJPH.94.4.651.

US Department of Housing and Urban Development. 2015. "Definition of Chronic Homelessness." https://www.hudexchange.info/homelessness-assistance/coc-esg-virtual-binders/coc-esg-homeless-eligibility/definition-of-chronic-homelessness/.

———. 2022. "HUD 2018 Continuum of Care Homeless Assistance Programs Homeless Populations and Subpopulations." https://files.hudexchange.info/reports/published/CoC_PopSub_NatlTerrDC_2018.pdf.

Ussher, Jane M. 2013. "Diagnosing Difficult Women and Pathologising Femininity: Gender Bias in Psychiatric Nosology." *Feminism and Psychology* 23 (1): 63–69.

Wacquant, Loïc. 2009. *Punishing the Poor: The Neoliberal Government of Social Insecurity*. Durham, NC: Duke University Press.

———. 2010. "Class, Race and Hyperincarceration in Revanchist America." *Daedalus* 139 (3): 74–90.

Wall Street Journal Editorial Board. 2021. "Refunding the Police in San Francisco." *Wall Street Journal*, December 16, 2021.

Walter, Shoshanna. 2020. "At Hundreds of Rehabs, Recovery Means Work without Pay." Reveal News, July 7, 2020. https://revealnews.org/article/at-hundreds-of-rehabs-recovery-means-work-without-pay/.

Walters, Dan. 2022. "Remember That Budget Surplus? Never Mind." CalMatters, November 21, 2022. https://calmatters.org/commentary/2022/11/remember-that-budget-surplus-never-mind/.

Ward-Ciesielski, Erin F., and Shireen L. Rizvi. 2021. "The Potential Iatrogenic Effects of Psychiatric Hospitalization for Suicidal Behavior: A Critical Review and Recommendations for Research." *Clinical Psychology: Science and Practice* 28 (1): 60.

Whitaker, Robert. 2010. *Anatomy of an Epidemic: Magic Bullets, Psychiatric Drugs, and the Astonishing Rise of Mental Illness in America.* New York: Crown Books.

Whooley, Owen. 2010. "Diagnostic Ambivalence: Psychiatric Workarounds and the Diagnostic and Statistical Manual of Mental Disorders." *Sociology of Health and Illness* 32 (3): 452–69.

Willse, Craig. 2010. "Neo-liberal Biopolitics and the Invention of Chronic Homelessness." *Economy and Society* 39 (2): 155–84.

Wolpert, Julian, and Elain Wolpert. 1974. "From Asylum to Ghetto." *Antipode* 6 (3): 63–76.

Yanello, Amy. 2011. "Two-Tiered Mental-Health System." *Sacramento (CA) News and Review*, September 15, 2011. Sacramento News and Review Archives. https://www.newsreview.com/sacramento/content/two-tiered-mental-health-system/3687288/.

INDEX

Page numbers in *italics* refer to tables.

224–25; depression and, 212; doctors and, 202, 224; Downtown and, 199, 201, 204–6, 215, 221–25; drugs and, 201, 206, 209–10, 213–17, 223–26; ecologies and, 201, 208; education and, 201; elites and, 207–8, 223, 226; encampments and, 203; eviction and, 199, 201, 203–5, 210, 213, 220, 223; 5150 code and, 221; food and, 204, 207, 212, 224; freedom and, 200, 207–13, 226; governance and, 199, 213, 225; "graceful exits" and, 205–6; harm reduction and, 199–202, 209–11, 216; homelessness and, 199–203, 213–16, 219, 222, 225, 312n8; hospitals and, 199, 201–2, 212–14, 219, 222–23; housing and, 200–208, 211–18, 221–23, 226, 311nn2–3 (chap. 8), 312n8; intervention and, 200–202, 218; IOP and, 200; jail and, 199, 212, 214–17, 221, 223, 226; law enforcement and, 221; legal issues and, 200, 210, 225; liability and, 192, 196–98; limitations of, 221–25; Los Angeles County DMH and, 200–206, 212–26; lunacy, trade in and, 207–9; medication and, 200–209, 212, 216, 222; mental illness and, 201, 208, 211–14, 226; missed opportunities and, 214–15; natural growth and, 214–18; nurses and, 203; outreach and, 201, 203, 219, 223; paternalism and, 201–2, 226; police and, 220–21, 224; politics and, 219; poor people and, 202, 207, 212–14; poverty and, 199, 213, 225; prison and, 214, 222; privilege and, 180, 214, 223, 227, 254, 293, 298; proposed solutions for, 263–64; psychology and, 200; psychosis and, 20; public safety and, 199; punitive, 192; racial

issues and, 222; radical ideas and, 199; recovery and, 211; redirecting behaviors and, 203–5; refusal of care and, 201–2, 204, 218, 220, 222, 224; rehabilitation and, 207–8, 212, 222–23; research methodology and, 293, *295*, 298, 301; rich people and, 209; rights and, 257, 260, 263, 272, 279, 315n26, 318n40, 319n41; safety nets and, 199; schizophrenia and, 204, 214, 218; shelter and, 199, 201; Skid Row and, 201, 212, 223; sobriety and, 200–201, 222–23; social issues and, 12–14, 18; social services and, 200, 224; social workers and, 204–5, 219–20; spatial, 12, 23, 199; SSI and, 207–9, 212; street diagnosis and, 52; therapists and, 216; trauma and, 17, 199, 210, 214; victims of, 218–21; violence and, 217; vulnerable people and, 214, 218, 222–23, 226, 312n8; wealthy people and, 207; white people and, 204, 214, 216, 222, 312n8
COVID-19 pandemic, 256–58, 267, 282
craziness: constraint and, 229, 252; containment and, 217, 223; family issues and, 83, 308n4; institutional circuit and, 136; madness and, 2, 13, 25, 40, 49, 64–65, 69, 83, 136, 217, 223, 229, 252, 279, *295*, 307n32, 308n4; rights and, 279; social issues and, 2, 13, 25; street diagnosis and, 49, 64–65, 69, 307n32; urban dilemmas and, 40
crime: constraint and, 229; containment and, 214, 222; courts and, 8, 12, 57, 86, 104, 106, 141–47, 192, 260; decriminalization and, 258, 301; drugs and, 44 (*see also* drugs); family court and, 144–47; family issues and, 86, 97, 102–7, 308n4; felons and, 27,